Hell-Fire Duke
The Life of the Duke of Wharton

MARK BLACKETT-ORD

THE KENSAL PRESS

© *Mark Blackett-Ord 1982*

All rights reserved. No part of this book may be reproduced, stored in a retrieval system, or transmitted, in any form or by any means, electronic, mechanical, photocopying, recording or otherwise, without the prior permission of The Kensal Press.

British Library Cataloguing in Publication Data.

Blackett-Ord, Mark

Hell-Fire Duke

1. Wharton, Philip, Duke of

I. Title

941.07'1'0924   DA501.W

ISBN 0-946041-02-4

Published by The Kensal Press,
Shooter's Lodge, Windsor Forest, Berks.
Printed in Great Britain by The Anchor Press Ltd
and bound by Wm Brendon & Son Ltd
both of Tiptree, Essex

Contents

Chapter 1	The Elopement	9
Chapter 2	Descent to Avignon	19
Chapter 3	Treason	29
Chapter 4	The Hell-Fire Club	37
Chapter 5	The Heir	49
Chapter 6	The Bubble	57
Chapter 7	The End of the Hell-Fire Club	65
Chapter 8	The Election	75
Chapter 9	Twickenham	87
Chapter 10	The True Briton	97
Chapter 11	Vienna	121
Chapter 12	The Invasion of England	131
Chapter 13	Rome	147
Chapter 14	Madrid	159
Chapter 15	Love and the Fall	169
Chapter 16	War	181
Chapter 17	A Dream of Home	191
Chapter 18	The Duel	203
Chapter 19	The Road to Poblet	215
Epilogue		225
Bibliography		229

Illustrations

Philip, Duke of Wharton. Rosalba Cariera: Royal Collection

*Philip's father "Honest Tom" Marquis of Wharton.
One of the Kit-Kat Club portraits. Sir Godfrey Kneller: Private Collection*

Ice-Fair. The frozen Thames early in 1716

Philip in his Ducal robes after taking his seat in the House of Lords in December 1719. Charles Jervas: Private Collection

The Frontispiece to the Constitutions of the Freemasons shows the book being given to Philip by his predecessor the Duke of Montagu

Gateway to Wharton Hall, Westmorland

Maria-Theresa, second Duchess of Wharton. Unknown artist: Private Collection

Philip's last portrait. The neck-tie, a quotation from Horace, translates "with love and jests". Unknown artist: Private Collection

PREFACE

What were the abilities that led Philip Wharton to be created a Duke at the age of nineteen? Why did he found the first Hell-fire Club: was it to rival or to parody the Freemasons, whose Grand Master he became? Could his opposition party ever have prevented Walpole from becoming Prime Minister? And could his planned Jacobite invasion of England have succeeded in overthrowing the Hanoverian dynasty? Was his life, which ended pathetically at the age of thirty-two, wholly wasted? This book tries to answer those questions.

I am chiefly grateful to Her Majesty the Queen for permitting me to have access to the Duke's correspondence in the Royal Archives at Windsor, without which an understanding of him would have been impossible. John Buxton and Canon G V Bennett referred me to them. I am further grateful to Her Majesty for gracious permission to quote extensively from the Jacobite State Papers, and to reproduce the portrait of the Duke by Rosalba Cariera in the Royal collection. I must also thank Sir Robin Mackworth-Young, Miss Langton and her staff in the Round Tower at Windsor, and Sir Oliver Millar. I received help from many in the London Library, the British Museum, Bodley's Library, the National Register of Archives, Lincoln's Inn Library, Christ Church College Library, Nottingham University Library, and the County Record offices at Carlisle, Durham and Hertford.

My family and friends have been invaluable. Other individuals I am chiefly indebted to are Major Malcolm Munthe, Bernard Bevan, Caroline Dawnay, Cressida Pemberton-Piggott, Betty Cuthbertson, Andrew Best, Peter Day, Frank Welsh, Felipe Fernandez-Armesto, Lucy Neville-Rolfe and my wife.

Warcop Hall
Westmorland
1982

NOTE

Except where otherwise stated, dates are given Old Style in chapters one to ten, which cover the period when the Duke was mainly in England, and New Style thereafter.

Members of the Church of Rome are throughout called simply Catholics.

"There is no life of the Duke save bookseller's trash."
Horace Walpole

This book is dedicated to the late Caspar Fleming and to all others who gave me encouragment.

CHAPTER ONE

The Elopement

> Farewell old bully of these impious times,
> True patron of the Whigs and of their crimes...
> The English Lucifer, whose restless pride
> Stopp'd by no bounds, both heaven and earth defied;
> Corrupt by nature, born to be the base
> Impatient leader of a factious race...
>
> Thomas Fifth Lord Wharton described in
> *Lord Whig-Love's Elegy* (London 1715).

Philip Wharton was born at Christmas-time in 1698. As the eldest child of Thomas fifth Lord Wharton, he was the heir to an ancient peerage, vast estates in England and Ireland, and considerable political power. The three godparents at his Christening on January 5th were King William III, the Secretary of State the Duke of Shrewsbury, and the heiress to the throne, Princess Anne. They sponsored Lord Wharton's son in spite of his shortcomings — which were many — because he was unswervingly loyal to the Whig government.

Philip was named after his grandfather the fourth Lord Wharton, whose eventful eighty-three year life had ended only two years earlier. From his young days at court, when James I had admired his legs, through the time of the Commonwealth when he had been a leader of the English "Presbyterians" and had sat on Cromwell's Council of State, and for thirty-six years after the Restoration as the last peer barred from a seat in the Lords because of his non-conformity, his Puritan principles had clashed oddly with his powdered face and lace- and velvet-clad figure. His collection of Van Dycks included fourteen full-length portraits and was probably the greatest ever to be assembled under one roof[1], the most important collection of paintings in Britain after the dispersal of that of Charles I. But with his love of art and show went physical cowardice. After the Battle of Edgehill when the regiment he led for Parliament fled without firing a shot he

9

The Elopement

was found hiding in a saw-pit, which earned him the unkind nickname, "Saw-Pit Wharton".

On the other hand for nearly half a century after Cromwell's death he bravely kept up the ideals of the Parliamentarians in a new hostile age, encouraging the development of the fledgling Whig party, and at home he tyrannised Miltonically over his family. His son Thomas, Philip's father, was terrified of him.

But Thomas Wharton was terrified of nobody else. Indeed Thomas's brash effrontery was often such that only his skill in duels kept him alive. He was a brilliant swordsman, who boasted that he had never himself given a challenge, that he had never refused one, that he had never fought without having his opponent at his mercy, and yet that he had never killed a man. Like many of his forward-thinking "witty" and rationalist contemporaries, he openly despised Clergymen. He could not fight them, but he abused them. A satire written on his death, called *Lord Whig-Love's Elegy*[2] recorded his treatment of one who asked him to sponsor a new church:

> "My Lord, who valued neither Church nor Priest,
> But turned whate'er was sacred into jest,
> Pulls out a sixpence — swears a bloody oath —
> "He's no regard to either Church or Cloth",
> Adding, "Good Sir, I am not so profuse
> To lavish more to such a foolish use;
> But if you'll build upon the self-same ground
> A bawdy house, I'll give you twenty pound."

He had once scribbled satirical verses himself. He had written *Lilliburlero* which (to Purcell's music) had become the marching song of William III's army in Ireland when James II had been driven into permanent exile in 1689, and so, (as he boasted) he had whistled a King out of three kingdoms.

He became the stoutest political warrior in the troubled Parliaments of William III and Anne, and the first to practice Parliamentary corruption on a grand scale. When an election was to be fought in an obscure county town he reckoned his own, he would arrive there in person loaded with gold pieces, to speak to the townsmen about Whig principles of liberty and the defence of Protestantism; he would remember their names, ask after their families, drink with them, invite them to feasts of roast beef and ale, and promise to use his influence at Court to find jobs in the excise for their sons and nephews. He seemed so straightforward that they nicknamed him "Honest Tom", and elected his Whig Parliamentary candidates in Buckingham, Aylesbury, Wendover, Malmesbury, Wycombe, Richmond, Appleby and Cockermouth. By the time that Philip was eight Lord Wharton had thirty followers in the Commons and had just been created Earl of Wharton, which gave Philip the courtesy title of Viscount Winchendon. Two years later, Queen Anne made the father Lord Lieutenant of Ireland.

The Tories loathed him accordingly. Swift, who met him in Dublin, called him "The most universal villain I ever knew"[3]. The new Earl treated Ireland rapaciously, taking £40,000 of gifts and bribes in a single year of office there. And whether in Ireland or England he remained as boyishly lewd in his private life as he was brazenly unscrupulous in public affairs. Once he was caught urinating against the altar and "leaving his other occasions" in the pulpit of the quiet church of Barrington, near Ilchester. Later after a dinner with the Duke of Kingston, he attempted to sexually assault Robert Walpole's sister Dolly, though he was over twice her age. "He early acquired" (according to Lord Macaulay), "the reputation of being the greatest rake in England..."[4].

His first wife, Anne Lee, whom he had married for her money, had died of grief (it is said) from her childlessness and from his infidelity. His second, Philip's mother Lucy Loftus, the lascivious daughter of an Irish Viscount who had died in action at the siege of Limerick, brought him wide Irish estates, a sharp tongue and morals as loose as his own. Philip was born to them after six years, followed by two daughters, Jane and Lucy. Then Thomas tired of her as she grew ugly, and took a mistress called Jane Peering, whom (it is said) he kept in a small brick tower in the garden of his mansion at Winchendon in Buckinghamshire.

Winchendon stood on the edge of the Western escarpment of the Chilterns about a dozen miles by carriage beyond Aylesbury, and looked out over the best grazing land in England to Quainton race-

The Elopement

course, which Lord Wharton regularly attended, for he enjoyed showing off the fleetness of his peerless horses. Season after season "Careless" and the others triumphed at Newmarket, or were sent to trounce Tory squires whose hunters had previously won every prize at their county race meetings. Once he raced a gelding of his in France, since it was unbeatable in England, and Louis XIV offered him a thousand pistoles for it. Lord Wharton, who disliked monarchs, foreigners and Catholics, took much pleasure in refusing the offer.

So Philip's childhood eyes opened to a world in which his father's gusto and importance were always apparent; and his father doted upon him too much to let him leave home for school or university. He learnt from expensive tutors, and from the literary and political élite who clustered around his father, and attended his crowded levees and assemblies. And most of all, he studied his father.

At Winchendon and in London as he grew up they were usually together. In London, they sometimes stayed at Danvers House in Chelsea, which Lord Wharton had acquired with his first wife from the Lee family. This large Jacobean mansion, containing a famous Renaissance bathroom ornamented with Ionic pillars, stood overlooking the river on the site of Sir Thomas More's house. Philip's father added to its amenities the forty-acre deer park he had inherited from his own father lying roughly between what is now the Fulham Road and the King's Road. But their elegant new brick house in Dover Street off the end of Piccadilly called Portugal Street, between Burlington House and Berkeley House (later Devonshire House), was more comfortable and convenient for Westminster than old Danvers House, so Lord Wharton usually stayed there as a neighbour of the Duke of Bolton, Dr. Arbuthnot and young Robert Walpole during Parliamentary terms. Although the festive din of Shepherd's Market still disturbed them twice weekly, and for a fortnight each May the May Fair turned the whole neighbourhood into a bazaar, at least the breeze from the country beyond Hyde Park kept their air clean and uncontaminated by the worst of the stench of old London.

From the Dover Street mansion's upper rooms Philip could look southwards across St. James's Park to the ruins of the great palace of Whitehall which had been burnt down in the year of his own birth and was never to be rebuilt. Northwards he could look across the fields of Mayfair to Oxford Street, then hardly more than a country road. Perhaps he could see where it passed Tyburn and the gallows where the felons from Newgate were hanged in batches eight times a year. His family's carriages and outriders passed there whenever they travelled the Aylesbury Road for Winchendon. Not that Winchendon was their only country house. They had other residences and estates in south Buckinghamshire at Wooburn, (a rival to the Duke of Bedford's Woburn Abbey in Bedfordshire), at Rathfarnham Castle near Dublin, and at old Wharton Hall in Westmorland. But Winchendon was his father's favourite; and there he took Philip as often as pressing affairs of State and Parliamentary business would let him.

At Winchendon Philip met Joseph Addison, who was his father's chief Secretary in Ireland. Addison liked pretty and precocious boys, and took him on walks to talk about literary subjects. Philip liked practical jokes. Once when walking together near where the racehorses grazed they reached a high paddock-gate which was locked in their path. Philip appeared very worried and apologised that he had left his bunch of keys behind. Addison said that they could easily climb the gate; and clad in his full wig, long embroidered coat, sword, and all the paraphernalia of a gentleman, he carefully ascended. Whereupon Philip produced the key to the gate from his pocket, unlocked it, and began swinging it mischievously to and fro to keep Addison stranded, ridiculously, on its top. Philip thought it a great joke; perhaps Addison thought so too; certainly all of the Earl's friends laughed when they heard of it. The eighteenth century loved "frolics".

His father spoilt him badly. The stud books of the famous stables of Winchendon have an account of the bloodstock he was given: "A chestnut mare", "a stone colt with four white feet and a bald face",[5] and in 1711 when he was only twelve, no less than three of the stables' eleven brood mares to start his own stud with.

His father made his tutors concentrate him on languages, history, the classics, Shakespeare and oratory, at the expense of mathematics, which was unfortunate for the heir to several fortunes. Worse, Philip never learnt to master swordsmanship. But when still very young he was fluent in French and Latin, was something of a poet, could read German, Spanish and Italian and could declaim rhetoric:

The Elopement

Now and then his father gave him speeches that had been spoken in the House of Lords, which he got by heart and delivered with all the graces of action and elocution... And the excellence of these performances was still heightened by the beauty and comeliness of his person.[6]

His rank and ability were already apparent to him when his father had gone to Ireland as Lord Lieutenant in 1709. But only a year later the political wind suddenly turned against the Whigs, and they lost the General Election of 1710. The Earl was ignominiously sacked from Ireland, and returned to England to find a Tory cabinet in power led by two able men:- Lord Oxford, a cultivated and generally respected statesman with antiquarian leanings, and the handsome, untrustworthy, amorous young Lord Bolingbroke. But the bluff Earl of Wharton was not alarmed by such as these. Supported by the other Whig magnates — called, collectively, the Junto — he threw himself into an attack on their government. So at fifteen Philip found Winchendon and Dover Street were always full of Whigs talking and plotting. Sometimes, when his father was out of town, Philip would preside over the dining room in his place. There he learnt that the new Tory government was in doubt about what to do when the ageing Queen died, and in particular what to do about the Pretender.

James III, as his supporters the Jacobites called him, was the eldest son of the Catholic James II who had been expelled from the throne by the "Glorious Revolution" of 1688. He was a melancholy, charmless young man, not at all an inspiring leader. He lived on Louis XIV's charity, in adequate comfort, at St. Germain-en-Laye, near Paris. The Act of Settlement decreed that on Queen Anne's death, the Crown would not pass to him but to the Electors of Hanover, who were understandably grateful to the Whigs for this prospect. Many Tories felt this was unfair, but none in England had dared openly say so, for anti-Catholic feeling was strong. Should the new Tory Government grasp this nettle, and even secretly invite James to be King in spite of his Catholicism when the Queen died, or should they rather try to befriend the other heir to the throne, Prince George of Hanover, their natural enemy? They spent four years enjoying the profits of government and quarrelling with each other without deciding this question. And when at last Queen Anne died in August 1714, they dithered. So Prince George hastened over from Hanover, took the Crown and dismissed them from office. He put Lord Oxford in the Tower on a charge of High Treason; Bolingbroke waited in England for a few months, then fled to France, where he kissed the hands of James as James III of England, and accepted his seals as the Secretary of State to the Jacobites. The Earl of Wharton and the other Whigs, relieved at his departure, bathed in the favour of the new King George I. And Philip's precocity soon became known at court.

During the winter of 1714-15, he had lost his boyishness and became something of a man. He was tall for his age, and looked older than his sixteen years. Thomas Herne the antiquary mistook him for twenty [7]. He had his mother's good looks and her light build, slim and lanky beside his heavy, muscular father, and had a pleasantly neglectful attitude to dress. His valets-de-chambre found it a struggle to keep him tidy. He was carefree, whimsical, over-educated and irresponsible, and if he was pampered and arrogant, he was never pugnacious. "He was ever free from an itch to contentious disputes" [8] wrote his first biographer, the anonymous author of *The Life of Philip Late Duke of Wharton by an Impartial Hand,* in the year he died. He was very susceptible to women. Whores, chambermaids and dowager ladies seemed the same to the adolescent Philip. Women were cheap in London in the early eighteenth century, and morals comfortably low. His earliest conquest is unknown, but by 1715 he was writing sentimental love verses and he had seduced a maidservant in a household in Highgate, and had settled upon her an annuity for life as a reward for her lost virtue, as he could well afford to do. Even in his vices he seemed to follow the father who had educated him so carefully.

His earliest surviving letter is one he wrote to his father reporting London news:-

22nd January 1715

Your Lordship will see by the posts that there is a strenuous opposition in the City but our friends are confident of success. Sacheverell preached a violent sermon on the 20th wherein he attributed the fire and distemper among the black cattle to the present administration. Sir Thomas Cross and Wortley Montagu are this day chosen without opposition for Westminster. They continue to talk of alterations in the Guards. We are all very well. My mama desires you would see what apples there are at Wooburn and Winchendon and order some of the best to be sent up. I am your Lordship's most dutiful son.

Winchendon.[9]

The Whig Lords of the Junto rewarded themselves in a manner they felt they deserved now that they had routed the Tories. The Earl was made Lord Privy Seal, and then on 15th February 1715 Marquis of Wharton and Marquis of Malmesbury. He was more powerful than ever. But much of the work of the government he now cast on the shoulders of the younger Whigs: Sunderland, Stanhope, Townsend and Walpole. He sought to end his days in peace. But it was not to be so. Just as his political success seemed most assured, his domestic happiness was ruined by an innocent mistress of Philip's.

Martha Holmes was the fifteen-year-old daughter of a Major General Richard Holmes. We know nothing of him at all except that he had probably been a friend of Lady Wharton's Irish soldier father. When Philip first met Martha, Lady Wharton was seeking a place for her as a Maid of Honour and had paid for the dress for her appearance at Court in February on the King's birthday. No portrait of Martha survives. But the effect that she had on Philip was catastrophic. Their courtship, at her father's London house and at Dover Street, was secret but rapid. She refused his dishonourable advances. He fell deeply in love with her. He sent her messages by his servants, sealed with his little seal engraved with the figures of Venus and Cupid and the words "Mon cœur est Vostre". His favourite valet-de-chambre, a blackamoor called Scipio, who was literate, married, and to Philip something of a confidante, now helped Philip take the only step in his relationship with Martha that seemed open to him. If she refused to be seduced he would elope with her.

So on March 2nd, clad in the dress his mother had bought her, she was stolen from her father's house in a hired carriage and driven down the narrow alleys to the outer precincts of the Fleet Prison.

The Elopement

There, in the lax days before the Marriage Act of 1753, unscrupulous clergymen could perform marriages without banns being called and without a marriage licence. And there Martha became Lady Winchendon.

Philip had not foreseen the consequences of his exuberance. As his first biographer wrote, "his Lordship was a person who never considered the consequences of anything" [10]. He sent a cheerful message from their secret lodging to his father at Dover Street the next day, telling him of the news. It arrived late in the March afternoon, and made the Marquis, who was ever choleric, very angry indeed.

Like his contemporaries, he regarded marriage as a business arrangement, not a matter of mere lust or love. He was insulted by the pennilessness of the bride that Philip had chosen. So he was soon in action, summoning his friend Nicholas Lechmere, the Solicitor-General, and obtaining warrants from the Lord Chief Justice. Then he ordered out his carriage and his footmen, collected some constables, and paid a call on Philip and Martha. It was after nightfall when they arrived, and Philip and Martha were in bed. As soon as the Marquis entered his bedroom, Philip saw how things were turning out. He tried conciliation, by kneeling before him and asking his blessing on the marriage. He did not get it. He was put in the custody of the Wharton footmen, who took him straight down to Winchendon, and the Marquis took Martha back to her father's house. There they arrived after midnight. Major-General Holmes had gone to bed. He refused to get up to see anyone. But the Lord Privy Seal and his warrants and constables were not to be thwarted. The Major-General's servants were soon paraded and two of them sent off to gaol for allegedly carrying messages between the lovers. Such tyrannical behaviour was as impotent as it was illegal. Nothing could be done to reverse the marriage.

So when the Marquis's anger had cooled and he returned home, the constables dismissed, to his bed at Dover Street, he was a sad man. Half estranged from his wife, his other children still in the nursery, Thomas Wharton had doted upon his son. Now, the heir to many generations of politically prosperous Whartons had thrown himself and his prospects away. In the days that followed the Marquis tried to get the marriage annulled, but to no avail.

The Elopement

He was sixty-six; he had done much in his life; Samuel Johnson, in his *Dictionary,* published forty years later, called a Leader "One at the head of any party, as the detestable Wharton was Leader of the Whigs" [11]. The shock of the marriage made him ill. With no more to live for, his life drew quietly to a close. Within six weeks of the elopement he was dead. On 12th April 1715, Joseph Addison wrote to Archbishop King in Dublin:

> Melancholy news of my Lord Wharton's death. He has said more than once that the affair of his son would break his heart. [12]

His funeral on 22nd April 1715 at Upper Winchendon Church, a building rather dwarfed by the huge house beside it, was held in an extravagant manner befitting the man. The Wharton bull's-head crest over an achievement of arms in the old style was raised above his tomb, with an ancient Greenwich helmet from the Wharton armoury renovated and erected to support it. And as the old rake was carried to the vault, the light failed melodramatically, and Buckinghamshire darkened under a total eclipse of the sun.

By his will old Thomas disinherited Philip of every penny of his fortune and every acre of his land that was not family property entailed upon Philip already. His last words to the new Marquis of Wharton were in his will which was opened after the great funeral:-

> I recommend it to my son to observe the advice of his mother and guardians, and to endeavour, by a dutiful and prudent behaviour, to make the best amends he can for the false step he has made. [13]

CHAPTER TWO

Descent to Avignon

>He no sooner found the reins which witheld him slackened, but, like a headstrong courser, he broke through all restraints, and ran into all manner of licentiousness...
> *The Life of Philip, Late Duke of Wharton* (London 1731).

So the world of Philip's boyhood had crumbled. The old Marquis whom he had loved would no longer preside over the great race meetings at Winchendon, Quainton and Wooburn, nor his supporters amongst the Whig magnates come down to Winchendon to dine and to admire the brilliance of Philip. Three of them, it is true, had been appointed his trustees and guardians by his father's will, but none was his friend. His mother, the old Marchioness, lived on at Dover Street, but she was to survive her husband by less than two years. Worse, because the world said that his marriage had killed his father, and he believed it, the death killed his love for his fifteen-year-old Marchioness. Before the funeral she heard of his father's death and came to seek him out at Highgate on the road to the funeral at Winchendon. When they met he said not a word. All the grief and guilt he felt for his father's death welled up again when he saw her, and he refused to speak. He left the room she had entered through another door, left the house in silence, and did not see her again for eighteen months.

We must guess (for none of his own papers survive from this period) that other matters too were a cause for his distress. Although his inherited Parliamentary power and an income of about £8,000 a year made him the most promising peer of his generation, yet he had responsibilities, both family and political, and he was a minor, not to be twenty-one for nearly five years. His land was heavily mortgaged and in the hands of his guardians, whose agents' incompetence or dishonesty was such that most of the income never reached them. And his father's cash and unentailed property, including many pictures and furnishings in his houses had been left to his small sisters. His men of

Descent to Avignon

business explained that all he owned was such income from his family's entailed land as his guardians allowed him, and the use of five ancestral mansions. Of these the oldest and most distant were Wharton Hall in Westmorland and Rathfarnham Castle near Dublin, both semi-fortified Elizabethan houses. The thought of their rugged "barbarousness" aroused a shudder in his urbane eighteenth-century heart. He could not live at either. Not that he often went to Wooburn, near Marlow. There he owned a large estate, a manor house, an old Bishop's palace, a race-course and, beside it, a curious tree-house in a beech-tree from which earlier generations of his family had watched races. The manor house was Philip's grandfather's favourite residence, and he had built on to it a gallery a hundred and twenty feet long to house his unparalleled collection of Lelys and Van Dycks, according to Lipscombe's *Buckinghamshire*[1]. George Vertue[2] says that the gallery and the pictures were always at Winchendon, but I regard this as unlikely since the fourth Lord Wharton's chief home was Wooburn. He had never modernised the moated Bishop's palace there, however, and only its gardens, with a bowling-green and "wilderness" were kept up.

At Winchendon too there was a bowling-green and "wilderness" but they were the least of the glories of the place. The gardens there were as fine as any in England. They were intersected with topiary and box hedges and elaborate trimmed beds in the formal style, and guarded with figures cast in lead or cut in stone. Three acres of kitchen garden with heated brick walls provided food for the household, and rare figs were tended in greenhouses and oranges in the large orangery which stood between the stables and the house. The stables themselves, where the Marquis had kept at stud old Careless, the fastest horse in England and ancestor of Eclipse, reflected the quality of his bloodstock. The wooden cornices inside the stables were carved; there was decoration on the mangers and racks, and even part gilding on some of the ceiling. From outside they were less spectacular, being of brick, and were easily outshone by the gleaming new white stone of Winchendon House itself, built in the plain pre-Palladian style. To the east of it lay the famous Dutch garden; behind was the view over the vale to Quainton, and in the garden beside the bowling-green was the small brick tower that Philip's father is said to have kept his mistress in, but which was actually a hunting tower built for gentlemen to take the air in without muddying themselves in the countryside. The grounds around were spaciously formal. To Philip's Augustan mind it was a paradise.

In London, on the other hand, neither Danvers House nor the Dover Street mansion were his to enjoy. Not being entailed Wharton property, they both passed under his father's will to his sisters' trustees. The deer park in Chelsea was bought by his cousin Lord Abingdon as a speculation, and Danvers House was demolished to build Danvers Street. Philip had to move into his grandfather's residence at St. Giles-in-the-Fields, between Denmark Street and what is now the Charing Cross Road. The district was unfashionable if not seedy, and the house ancient, having been the "capitalis mansio" of the pre-Reformation hospital of St. Giles, but it possessed a sizeable garden. His sentimental attachment to the place stopped him ever moving to Mayfair. Within a few years he was commissioning Laguerre to paint the ceilings. Vertue[3] says that Philip also commissioned Louis Chéron the historical painter who had worked at Chatworth and Boughton to decorate the interior of one of his houses, but whether it was the house at St. Giles is unknown.

Here he came after his father's funeral. London was the natural home of a young nobleman seeking amusement or debauchery. He went to the opera to ogle King George, and dawdled in the coffee houses, Pontacks in Lombard Street to talk Whig politics, and Buttons or the St. James's coffee house where the fond couple Addison and Steele held court. Addison was now a Secretary of State, and Steele sat in Parliament for one of the Wharton boroughs, and was writing a short but laudatory life of the late Marquis.

Or Philip would seek lower company, for the manners of London Society were still extremely coarse. Although brothel-keeping was illegal, and occasionally pimps were whipped, whores were common and were blatantly used by the better class of citizen. Some of the most famous of their convenient and comfortable salons were now in their heyday. It was almost an honour for a pretty country girl to be picked up by Mother Needham and employed by her in her rooms in Park Place, St. James's. Never had this trade been so well organised before.

Worse vice attracted young decadents. Titillating homosexuality and sodomy were practised, though never mentioned openly. Veiled hints by contemporaries suggest that Philip was happy to enjoy anything extravagant, sensual and perverse.

His cleaner friends passed their days in coffee houses, chocolate houses and little clubs, talking a great deal about duels, love and politics, and complaining about the decline of letters and the growth of new commercial wealth. They paid calls on one another in their sedan chairs, drank, took plentiful snuff (a recent innovation), gambled with cards and dice, complained of boredom and thought about dress. Clothes were richer than at any date since. Men of wealth wore heavily embroidered great coats with huge sleeves and gilded braid buttons. Lighter frock coats were not yet in fashion. It was an age of manicured hands, plucked eyebrows and much make-up for men. Their shoes had high heels; their linen cuffs and cravats were elaborately edged with lace, their sword-hilts were gilded, and their long, many-buttoned waistcoats were wrought with embroidery. On most occasions a full-bottomed wig, spreading over the shoulders, would be worn. But for an informal morning visit the coat and the wig was dispensed with in favour of a bright dressing gown of embroidered Indian silk and a night-cap or silk cloth wound round the head like a turban. Dress, and not manners, distinguished the gentleman from his servant.

In society Philip saw as little as possible of his three guardians, who were not congenial men. The Duke of Kingston's chief interest is that he was father of Lady Mary Wortley Montagu who, years later, called him "A man of pleasure, far too fine a gentleman to be a tender or even considerate parent"[4]. Charles, Earl of Carlisle, had been appointed First Lord of the Treasury on the Accession of George I. Vanburgh was building Castle Howard for him as a stupendous statement of Whig wealth and self-satisfaction. Concern with the work there left Carlisle no time to share with Philip their mutual passion for hunting. Nicholas Lechmere was the small but self-important Solicitor-General who had found Philip and Martha in bed together that unfortunate night in February.

Philip, finding himself controlled by these three old politicians, sought legal advice, hoping that his marriage would have ended their power over him. But it hadn't. So he and they considered what on earth should be done with him. Their deliberations were watched by many, for the Wharton connections were wide. The family of Smailes, attorneys of Richmond, Yorkshire, who were hoping to continue as the Whartons' agents in the North, wrote lengthily to one another about their new master:

> My Lord Marquis is very kind and promised me anything he can do for me. It is not yet known what will be done about him, whether to travel or to go to Cambridge, but I hear the latter (though it is a secret) for he told Jack he would go to the University and offered brother Robin to be his chaplain [5].

They and many a hopeful young Whig politician admired him. The Tories hated him as a spendthrift and a roué. "Mr Palmes tells us Lord Wharton is excommunicated" wrote dull Sir Thomas Cave, who hated Whigs, barely two months after Philip became a Marquis, "'Tis but what the whole tribe deserve" [6].

The year 1715 drew to a close with party feeling once more disturbing Britain. Half of the nation was in rebellion for the cause of the "Pretender", James III. The 'Fifteen was a belated Jacobite protest at the accession of George I the year before. The standard of James Stuart was raised in Scotland at Braemar by Lord Mar, lately Queen Anne's Secretary for Scotland. But he was no soldier, and he infected the rising with his own incompetence and indecisiveness. Lord Oxford was arrested in London just before the rising; the affable Duke of Ormonde, a popular commander, fled the country; Lord Bolingbroke was already in France as James III's Secretary of State. So all over Britain, where little rebellions broke out, they were unco-ordinated and virtually leaderless. And in the face of it, the Whigs acted with their customary efficiency. They suspended the Habeus Corpus Act for a year, detained numerous Tory members of Parliament and Jacobite leaders, and borrowed Dutch troops to strengthen their small standing army. After two battles on the same day, Sherriffmuir and Preston, the rebellions in Scotland and England respectively were ended. James himself arrived in Scotland, late as usual, for Christmas, and stayed long enough to give credit to the rumour that he was crowned at Scone. Then he was persuaded to flee and save his life to preserve his cause. He spent less than six weeks on the island he had not visited since he was in the cradle.

Only in Westmorland was Philip affected by the Jacobites. At Appleby, twelve miles from the crumbling towers of Wharton Hall, the leaders of some rebels found Philip's local bailiff, a Mr Bains, and tried to discover from him where the town's excise money was hidden. When he could not or would not tell them, they locked him in the Moot Hall and left him there.

The Whigs in London exacted revenge for having been frightened by the 'Fifteen. They and King George were determined to teach the Jacobites the lessons of rebellion. Nicholas Lechmere arranged the prosecutions. In the following months, nineteen Scottish peerages were forfeited by attainder. Lords Kenmure and Derwentwater were beheaded. Many a lesser Jacobite suffered much, dozens were hanged and hundreds transported, and all had their land confiscated. And while the ragged bands of the humbler captured rebels, whose chief crime was ignorance, were brought in chains to London, they suffered the worst winter of the century. The Thames froze over, and a jolly fair was held on the ice. Almost anything could be bought there, from great haunches of beef to little printed souvenirs of the Ice Fair. It was almost as popular for Londoners — including Philip presumably — as the spectacle of the execution of Scotch Jacobites.

Philip was left to his own devices this winter whilst his guardians chastised Jacobite rebels. But they then decided that he should go abroad to finish his education. His father had mistrusted English universities, so he was to go to Geneva with a learned Huguenot tutor called Dusoul and an allowance of a thousand a year, which Philip thought a trifling sum, but it was the size of the income of a rich gentleman. Otherwise he approved the plan. He enjoyed learning and had never been abroad. So he, Dusoul, Scipio and a few other servants set off as soon as the bitter weather permitted them.

They sailed from Dover, arrived in Holland and crossed the Low Countries into Germany. But soon he was irked by his dull and dictatorial tutor. So he hired a long train of servants to dilute his company — footmen to stand on his carriage, and running footmen to jog beside it — and took to calling Dusoul his "secretary". His throng of lackeys and his two sets of coach horses amused the Princes of the little states of eighteenth century Germany. They liked ostentation. And they knew that England was ruled by a few noblemen, and that one of the greatest, a friend to the Hanoverian succession, had been called Wharton. Philip was given a knighthood. He wore its insignia and sash every day, until it was suggested to him that doing so was slightly absurd. The Landgrave of Hesse gave him some horses and a gold snuff box. In Hanover he met the Czar of Russia, Peter the Great, a huge, wild, courtly and clever barbarian who ate with his fingers and was in love with his wife — both of which were unusual — and who was addicted to war and travelling. Within two years the Czar had tortured his son to death. He was on his way to besiege the town of Schönen, and was inspecting Hanover whilst George I (who owned it and disliked him) was absent.

Philip did not care that the Czar was unsuitable company for an English Marquis to be seen with, but was hugely impressed by him. He offered his services in the Czar's attack on Schönen. Luckily, since he was not brave, he was refused.

By now he had decided that life in Geneva with Dusoul would be intolerable. His thoughts turned towards France. Paris was the centre of the civilised world; and France was prohibited territory to his Huguenot tutor. So, as summer was beginning he took an abrupt leave of Dusoul on the frontiers of Switzerland, crossed Lorraine and Champagne, and by the end of July he had arrived at Paris with his servants and with a bear cub he had bought on the way.

Paris was full of Jacobite exiles from the time of the Revolution — mostly Irish — and rebels who had fled after the 'Fifteen — mainly Scots. Harry Bolingbroke, lately James's Secretary of State was still here, but had been sacked by James for revealing secret Jacobite plans for the 'Fifteen to an ex-nun called Claudine de Tencin whilst enjoying her bed, since her other lovers had passed them on to London. Bolingbroke's hobby was now to tell anyone who would listen how hopelessly incompetent the Jacobites were. But everyone else that Philip met in the English Coffee-house seemed to support the Jacobites. To Philip, whose Whig education had taught him that James's followers were adherents of the devil, this was all very strange and new.

He was soon intimate with Thomas "Penny" Winnington, out from Christ Church on secret business for his uncle, Lord Oxford. According to a slightly unreliable contemporary report, Philip "Does not leave him for one minute by day, and lies with him by night" [7].

Probably through Winnington he met the Jacobite Mr Gwynn, who was one of the host of spies, agents and political informers who operated a web of intelligence across Europe, working more widely and as efficiently as the post office. He told Philip how good, how wise and how misunderstood the Pretender was; how James was a true Englishman, George I a foreigner; how the throne was James's by hereditary right, whereas George had usurped it, how England was governed by a corrupt party system and not by the will of the people, and how the ancient liberty and honesty of England and Englishmen could only be restored by James III.

The novelty of these ideas (which echoed those of everyone he met) thrilled Philip. He was converted, like many English continental tourists less romantic than he. Or at least he was flattered by Jacobite attention to him and rather intrigued by their cause. Within a month of his arrival he had written submissively to King James and he asked Gwynn to arrange an audience for him at Avignon, where the Court now loitered.

The news of the apparent conversion of the only man of rank to have joined the Jacobites since the disastrous failure of the 'Fifteen soon spread around Paris. He helped to broadcast it himself. He was dangerously indiscreet.

Once after dining at the Duke of Leeds' Paris house, he yelled merrily to Scipio that he was agreeing terms with the Jacobites: "You shall be a Page of the Backstairs to the King", he called, "and I shall be a Duke, and have the Garter" [8]. This tactless remark so embarrassed everyone who heard it that he soon had to give a hundred French livres to help destitute fugitives from the 'Fifteen to save his reputation with the staider Jacobites.

Soon Harry Bolingbroke invited him to dinner to persuade him to change his mind and leave them. But his bland talk did not quench Philip's new zeal. The glories of James's cause and of his empty titles and honours had been too strongly impressed on his imagination by Gwynn. He knew Bolingbroke had failed the Jacobites, and said so.

He felt that he himself could do better.

Lack of money broke his Parisian reverie. His income was controlled by Dusoul, who still fretted at Geneva. So he set out thence to bully or charm him into giving him more money. He succeeded almost as soon as his train of followers (who included Winnington) had reached Switzerland. Perhaps Dusoul hoped to buy back Philip's respect. He failed. Education at Geneva looked duller than intrigue in Paris; so Philip immediately set out for France once more, leaving his tutor with the bear cub. "That you may not want company", he said, "I have left you the bear, as the most sociable companion in the world that could be picked out for you".

On the road back he received gratifying letters. Mar and Ormonde, James's "Ministers" at Avignon, and then His Majesty James III himself, had graciously replied to the ingratiating letters of the seventeen-year-old son of their great Whig enemy:

> Your sentiments well deserve not only an ample forgiveness of what's past but an entire forgetfulness of all the mistakes of your family [9].

So Philip turned the coach-and-six off the Paris road to head for Avignon. But he did not tell anyone, even Winnington, their destination. To be known to visit Avignon, and to be seen amongst the penniless Jacobite exiles there, was a crime punishable in England by death, and Avignon was full of Whig spies. So the party stopped at Lyons, and from there Philip wrote to King James and Lord Mar, asking for a secret interview. He sent a stallion as a gift, and reminded them of his considerable influence in England; he said he could have fourteen of his followers returned to the House of Commons in James's interest, and that he could raise men in Buckinghamshire, Westmorland, Wiltshire and parts of Yorkshire to fight for him, armed (ironically), with the swords and muskets at Winchendon that had been used against the Pretender's father in the Glorious Revolution of 1688. With the enthusiasm of a convert he swore:

> I do solemly declare and take Almighty God to witness, that I will always to my last breath serve nor know no other King

of England but James III and his lawful heirs. Whenever I depart from his interests, which now are, and, I hope, always will be, inseparable from those of my country, may the same God Almighty pour his most chosen curses on me and mine. I beg this letter may be kept with care, that if ever I should depart in the least from my present sentiments, it may rise up in judgement against me, and show me to be the least of mankind [10].

These generous protestations were marred, however, by a final request that he should be made a Knight of the Garter as a reward for his loyalty. But refusing Jacobite requests for James's honours was a common enough task for Lord Mar. He told Philip that until the King was once more on the throne of England it was his policy to give no Garters. But he gave Philip a commission as Colonel of Horse in the army that would (in theory) rise in England to restore James when the time was ripe. And an ADC called Erskine was sent to his lodgings at Lyons to bring him secretly to pay his respects to his new-found Sovereign at Avignon.

With Erskine he left Winnington and the band of servants and sycophants and travelled to Villeneuve, which lies beside the Rhône on the opposite bank to Avignon. Here Erskine and he took lodgings. But their beds were not slept in. That night they engaged a discreet boatman to carry them over the river. There, in the old Palais des Papes, Philip was allowed interviews with Ormonde and with Mar. Then on October 5th 1716, he was shown into the presence of James Edward Stuart, James III of England and VIII of Scotland.

CHAPTER THREE

Treason

> I begged an alms, as a poor Peer,
> And nicked the credulous Chevalier;
> What better service could I render
> Than out-pretending the Pretender?
> *The Humble Petition of Philip Duke of Wharton* (c. 1730).

Although he was still only in his twenties, King James had not weathered well. Philip saw his years of exile, hope, hard work and dashed expectations marked clearly in his face. But if the face was sad, it was also noble, and almost kingly. Philip thought James looked like Charles II. But in character he was very different. James was not a merry man; he was weak-minded, quite conscientious, rather self-absorbed, and devotedly Catholic. He had the solemnity and stubbornness of his ancestors, but not their fire. But Philip charmed him. Most Stuarts were susceptible to flattery by good-looking young politicians: James had once been taken in by Bolingbroke. Philip talked to James about elections, parties, votes, armies and invasions, and James was verbally seduced. Before their audience was half through he had agreed to make him Duke of Northumberland, that title having lately become vacant.

So, even before his eighteenth birthday, Philip was to be created a Duke. Now, in addition, James was offering him a job. He wanted someone of high rank to go as his representative at Cassel to investigate whether the Landgrave of Hesse's daughter might be available as a wife for him, and Philip seemed the man. Philip knew that political employment meant political power, and accepted keenly. James said he could take a Jacobite Secretary with him as "A kind of humble companion," in Lord Mar's words [1]. Who should this be? He rejected an English Protestant veteran of the 'Fifteen called Mr Alexander in favour of a French Catholic called M. Panton.

With him he retraced his steps to Lyons, where Winnington and the servants had been waiting, and then hurried towards Paris to prepare for his vist to Cassel. Lord Mar sent letters to him full of advice urging him to keep his visit to James a secret. Philip wrote back feebly, admitting that Winnington "fancies I have been at Avignon, but it is only a fancy"[2]. An angry letter from his tutor at Geneva which reached him on the road failed to dampen his high spirits.

At Paris the unkept secret of his visit to James, his new title and his proposed embassy, made him a great figure amongst the Jacobites. Bolingbroke wasted no time in sending him a note, recommending a servant to him. Philip told Avignon, "My answer was I would take no spies in my family"[3].

He did not set out for Germany immediately because King George was at Hanover, and he refused to pay the public respect that would be required of him if he passed nearby, to a monarch he had just renounced. So he stayed in Paris in October, warning the Landgrave of Hesse's chief Minister, General Rank, by letter, of his impending arrival. Rank replied, "Venez donc nous joindre"[4] and Philip waited impatiently to set out.

But his antics had been noticed by the Whig world. His new friends were frightened by his indiscreetness. "If he continues talking as he does now" wrote the exiled Jacobite Lord Southesk from Paris to Lord Mar, "He can't fail of being soon in our condition, which were a great pity"[5]. Philip even quarrelled with King George's Ambassador in Paris, Lord Stair, and played practical jokes on him. He merrily smashed the lantern hanging outside the Embassy because it was (naturally) unlit on the Pretender's birthday, and snubbed him publicly when he tried to extract Jacobite secrets from him. Then after a dinner with him on the birthday of George Prince of Wales he lured two of his ADC's to the English coffee house where they were obliged by him to drink "Confusion to the Whigs" because, (as he said) "The Tories are too many for you to drink any other health". But wild behaviour was proving expensive to him. When he had spent the money that Dusoul had given him in Geneva, he borrowed £2000 from the kindly old Queen Dowager Mary of Modena at St. Germain. But on the 19th November he was out of money again. His guardians in England refused him more funds, alarmed by his behaviour: London Society had heard that, "all the news here is about the young Lord

Wharton having changed these principles which the late Earl took so much care to instil early in him."[6]

So he had no choice but to write glumly to King James to tell him that financial pressures forced him to postpone visiting Cassel. Then he spent a week taking his leave of Winnington, Queen Mary and Paris and exchanging abuse, for the last time with Lord Stair. The latter summoned him at the moment he intended departing. The invitation was surprising. The two were not on speaking terms. But Philip was never one to hesitate, and as he thought that Lord Stair could do him no harm, he drove promptly to the Ambassador's house. Lord Stair was still in bed. But at his levee that cold dawn he was prepared to surprise the young Marquis. Philip was shown in to see him.

Was Lord Wharton aware, asked the Ambassador, that warrants had been issued in England for his arrest? Was he aware that he was to be charged with treason the moment he arrived home? It would be best, the Ambassador went on, if Wharton stayed on in Paris, and there he would be safe: he could receive an allowance from the Whigs, and tell him, in exchange for a free pardon, all about the activity of the most notorious Jacobites.

Philip had been caught out by the Whig secret service. But he followed his instincts and this at this tricky moment, and he was right to do so. He guessed that Lord Stair knew nothing of importance about him or about his Jacobite activity. So he smiled down on the night-shirted Ambassador. He never listened to gossip, he said, nor cared what the vulgar said about him, and Lord Stair should do the same. He would not delay his departure for London. But he would help Lord Stair, he said, by setting out especially early, in order that Lord Stair would have the first opportunity of alleging these crimes in their proper place, if he dared:— in an English court of Law.

"I am sorry for you," the Ambassador said, as Philip took his leave: "You are very bold."

Early in the morning of November 26th his post-chaise, closely followed by others containing Panton, Scipio and his servants, began a leisurely four day journey to Calais. There he bid an emotional farewell to Panton whilst waiting for a favourable wind, and smelt out an ill-disguised secret agent of Lord Stair's called Colonel Boyes who had booked a berth on the same small vessel to keep an eye on him. To avoid any risk of being discovered Philip handed back to Panton all his incriminating Jacobite papers before embarking. And the short voyage to Dover went peacefully. Thence they clattered and jolted for two days over the horribly muddy roads of Kent, arriving a fortnight before Christmas 1716, and Philip's eighteenth birthday, in London.

There he conscientiously befriended the principal English Jacobites, old Lord Strafford, John Menzies, and his own Scotch cousin, George Lockhart of Carnwarth. He wrote regularly to Lord Mar, and he told him that he was still prepared to proclaim James III at Cheapside when asked to do so. But on the other hand, he dealt firmly with the stories about his disloyalty sent to London by Lord Stair, complaining about him to Addison and the two of his guardians who were in the government. He said, "I have laid the fault of everything upon Lord Stair's behaviour, and have heaped many coals upon his head." [7]

Wiser men kept out of London during Christmas week, for the dirty capital was in the grip of smallpox. Philip's ugly old mother, the dowager Marchioness, went down with it at Dover Street. Lady Mary Wortley Montagu, who was now in Constantinople with her husband the Ambassador, had already learnt there of smallpox inoculation, but she returned to England too late to help Lady Wharton, who by 5th of February was dead at Aylesbury on the road for Winchendon. She did not leave Philip a penny, though on her death her Irish estates passed to him and raised his income to £14,000 a year. He was oblivious of this, for he himself had caught smallpox and was dangerously ill. But after a few days his fever passed, he broke out into great scabby spots and his expensive doctors announced that the worst was over; though his complexion was damaged, his life was safe. A few days more, and he was visibly recovering. He began a long convalescence.

Meanwhile Martha, his titular Marchioness, was living off £500 a year from his estate, and keeping a coach of her own with the Wharton arms on it. Hearing he was ill she suggested that she should come to London to nurse him. "She sent for leave to come to him, though she never had the Smallpox", a contemporary wrote on 8th February. Philip "sent her word she might, that he hoped she would catch them and die, for that he wanted to be rid of her." [8] Wisely, she stayed away in the country.

When the spring of 1717 had turned to summer he was sauntering out to coffee-houses and attending Court functions again. On 17th July Handel's *Water Music* was performed for the first time and he was doubtless at Greenwich to hear it. His frivolity and friendship for Whigs were observed with distress by the Jacobites. His letters to Avignon had grown few. "He minds nothing but the pleasure of the place he resides in," George Lockhart told Avignon. "There are other strange contradictory stories related to him; what to credit I know not, but I dread the worst" [9]. By the height of the summer when he retired to Winchendon to avoid the dusty stench of London, Philip had given up the pretence of being a Jacobite and was concerned only with making arrangements for a departure for Ireland to see his new Irish Estates. The new Lord Lieutenant of Ireland, a neighbour of the Whartons in Dover Street, the middle-aged Duke of Bolton, whom Swift called "A great booby," [10] was going to Dublin, so Philip joined his party, and from Winchendon they set out together along the rough roads to Holyhead in late August thronged by grooms, footmen and bodyservants. Philip's jocularity on the way caused comment. Eustace Budgell, the Controller General of Ireland, told Addison "He did several things at the places where they lay, and in the gaiety of his heart, which some think had well been let alone." [11]

At Holyhead in Anglesey they left their carriages and embarked on the Viceregal yacht. Within the day they were at Dublin, where the notables of the city and society met them on the quay to be impressed by the company Philip was keeping. They remembered his father, and after he had displayed his wealth and his wit to them during the next few days they paid him the unusual honour of admitting him to the Irish House of Lords, although he was more than two years short of twenty-one. He took his seat at the same time as the recently created Whig Viscount Hillsborough, who was older and so entitled to his place, but was almost as notorious a rake. Thomas Hearne described Hillsborough soon afterwards as "A very handsome man, and is one of those wanton immodest gentlemen that a year ago used to ride naked, and make strange work with young women." [12] Like the Duke of Bolton he owned a house in Dover Street.

Hillsborough was rich and as famous as a seducer of women, but rather feeble-minded under his flamboyance, and he was soon ready to follow Philip everywhere. Perhaps it was he who introduced Philip to the literary men of Dublin who assembled regularly at Jonathan Swift's Deanery. Here Philip met Lord Molesworth, an independent-minded old Whig who had known his father, and Edward Young, the sharp but melancholy scholar of 38 who was later famous as the author of *Youngs Night Thoughts,* and Dean Swift himself, who was now working on *Gullivers Travels.* Swift was a bitter man, condemned to castigating the British government (whose favour he would have liked) on behalf of Ireland, a land he despised. He was not a Jacobite but called himself a Tory, and carried on a correspondence about the moral decline of Britain with other Tories like Pope. He and Young were not entirely won by Philip's wit and love of reading. They disapproved of his heavy gambling and the wild masquerades he and Hillsborough were soon giving in Dublin and at Rathfarnham Castle, the chief mansion of his mother's inheritance. This stood amid Dutch gardens and greenhouses, said to rival those at Hampton Court, a mile or two south of the city. Once Swift publicly rebuked him for playing practical jokes, his famous "frolics": "You have had some capital frolics," the Dean remarked;[13] "Take a frolic to be virtuous; take my word for it, that one will do you more honour than all the other frolics of your life."

Philip admired Swift and liked Edward Young a great deal, but paid no attention to the good advice they gave him. As Marquis of Catherlough (his Irish title) Philip toured his wide lands in Meath, at Catherlough itself and around Rathfarnham Castle, demanding his rents from the tenants. That he was not entitled to the rents because he was not yet of age did not deter him. Parliament said he was of age, he (inaccurately) declared, and who were they to argue? Irish Society was amused by this even if his tenants were not.

In the Irish House of Lords — whose attendance was so low that it generally met in a room no bigger than a drawing room — his eloquence surprised even his friends. Reports of the speech he had made in support of the Whigs immediately after taking his seat delighted Addison in Whitehall as much as it dismayed James's Ministers at Avignon. His youthful ridiculousness was changing into something more like brilliance. In September he was made a Privy Councillor of Ireland. In November he was elected Chairman of the Committee that drew up the congratulatory address to the King upon the birth of a grandson. He was the highest-ranking peer to attend regularly at the House. He knew that if he was an energetic enough supporter of the British governors of Ireland, they would have to reward him.

But as well as recognising that he was clever and spoke finely, the Whig Lords of the English Government saw that he was dangerous. His guardians had endured enough trouble from him already. He was very young, self-important and unreliable. They decided to reward him in a way which would not give him government office or bring him into their midst. They did not give him a political job. Instead they made him Duke of Wharton.

It is an honour unparallelled since the Fifteenth century for the Government to make a Duke of one who is not of Royal blood and not yet even of the age of majority. Some comment on this was made at the time. It was said by some that King George had always intended to give old Thomas Wharton the Dukedom, and that he had been forestalled by the latter's death, so Philip was honoured on his father's behalf. This was implied from the terms in which old Thomas was described in Philip's new patent of nobility. But on the very day he died, the old Marquis of Wharton had been made Marquis of Malmesbury and of Catherlough, in addition to his earlier title, Marquis of Wharton. So King George had every chance to have made him a Duke had he chose. It was clear that Philip's merits alone were being rewarded now. A cryptic letter of Addison's, written in October 1717, to the Duke of Bolton, confirms this:

> "I have since, with great pleasure, taken the first opportunity to lay before His Majesty your Grace's request on the subject with regard to the Marquis of Wharton. I am to acquaint you that the King has very readily complied therewith in consideration of the great zeal and duty that Noble Lord has shown in His Majesty's service [14]."

Just after Philip's nineteenth birthday, his patent was sealed.

Now he stood in the first rank of the Hanoverian as well as (secretly) the Jacobite peerage, although he was still almost two years short of the age of majority.

Success made him yearn for London once more. So, knowing that the Viceroy was leaving for Holyhead on 8th January, he arranged berths for himself and his new intimate Edward Young aboard the Viceregal yacht, and sailed from Dublin, leaving a surprised Swift with the information that Philip had left the Whigs in spite of his dukedom, and would henceforth be a Tory.

CHAPTER FOUR

The Hell-Fire Club

> His free manner of life, and an education rather polite than learned, with a ready turn of wit which he was master of, did not fail of getting him many admirers.
> *Life of Philip late Duke of Wharton* p.7.

Three days later he and his party were back in London, anticipating that his social and political success would be as great there as they had been in Dublin. But awaiting him the new Duke found several creditors' duns, no cash to pay them, and the necessity of redeeming all his furniture from his sisters' trustees to whom everything of his father's, except entailed land, had been left. Not wishing to sell the old Marquis's furniture (and in particular his pictures) the trustees were pawning it to an unpleasant man called Colonel Francis Charters; and in recovering it Philip became deeply in debt to him.

Francis Charters, who vied with Thomas Guy (founder of Guy's Hospital) as the meanest man in London, was a Scotsman who had followed the haughty but slightly impoverished Scottish peers to London after the Union in 1707. To these, who were too proud to be outspent by the rich English gentry and nobility, he became necessary as a money-lender. His house which stood starkly alone between a stable yard and some vacant building land at the newer end of Bond Street was often full of them. Lord Stair, Philip's old enemy the Ambassador in Paris, paid most of the expenses of his Embassy with Charters' gold. Charters was an unpleasant but remarkable man. Only once was he worsted, and then by a London Jury. They found him guilty of rape, though he was universally known to be impotent: he only escaped hanging by paying an enormous bribe to the Government for a pardon.

The Trustees chose to pawn the furniture at Winchendon and Wooburn to Francis Charters rather than to sell it. The reason for this was they wanted Philip to be able to redeem it, one day, for himself, to refurnish those houses. It was a kind thought. But Philip himself was at present in no condition to redeem anything. And Charters was a hard man to be indebted to, as Philip was soon to learn.

Many of Philip's rents were not being paid. His agents made the most of the fact that he was a minor and so had no legal redress against them. Those in the North, the family of Smailes, attorneys of Richmond, were typical. They managed the estate around Wharton Hall in Westmorland, his lead-mines in Swaledale, and in Richmond (Yorkshire) the forty "burgage" houses which his father had bought because their occupants had votes in the borough Parliamentary elections.

The Smailes's sent Philip an annual account of the rents and outgoings. It varied little from year to year. In 1720 fifteen houses were described as "in decay", and so yielded nothing. The rent from the others was £87 a year. But some was unpaid; only £58.12.0 was collected. Out of this, the Smailes's incurred expenses; bricks £3.12.0, workmen's wages £7.15.0, the Smailes's own expenses of £5.0.0, and salary of £8.0.0, totalling £57.12.8. So of his £87 a year rent due Philip received less than one pound. Or rather he did not receive it. It was not worth the Smailes's while to send such a trifling sum up to the Duke in London. He got nothing [1].

And he could not sell his entailed land to pay off the ever-mounting debts because he was still a minor; and because his guardians gave him as little money as they could, and because he was now a Duke and very extravagant, he quickly ran up prodigious debts.

He consulted the most eminent counsel available, William Peer Williams, who was later to become a very rich Member of Parliament and the compiler of Peer Williams's Law Reports. At the consultation Philip indulged in one of his famous "frolics". He found the lawyer being shaved. Would His Grace be shaved also, asked the barber? He would, said Philip. But when it was done he searched his pockets for some money, and found he had none, not even sixpence. The barber protested effusively and probably truthfully that it was an honour to shave a Duke; he would not dream of taking payment for it. Philip said that he would repay him; he sat the barber in Williams's chair and shaved him himself, very badly, in a manner indicating his superiority to such things. The barber was thus paid.

On February 12th Williams sent his written opinion to Philip. He said that he needed a private Act of Parliament to enable him to sell his entailed land whilst still a minor. It would be terribly expensive. But Philip was desperate, and he asked Williams to press ahead with a draft Bill.

Usually only the sharp spur of extreme necessity would induce an early eighteenth century nobleman to take an interest in his own financial affairs and in this Philip was typical of his time. To the man of fashion, wealth was not to be nurtured but to be enjoyed lavishly and even wastefully, for this was the age of splendour. Although only twenty years later a landowner might encourage the agricultural use of lime or the cultivation of turnips, in the first quarter of the century he still thought any pastime more rural than severe landscape-gardening was vulgar. The ostentatious baroque architecture of Vanbrugh, Talman and Hawksmoor had not yet been replaced in his favour by the restrained pastoral classicism of the Palladians; similarly his long wig, heavier than those of any of his European contemporaries, his pompous gold-buttoned coats and the velvet liveries of his numerous footmen proclaimed that dress was still a matter of show rather than elegance. He was a townsman rather than a countryman: even if the last centralised British Court on continental lines had fallen with the charred walls of Whitehall twenty years before, it had been replaced as his chief place of resort not by his country house but by any of the three thousand London coffee or chocolate houses and the little clubs that sprang up in them. He was distinguishable from the rural gentleman by his wealth, by probably being a Whig rather than a Tory, and by holding religion in some contempt, though he would seldom admit to atheism or miss church on Sundays. Church, like any ball, assembly or masquerade, provided him with a chance to ogle and flirt with a lady whom he might want to marry if she was rich and a virgin, or seduce if she was already married. His advances would often be accepted. An unmarried girl (as Lady Mary Wortley Montagu complained) lived a desperately dull life under close domestic supervision, her parents' chief concern being to preserve her virtue so that she could marry well, and her own chief desire being to marry so that she need no longer be virtuous. Marital unfaithfulness, though never approved in society, was everywhere tolerated, and was made both more time-consuming and more titillating by the rigorous standards of outward behaviour that gentility demanded. Conventional respectability prevented a lady from speaking to a gentleman in private except on an afternoon when she was known to be accepting calls and therefore might be interrupted at any time. Many innocent drawing-room relationships were therefore practically forced into becoming full-blown bedroom affairs. But a married lady had little enough else to entertain her: cards, gossip, and the acquisition of a monkey, a parrot, a blackamoor page, expensive jewellery, lace or silk dresses passed her hours until the evening brought relief with a ball or a box at the opera.

Her lover, also spending from October to June in London or "the Town" as he called it, would pass most of the day with his own sex. He woke at ten in his house or lodgings in St. James's or in one of the newer streets, mostly off Piccadilly, and after being dressed and shaved by a servant or two and fending off any tradesmen or welcoming any humble friends who were waiting for him below, he would at once walk or be carried in his sedan chair to the particular coffee-house his friends patronised. Here his arrival would coincide with that of the daily and weekly newspapers, which he would read and discuss through the rest of the morning in an atmosphere of congenial pipe-smoke, warmly insulated from the smell and thievery of the lesser Londoners, bustling, sometimes gin-sodden, often desperately poor, down the narrow and ill-paved alleys outside. They would bow or bare their heads to him and give him the clean edge of the lane if he walked past them to call on a late-rising friend nearby, or to take the air and look for acquaintances in St. James' Park. Soon after 2.00 he returned to his own house or to a friend's to dine with the family. His afternoon might be spent gaming, secretly seeing a mistress, sedately playing whist or cribbage in genteel company, or visiting a brothel, according to his inclination. Whether at a house of ill-fame or in Lady Strafford's notoriously respectable drawing-room he would be served tea and meet friends. Then, if there was no private ball or public assembly with music and dancing to which he had the entree that evening, he might visit the opera (now dominated by Italian artistes) or the theatre (a tragedy by Addison or some of Wycherley's bawdy) at the Haymarket, Drury Lane, in the little piazza theatre in Covent Garden, or at the new one in Lincoln's Inn Fields. Otherwise he attended a club meeting at a coffee-house or tavern. His club was a group of friends bound together by any common interest — political, convivial, theological, debauched or actually violent — and might have rules as formal as those of the Order of Freemasons, whom Philip was soon to join, or as few as those of Sir Roger de Coverley and Will Honeycombe's fraternity described in *The Spectator*. With its members he supped at about ten, and afterwards he returned home, or, if he was a wild young "gallant", arrogant and pugnacious, he practised merry and barbarous pranks, breaking windows and the heads of elderly night-watchmen, before returning to his bed in the early hours with his coat soaked with brandy or blood.

But in many ways Philip was not typical of the young man of fashion. Primarily his concerns were of more social and political importance and (when he was sober) on a higher intellectual level than those of most coffee-house wits. A roomful of men of literary repute waited for him to rise in the mornings; if not Sir Richard Steele or John Gay themselves, then Dr. Freind or Dr. Arbuthnot (each of whom lived in Dover Street where Philip had been brought up) or Ned Ward or Colley Cibber, the convivial Poet Laureate so decried by Pope. The principal London hosiers, tailors and bootmakers would also have called on him early, anxious for the honour of his patronage. And at his levee which the throng of callers and miscellaneous servants would have turned into a busy affair, one or two Members of Parliament might be seen trying to obtain his instructions as to how they should vote that day in the House. When at last in spite of the confusion his toilet was completed and all creditors and those who had not been admitted to see him were turned away with the information that His Grace was not at home, he was ready to set out to pay a call, to visit a coffee-house, to drive in his coach or to walk in the Mall. In any event he would not step outside his house alone, but surrounded by friends and servants, and seldom on foot. Although he might be conveyed just a street or two in his sedan chair, he would usually travel by carriage, with footmen standing behind the coachman and running-footmen jogging beside the horses. To travel in less style, whether in a light "chariot" or in anything less than a coach-and-six was a betrayal of dignity.

But often enough his dignity was betrayed in other ways. At five o'clock his well-attended coach was more often outside Mother Brett's house of expensive ill-fame or at a club where he would play Faro, Loo and mere dice for fabulously huge stakes, rather than outside the drawing-room of a respectable hostess whose day at home it was. And in spite of his literary interests and the inevitable patronage of the theatre and opera that this and his wealth gave him he preferred to spend the evening riotously drinking with his cousin Lichfield or with Hillsborough (who was now moving his household establishment from Dover Street to a vast new mansion beside the Duke of Montrose's on the West side of Hanover Square) rather than quietly at a playhouse. Many a night his tired servants brought him home insensible, his sumptuous clothes filthy.

In his daytime company he liked to mix poets, lords and politicians; and the Oxford friends of delicate Edward Young rubbed shoulders in the old mansion at St. Giles's with liveried thugs who carried his sedan chair and with Figg, the brother of the prize-fighting champion, who was Philip's amiable but ungainly bodyguard. Philip needed Figg to protect him not only from street-violence but also from duels with quarrelsome men skilled in swordsmanship. To be called a coward by them as a consequence was unpleasant, but to be run through with a rapier was worse.

Such an attitude was excusable only in a Duke. Only Philip's semi-regal status permitted him thus to ignore the usual rules of honour. Early in George I's reign England had only twelve dukedoms, and their holders were venerated accordingly. Each had an income ten or twenty times that of a country squire, and treated such rather as they treated their tenants. When the yeoman's furniture was of oak and the squire's of walnut, the Duke's was gilt. He wore silk, they wool; he wore jewels, coats embroidered in gold, brooches in his clothes and diamonds on his fingers. In any other country he would be a Prince; his acres and wealth were larger than those of some European monarchs. Philip's lands were over half the size George I's had been when he was Elector of Hanover.

Moreover the English peerage as a whole was now at the height of its power. It controlled the government. And in early 1718 the peers were preparing a Bill which, had it not been defeated under the effect of Walpole's spirited eloquence in the Commons the following year, would have ended the creation of new peerages to dilute its ranks. Aristocracy now seemed all-powerful. And so the young Duke had not been in London a year before he was an established leader of society.

Respectable members of society were pleased to hear that he next mastered his unfair aversion from his wife, and that his large household was suddenly put under the control of the efficient young Martha, Duchess of Wharton. Cynics suggested that because she was already keeping a house and a coach at his expense, he thought that he might as well enjoy her beauty:

> He brought her to his house: but love had no part in his resolution. He lived with her indeed, but she is with him as a housekeeper, as a nurse [2].

But at the end of the summer, the Duchess was pregnant. He was delighted and became more attentive to her than before. When he was not with her, he was usually reading, debauching, at a coffee-house or at a club.

Since Whitehall had been burnt down in 1698, London life ceased revolving round any royal residence, and the London gentleman's club was born. By the time that Philip was living in London, there were clubs for every taste: political, philosophical and literary clubs, loosely-constituted clubs for gangs of drunkards and duellists, and prim, formal clubs for the moral and pious. Some had permanently-established club-rooms. Some were so hazily constituted that they never even had a name.

Philip, as well as being clever, was also self-possessed and vain, and he had a taste for satire. He, therefore, became one of the founders of a club which primarily ridiculed religion. It was something more than an atheist's club: it was a blasphemer's club. He caught on to the current religious speculation by making a mockery of religion. Probably during 1719, in London, the Hell-Fire Club was born. He was the principal member. It was begotten of satire, Deism and arrogance.

Amongst the many London clubs already existing were some free-thinking or philosophical clubs. Religion, generally, was declining in England, and Rationalism increasing. Deism — the belief that there is a non-intervening God, not a personal one — was widespread. Its gospels were the writings of John Locke and Newton, and its prophet was to be the poet Pope. Philip's only theological gesture on his return from Dublin was to found or help to found the Hell-Fire club. It was a society about which much nonsense has been written, but about which it is not possible to say much with certainty because none of its papers (if it had any) nor any referring to it and belonging to any member has survived. Like so many other aspects of Philip's life at this time its details are extremely obscure. We can only form a picture of them (through a fog of legend) by collecting together remarks about them made by contemporaries.

The club of the Hell-Fires was founded in about 1719 by Philip and a handful of others — probably Philip's immediate friends Hillsborough, Lichfield and Sir Ed. O'Brien. It was a club for ladies and gentlemen of the highest circles, to promote sacrilege. It has been said that the Duke of Wharton was its President, but this is not so. The President was the Devil. During meetings a chair was kept for him at the head of the table, presumably vacant. The meetings of the club were usually on Sundays in the Greyhound, a small tavern in Bury Street, near St. James's Square, which they made hellish by filling with the fumes of burning brandy and sulphur. Three members called themselves Father, Son and Holy Ghost and others were patriarchs, prophets and martyrs. But their purpose was not a particularly serious one. They performed no ceremonies and they prayed to no devils. They presumptuously said that they were devils themselves; when one died, they said that he had gone to be their ambassador in Hell. Meantime, they gambled at dice, quadrille and newly introduced Faro, and ate "Holy Ghost Pie", "Devil's Loins" and "Breast of Venus" all provided on the premises, and drank a concoction called Hell-fire punch.

Because ladies, even Hell-fire ladies, could not be seen in a tavern, the club sometimes met in a riding academy nearby, where Philip used to take horse-exercise. Otherwise the club assembled in members' houses in Westminster or in Conduit Street, near Hanover Square. It is even said to have met in the Royal palace of old Somerset House, on the Strand, which is not impossible. Or it split into two or three small groups and met separately. By 1721, a couple of years after its foundation, it had three or four dozen members.

Ladies (but not whores) were always admitted as easily as men, and were as enthusiastic as any, according to an appalled letter of complaint about the club written to the Archbishop of Canterbury:

> There's some ladies among them sometimes, which are as bad as the men, only they don't go to the Tavern.... There was one of them put a pillow under her coats, and being asked by a gentleman if she was with child, she answered that miracles were not ceased; nor was she not the first Virgin that has been with child, and that she would soon bring forth her first-born, that he should wrap it up in swaddling clothes and lay it in a manger. Many other things I've heard of them, but cannot write of them, they are so shocking to human nature[3].

But not a single contemporary suggests that any sexual orgies or Satanic rituals took place, as has been suggested. It is as we would expect; whores were too cheaply obtainable down St. James's to be wanted at jocular club meetings. And Satanic ceremonies would in practice be as boring as church, which was what the Hell-Fire Club members met on Sundays to avoid.

Legends about Philip's club have been transformed into stories about the activities of a group that met thirty years later under Sir Francis Dashwood, and Lord Sandwich. About the last a contemporary poet, Charles Churchill wrote —

> Nature designed him, in a rage
> To be the Wharton of his age;
> But having given all the sin,
> Forgot to put the virtues in.

It is said that in the 1750's Sir Francis Dashwood started a Hell-Fire Club which met near West Wycombe in some caves (now open to the public and called "The Hell-Fire Caves" by the present owner) where the Black Mass was celebrated by the club members, who included John Wilkes, Sandwich, the Duke of Queensberry, George Selwyn, Bubb Doddington and Hogarth. And in between and during their satanic ceremonies, it is said that they performed indecencies on ladies dressed as nuns.

But all this too is a myth. Sir Francis Dashwood indeed founded a pseudo-medieval club for his elderly political cronies, and John Wilkes, when he wanted to attack Dashwood in Parliament, pretended that it practiced all kinds of immorality. But it was never called the Hell-Fire Club by anyone. There is no evidence to suppose that any of the famous "members" listed above (except Sir Francis) had anything to do with it, nor that anyone indulged in its reputed naughtinesses. Black Masses were unknown in its day, and wild sex was never practiced in semi-public discomfort by portly politicians who could buy it more conveniently in London. The caves at Wycombe were not a subterranean sexual paradise, but merely Sir Francis's disused chalk-mines. Some stories of the debauched doings of the club there and elsewhere have recently been invented by the writers of dirty books, and the rest are a compendium of garbled pieces of social history from other ages, misquoted anecdotes from Rabelais's *Gargantua,* Sade's *Justine* and Ned Ward's *Secret History of Clubs,* and half-remembered old stories brushed up and stitched together by energetic and credulous historians and historical novelists of the nineteenth and twentieth centuries. Their chief or only interest lies in the fact that the name which has been stuck to Dashwood's is the name of Philip's "satanic" club.

Philip's friends in the Greyhound who had first coined the phrase "Hell-Fire Club" pretended to regard their brotherhood as nothing but a joke. But the fact that they bothered to found it at all in the face of predictable public abhorence (for they never tried to keep its meetings secret) shows that they had a more extrovert purpose than mere private amusement. The club existed less to gratify its members' personal whims than to shock the outside world of ordinary churchmen and clubmen by shamelessly mocking and satirising them. So Philip and the other Hell-Fires, though they would never have admitted it, had some sort of serious purpose in founding the club: they wanted to proclaim a profound contempt for established morality, thought and theology.

The Hell-Fire Club

Perhaps the inspiration for Philip's Club came from the man who was becoming his closest friend in the year that the club meetings began, the discontented mystic Dr. Edward Young. He had returned from Ireland to continue tutoring the Earl of Exeter's young son at Burleigh House. The Duke had found him at work when he went to stay there sometime in late 1718 or early 1719, and he urged him to leave and come and join his own great household in London. Young, who had a secure job at Burleigh, refused. Philip insisted, promising to give him an annuity of £100 per annum for life. Young weakened, and at last agreed, and soon found himself the odd mixture of tutor, companion and jester to the Duke. He flattered and amused him, and kept his Latin polished. Joseph Spence, who had been at Oxford with Young, recorded [4]:

> The Duke's most vehement ambition was to shine in the House as an orator. He therefore drove Dr. Young down to Winchendon with him, where they did nothing but read Tully (i.e. Cicero) and talk Latin for six weeks — at the end of which the Duke talked Latin just like Tully's. The Doctor, (on some other occasions as well as this) called him 'a truly prodigious genius'.

Edward Young shared with Philip a taste for poetry and politics, as well as for the classics. But Philip was fifteen years younger than he, and did not enjoy his feeling for sentimental melancholy which gave him a weakness for graveyards and which constantly intruded into his poetry. Otherwise their writings — for Philip too was writing poetry — were often so similar as to be indistinguishable. During 1719 the Doctor was working on a tragedy, his most successful play, ultimately dedicated to Philip, called *The Revenge,* and he acknowledged as Philip's some lines in it:

> By this — thy partial smile — from censure free:
> Twas meant for merit, though it fell on me...

His *Night Thoughts,* a long, fine, gloomy poem of which Sam Johnson approved about the hopelessness of human aspiration, was written and

The Hell-Fire Club

became famous throughout Europe after Philip's death. It is said, rather surprisingly, to have been Robespierre's favourite reading. Its principal character Lorenzo, a grand decadent cynic with no sense of things eternal, whom the author seeks to convert to a wiser outlook, is said to be drawn from Philip:-

> Lorenzo, hast thou ever weighed a sigh?
> Or studied the philosophy of tears?... [5]

Though the poem contains no internal proof of Lorenzo's identity, Philip was the nearest man to Lorenzo that ever lived.

CHAPTER FIVE

The Heir

> Where boasting ends, there dignity begins;
> And yet, mistaken beyond all mistake,
> Lorenzo's proud of being proud;
> And dreams himself ascending, in his fall...
>
> Edward Young. *Night Thoughts,* 8.

On March 29th 1719 to Philip's delight Martha gave birth to a son. She was given complete control of the child, and was encouraged to keep him under a throng of nursery-maids at Winchendon where the air was good, and where Philip was constantly with them. The boy was called Thomas after his grandfather, and styled the Marquis of Malmesbury. And his chief godfather at his splendid christening was the King, George I himself.

For Philip had changed his mind about opposing the Whig government. The Whigs, after all, seemed fairly strongly established in power, so he associated himself with them. And accordingly in May, two months after the boy's birth, he left Martha and set out to seek court favour on one of George I's expeditions to Hanover. He joined a bevy of ministers, lackeys, placemen and mistresses to trail across a surprised Europe, and only left them at Rotterdam before they were about to enter the German states which had once known him as a Jacobite. He thought it wise not to risk being unmasked in their company. Instead, staying at Rotterdam, he made two new friends. One was a lady called Madame Vanhutyt, whom he seems to have seduced; but he was obliged to pay her a pension for it. The other was Lord Spenser, the literary son of George I's favourite minister the Earl of Sunderland. When after a week or two Spenser left for Utrecht in pursuit of the Royal party, Philip excused himself from accompanying him by saying that he wanted to go to Italy, and actually returned to England, summoned by the ill news of the death of his patron Addison. And back in London his uncertain financial prospects

The Heir

required his immediate attention.

By the spring of 1719 counsel had settled the final draft of his private Act of Parliament, and after large fees had been paid for its promotion in Parliament it had received the Royal Assent on April 18th. The Act vested most of his Yorkshire land in trustees who were to sell them to raise cash for him to buy certain "estates from which the said Philip Duke of Wharton takes part of his honours and titles," and to redeem certain "goods, pictures, householdstuff and furniture in or about the Mansion Houses of Winchendon and Wooburn." In theory, therefore, he was to repurchase or redeem from Colonel Charters the Wharton property of which the old Marquis had disinherited him. Unfortunately, however, as soon as any of the land was sold, he spent the money on himself rather than on redeeming any of his debts.

He was distracted by matters of state. King George's principal English advisers were now Lord Stanhope and Spenser's father, Lord Sunderland. Stanhope, a soldier, had been the old Marquis of Wharton's Member of Parliament for Cockermouth and then Wendover. He had been First Lord of the Treasury and Chancellor o. the Exchequer, and now would have been almost Prime Minister were it not for the King's ill-justified trust in the artful Sunderland, once a son-in-law of the Duke of Newcastle and now a son-in-law to the Duke of Marlborough. He had lately exchanged offices with Stanhope to become First Lord of the Treasury, and since Addison had died and Lord Cowper the old Lord Chancellor had resigned, he shared royal favour only with Stanhope.

But they were not confidently secure in power. In March 1719 a Spanish fleet had actually sailed for England intending to invade on behalf of James III. Had not the Highlanders who had risen to support it been dispersed at a skirmish near Glenshiel and the fleet been dispersed by the weather, this threat to the Hanoverian dynasty might have been more serious than either the 'Fifteen or the 'Forty-five. As it was, it merely left the British Jacobites with some improbable legends, their excellent songs, and a few more martyrs.

A greater threat to Stanhope and Sunderland came from within the Whig party in Parliament itself. There Lord Townsend and his brother-in-law, Robert Walpole, each of whom had lately been in the

Government, plotted against them. They had discovered that their best ally against the King's Ministers was the King's son, George Prince of Wales, who was no cleverer than his father, but who had the advantage of an ambitious wife who could dominate him. The King found the Princess Caroline too attractive and too intelligent by half, and he hated her as much as he hated his son. In November 1717 he had driven them both from the claustrophobic atmosphere of St. James's Palace to set up an independent household in Leicester Fields, (now Leicester Square), where those Whigs who were out of favour at Court such as Walpole, Townsend and Lord Cowper, assembled around them. Lady Cowper, a former lady-in-waiting to the Princess, kept a diary of all they did, and in particular how Walpole and the formidable Princess handled the Prince:

> Walpole let the Prince lie with his wife, which both he and the Princess knew, [1]

she icily reported.

Although Philip was too young by one month to enter the British House of Lords when the Parliamentary session began on November 23rd 1719, he began attending this busy little Whig opposition court around the Prince and Princess of Wales. He principally admired the old Earl Cowper, who had been an ally of his father as Lord Chancellor both under Queen Anne, and, for a time, under King George, and before that the youngest Lord Keeper ever. Cowper was an oratorical Whig of the school of the 1688 Revolution, who now felt that political corruption was souring the idealistic principles which he associated with the Good Old Cause. His generosity and wisdom contrasted with the shady self-interest of others around the Prince of Wales. Philip, who had no quarrel with the Ministers on any point of principle, but had joined the Leicester Fields group because it simply gave him a political niche, became Cowper's political apprentice, and was constantly in his company at Leicester Fields or at Cowper's House in Great George Street.

So it was as an opposition Whig that Philip on 21st December, 1719, immediately after his twenty-first birthday, entered the British House of Lords. He was introduced by his former guardian the Duke of Kingston and his friend from Ireland the Duke of Bolton. He found most peers had retired for the short Christmas recess, but this did not deter him from commissioning a full-length portrait of himself in Parliamentary robes clutching a copy of his Private Act, to celebrate the occasion. The painter was probably Charles Jervas, the over-fashionable court painter. But Christmas passed before Philip could practice his famous rhetoric and display in Parliament the classical learning that he had lately been brushing up with Dr. Young and the Duchess at Winchendon.

On the first business day, February 4th, he was appointed to a Committee to investigate a scurrilous pamphlet, *Mr. Higg's Merry Arguments from the Light of Nature* containing a lewd story about an apple-woman and some pippins. The Committee, chaired by the Archbishop of York, met regularly, to express its indignation, for a fortnight. But when on the 17th it had failed to trace the author or the printer of the pamphlet, it had to be content with ordering all copies that it could find to be burnt by the common hangman in New Palace Yard and in front of the Royal Exchange, and with summoning the Judges to ask them how the writers and printers of scurrilous pamphlets could be found and punished. The judges evasively retorted, "There are very good laws against profaneness and immorality... The chief grievance is their not being put into execution."[2] This being agreed upon, the Committee met no more.

Philip was struck equally by the prudery and the ineffectiveness of the Committee. Like the Government itself, it had no instruments of detection except informers and rumour. It could not even find the printer of a pamphlet which had been published within a mile or two of Westminster. He realised that serious plots against the Hanoverians could be brewed without detection under the noses of the government.

He had also been attending the Lords' debates, opposing a Government Bill to give the House power to decide appeals from the Courts of Ireland. The Irish House of Lords had always been the supreme court for Irish appeals, and Irish Lords like his friend Lord Molesworth (who sat in the British House of Commons) were understandably annoyed at the British government trying to take the right from them. Philip, as a member of the Prince of Wales's opposition clique, was delighted at the chance of opposing the Government with them. He fought the Bill vehemently, and so was suddenly hailed by the Irish as their champion. The Whigs of the Government and those who supported the English domination of Ireland such as Bishop Downes, the English bishop of Killalla, were correspondingly disgusted:[3]

> We foreigners and our foreign friends are railed at by the natives... The Archbishop of Canterbury himself is not now half so much in favour as the Duke of Wharton... though the one has done them more service than ever this Duke will do.

By the end of February he had not missed a day's work at the House. He was beginning to make a mark at Westminster and in the world at large as an irritant to Stanhope and Sunderland. Then domestic disaster struck him.

His small son, Thomas Marquis of Malmesbury, the godson of the King, was now eleven months old. In February his parents had been preparing to bring him with them from Winchendon to London, where the Parliamentary session was beginning, but news had reached them of an outbreak of smallpox in London. Philip himself was not at risk, but neither Martha nor the boy had had the disease, so to let either come up to London with him was out of the question. Although Martha, who distrusted him when he was away from her, had begged to be allowed to come with him, he had required her to stay with the child and had left for London alone.

But a month in the country without Philip had proved too much for her, and contrary to his orders she drove up to London with the boy to be reunited with him. Then the boy caught smallpox, as he had feared. The most eminent doctors were helpless. By the end of February the child was dead.

There was a pathetic funeral at Winchendon on March 4th. The boy was buried with almost as much state as his grandfather had been less than five years before. On the brass plate on the child's tiny coffin in the church are inscribed the words,

The Heir

> The Right Honourable Thomas Marquis of Malmesbury, died 1 March 1719/20, aged 1 year wanting 7 days.

Philip's fury was terrible. He blamed Martha for the death, and since he loved her little and perhaps resented being tied to her, he treated her heavily. She was only allowed to stay near him until the funeral. Then he banished her to the house he was least likely ever to want to visit, his ancestral seat, Wharton Hall in Westmorland. Even his father had only stopped there on occasional election-tours of the North. Daniel Defoe, who visited Westmorland in this very year, described the county as, "the most barren and frightful in England".[4] Philip provided her with £500 a year by a deed executed in May 1720, "upon her going to reside at Wharton Hall"[5]. For nine months we hardly hear a word of her. To the pale young London Duchess the lichened peel-tower with its strong gate-house, its old banqueting-hall and its great kitchen, must have seemed another world from the drawing-rooms of London. No alternations had been made to its gaunt walls since the days of Queen Elizabeth. No member of its owners' family had visited it for nearly ten years, and it probably had not seen a Wharton lady since the time of the Civil War. Its chambers were covered with tapestry and panelling and mould and Cromwellian armour from the days of the fourth Lord Wharton, Philip's grandfather. The servants there were uncouth and their language almost incomprehensible. The local gentry who came to gaze at her beauty and hunt in the great deer-park must have seemed no better. The only neighbour she might have met in London was Sir "Kit" Musgrave, the Tory M.P. for Cumberland. He passed by frequently, for he was demolishing his own castle at Hartley, a bare two miles from Wharton Hall, in order to move the stone from it twenty miles northward to where he was improving a more suitable mansion for himself at Eden Hall near Penrith. The distant melancholy sound of the demolition of Hartley Castle must have seemed to Martha to emphasize her loneliness.

Philip hid his relief at her departure and his grief at his son's death in brandy, gambling, women and politics. He found it easy to be busy. On April the 4th 1720, exactly a month after the burial, there was a debate in the House of Lords on the first reading of the most disastrous enactment of the age. It was called the South Sea Bill.

Early this year a scheme whereby the whole of the British national debt would be taken over by the South Sea Company and paid off out of its profits had been suggested to the Ministers. It looked plausible and highly desirable. On February 1st the Commons agreed to it in principle. The price of £100-worth of stock in the Company rose accordingly to £160, on the public expectation that the purchase of such stock would be an excellent speculation. Now, when the South Sea Bill came to be debated in the House of Lords, Philip's friends were aghast at the possibility of its success. If such a financially miraculous scheme was allowed to work, then the government would become immensely popular. And the members of the opposition, whether Tories or renegade Whigs around the Prince of Wales, would be in a hopeless situation. So at the debate, Philip's speech — which was reported at length — attacked the whole scheme. The true reason he did so was not because the scheme would be bad for the country, but because it would be good for the Government. He was supported for the same reason by Lord Cowper, and by the Tories led by the old general Lord North and Grey, a secret Jacobite. But in spite of them the South Sea Bill passed the House of Lords, and the price of stock soon stood at £300. Philip retired from Westminster in disgust and spent the rest of April gambling and drinking vilely at Newmarket, where his expensive race-horses were running.

He was not the only person to notice what a weak position the political clique of the Prince and Princess of Wales at Leicester Fields was in. The Prince was also uncomfortable about his relations with the King, who hated him so much that it was possible an Exclusion Bill might be passed, barring his succession to the throne. But the Leicester Fields party had still one hope. Walpole's power over the House of Commons alarmed the Ministers. So while Philip was squandering guineas on his race-horses and Cowper was enjoying in Hertfordshire the well-earned Easter rest of an elderly man, Walpole and the Prince of Wales struck a deal with the Ministers. Walpole agreed to allow them all of his Parliamentary influence in support for their Government and the Scheme, and would help to arrange a rapprochement between the King and the Prince of Wales. In return, he and Townsend were to be admitted to the Government. But their supporters — notably Philip and Cowper, who were respectively regarded as too young and wild and too old and idealistic — were to be left out in the cold, because there was unfortunately no room for them in the Government. The news of this Whig reconciliation and his own betrayal came as a complete surprise to Philip. As he wrote desperately to Cowper:

> 24th April 1720   Newmarket
> My Lord...
>   The reconciliation in the Royal Family is so sudden... Your Lordship may easily judge the consternation which I am in at present, who have so lately flown in the face of the Ministry and attached myself to the Prince...[6]

Having been out-manœuvred in politics, he now lost heavily on the turf. Cowper's wife recorded in her diary on May 4th that "Wharton at Newmarket has lost a great deal of money. Some say £13,000."[7] So he was thoroughly grumpy when he returned to see Lord Cowper before the Parliamentary session began on May 9th. But Cowper had little cheer for Philip. His own serious political career was past, and he sought no rewards from the present Ministry, which he regarded as irredeemably corrupt. Philip, on the other hand, sought power. He once more appeared regularly at the Lords' debates in the first two weeks of the summer session. Then, after May 20th, he attended less often. Both he and the English public had lost interest in the squabbles at Westminster. They thought only of the stock-jobbers and share-brokers who crowded Exchange Alley, and of the ever-rising price of South Sea Stock.

CHAPTER SIX

The Bubble

"Ask you why Wharton broke through every rule?
'Twas all for fear the Knaves would call him Fool..."
Pope. *First Moral Essay* 206-7.

The value of South Sea Stock rose another £100 to £430 during April, and was still rising inexorably at the start of the 1720 summer Parliamentary session. Philip had always opposed the South Sea Scheme; but now that it seemed that it was working, he succumbed to buying stock. Together with two of his old guardians and four other Dukes, some Tories like Lord Orrery and many Whigs like the new Lord Chancellor Lord Parker, he subscribed for £2000-worth of stock on June 17th. And like them also he began to speculate in the large amounts of stock which was already on the public market. He ineptly punted tens of thousands of pounds on over-priced South Sea Stock throughout the summer of 1720.

Being as short of ready cash as always, he had to borrow to pay for it. His debts and the interest he owed upon them soared, until his huge indebtedness became generally known, and his ducal word was no longer enough to gain him credit. Then he had to sign notes of hand and execute bonds for his borrowing from such as the Rev. Hilkiah Bedford, the nonjuring Bishop, on June 22nd. By then the price of stock had reached £890, and everyone who had invested in it now believed themselves to be many times richer than they had been before. The wise sold out. Others, like Philip, borrowed more money on the strength of their notional wealth and enjoyed themselves. Ostentation and extravagance spread everywhere. New carriages filled the narrow dirty lanes of the fashionable town and the crowded thoroughfares to Change Alley in the City.

Not until July did Philip realise that he had over-spent to such an extent that his debts could only be repaid if he sold land. And the general inflation had at least increased the value of his manors and

The Bubble

farms. He decided to sell his Irish estates first.

Accompanied as usual by Edward Young, Scipio, and a train of servants, he sailed for Dublin at the beginning of July. Within a week, before Dean Swift and old Lord Molesworth had recovered from their surprise at his arrival, he had found buyers for all his land:

> Lord Wharton came over on Sunday last, and has sold all his estates in this kingdom. I hear Lord Chetwynd has given him eighty-five thousand English pounds for Rathfarnam; General Wynn sixteen thousand English pounds for his estate in County Cavan; and Mr. Wesley thirty thousand pounds for that in the County of Meath. [1]

Although the sale to Lord Chetwynd of Rathfarnham Castle, his chief Irish seat, was cancelled, Wesley paid for the land in Meath, which ultimately became the principal estate of the Earls of Mornington, forebears of the Duke of Wellington. With the forty-five thousand pounds from Wesley and General Wynn Philip planned to return immediately to England. He sent a note to Swift:

> Dear Dean   Monday Morning
>   I shall embark for London tomorrow. It would be necessary for me to take leave of Lord Molesworth on many accounts; and as Young is engaged in town, I must infallibly go alone, unless your charity extends itself to favour me with your company there this morning.
>   I beg you would send me your answer, and believe me sincerely
>   Your faithful friend and servant
>   Wharton
> P.S. If you condescend so far, come to me about eleven of the clock. [2]

Meanwhile, the price of South Sea Stock, in which Philip had invested so much of his wealth, had reached a new peak in London. In late June it was at £1000. And still it gradually rose. Then it stopped and began to waver. The news from France was bad. John Law, the

Scotsman who controlled the finances there, was in great distress. The inflation he had caused with paper money was destroying the purchasing power of the notes he had floated. Inflation, even greater than that which England was suffering from, had undermined his elaborate schemes. The value of his stock was to fall disastrously. In London, a few people were wise enough to learn caution from what was happening in France. They sold their stock, and caused the price to slip slightly down from £1000.

Once on board ship again bound for Holyhead, Philip's thoughts turned to Oxford. Young had shown him his college there, All Souls', sometime earlier in the year, and had pointed out that work on the new buildings designed by Hawksmoor for the great quadrangle there had been left uncompleted. William Steuart, a son of the Earl of Galloway, had stopped financing the work when he had paid for only one tower, although he had grandly commemorated himself for this inadequate generosity by setting a plaque to his own praise in its wall. Philip, wanting to emulate the late Dr. Radcliffe, who had recently left a fortune to clear a new quadrangle adjoining All Souls' for building the new "Camera" there, had suggested that he himself might pay for the range of buildings to be finished. The fellows had not taken him very seriously. But now as his carriages, loaded with cash, jogged across Anglesey on the road to Bangor and England, he declared that he would make his word good.

He agreed the details of the work with a builder at Harwarden where they stopped to visit the rectory of a fellow of the college named Gardiner. For the new structure Hawksmoor's design was to be followed in detail, provision even being made for "finishing the staircase in Bletchingdon," a sort of local marble.

The college was appropriately grateful when they heard of Philip's proposed generosity, and showed it when Philip's party reached Oxford a day or two later. Oxford, so far as its leisure-loving dons held strong views on anything, was a Tory stronghold. It had been Charles I's capital in the Civil War; it had only been held down by force at the time of the Jacobite rising in 1715; its Earldom was held by the last Tory Prime Minister, Edward Harley; and it was full of angry high-churchmen of the school of Francis Atterbury, frustrated at being overtaken in the race for Bishoprics by low-church Whig

The Bubble

clergy. But although Philip was a Whig, the well-fed fellows of All Souls' liked what they saw when Young introduced Philip to them; and liked him even more for his opposition to the government than for his wit and generosity to them. They accordingly ordered a stone to be cut and placed high up in the wall of the proposed building, where it rests today, bearing a laudatory inscription in Latin which reads, when translated,

> The Most Noble Prince Philip Duke of Wharton caused this building to be erected at his own expense, to adorn with his munificence the Muses he had cultivated with scholarship and affection, in the year of our Salvation 1720.

The work at All Souls' was the only building he ever commissioned; his short and hectic life allowed him no other chance to patronise architecture. His extravagance prevented him from even repairing the houses that his ancestors had erected. So the All Souls' building is the only surviving edifice to his memory.

In return for the inscription and the promise of a Doctorate of the University, all he had to do was to pay for the building costs. £250 was duly received by the college before he left Oxford. But after this he was unfortunately never in a financial position to spend another guinea on the erection of his building. Years later the college had to sue his executors to obtain the balance of what he owed them.

While his mind was on architecture, the Lord Lieutenancy of Buckinghamshire had become vacant. Philip thought that the office should be his, as it had been his grandfather's and father's before. But in the two and a half years since the Whig ministers had made him a Duke, they had profoundly changed their view of him. He was no longer the spoilt child of the Whigs. They did not make him Lord Lieutenant of Buckinghamshire.

So he left Oxford in August indignant at this, and intent on fighting the Ministers harder. He saw that to do so he must arrange some sort of union between the Tories and the party of himself and Cowper — who had been dubbed "the Grumbletonians" — the old Leicester Fields Whigs who had been deserted by Walpole and Townsend. The Tories knew he was in this mood. On August 2nd,

The Bubble

Edward Harley the connoisseur son of Queen Anne's Minister wrote:

> Duke Wharton is again turned Tory... He has promised to be the friend of the Church and University, says his family have too long been enemies to both, and that he will endeavour to make amends for what they did.[3]

In fact Philip merely wanted to ally with the Tories not to join them. However vigorously he opposed the Whig government, he still thought of himself as Whig and a follower of the fortunes of the deluded Prince of Wales. He hoped that the Prince and his ambitious Princess might one day shake off Walpole's baleful influence and become leaders of an independent opposition Whig court once more.

Pondering these things, Philip travelled back towards London. The road along which his coach-and-six lumbered was thick with dust. A heat-wave anticipated the spacious summers and great harvests of the later years of the 1720's. In London itself the streets were sticky with decaying garbage and rank with the smell of the poor. The great men of England had dispersed from the humid centre of the capital. Sunderland was still in Hanover with the King. Most others had houses on the outskirts of London, as well as seats in the country and houses in town. The Prince and Princess of Wales were at Richmond. Lechmere was at Campden House, on top of the hill above Kensington. Secretary of State James Craggs the younger had found quiet as a neighbour of Lady Mary Wortley Montagu and Pope in the newly-fashionable riverside village of Twickenham. Robert Walpole, when he was not in Norfolk, was at Orford House, beside Chelsea Hospital. His gardens too ran down to the river. The breeze off the Thames, though filthy with the language of watermen, at least wafted air that was cool and free from dust.

Philip had come to London at this unfashionable time to spend some or most of the forty-five thousand pounds that he had raised in Ireland on South Sea Stock, which in late August stood at around £800. When he had done this he went to Winchendon.

The price of stock would never be so high again. The bubble was breaking. The Company had never begun to trade seriously, but had issued vast amounts of stock of no inherent value. When there were

The Bubble

no more new buyers for it the price stopped rising, and when some prudent stockholders began to sell, the price slipped downwards. Soon it fell as steeply and as steadily as it had once risen.

But Philip had fled from the stench of the metropolis before the fall became apparent. He passed the new few months entertaining and gambling on a Ducal scale at Winchendon, which was large enough to accommodate the whole Hell-Fire Club. On September 19th there was, "A great foot-race at Woodstock for £1,400... between a running footman of the Duke of Wharton's and a running footman of Mr. Dilston's of Woodstock, round the four mile course..." [4] The Duke of Wharton's man lost.

In London throughout the autumn the price of South Sea Stock fell lower, and the cries of the thousands who had punted upon its success grew louder. All felt, with some reason, that they had been fleeced. When Parliament met on December 8th and stock was worth less than £150, their aimless murmuring took a more coherent turn. The Members of Parliament blamed those who were closest to the centre of power in the State, and especially Sunderland, for the disaster. Robert Walpole, on the other hand, who had joined the supporters of the Scheme very late, who had spent most of the hectic summer quietly in Norfolk, who had himself lost (mildly) from the Bubble and from bad debts including one of £9,000 owed to him from the now nearly bankrupt Lord Hillsborough, Philip's debauched friend, looked different. He seemed to be the single member of the Government who was unsullied by the incompetent and dishonest management of the Scheme.

Philip heard glumly of the crash of his own fortune and the rise of Walpole's popularity. He detested Walpole not only for deserting him and Cowper and the other opposition Whigs, but also for temperamental reasons. He hated him as only a proud, elegant and thwarted young Duke could hate a successful, unscrupulous and very fat Norfolk squire; and one of his driving passions from the time of the betrayal of the Grumbletonians was this hatred.

Parliament sat for ten days from December 8th. Lord Molesworth said in the English House of Commons that the Directors of the Company were the butchers of their fatherland, and should be sewn up in sacks and thrown into the river, as the Romans had treated people guilty of patricide. In the House of Lords Philip opened the first debate, calling for the Scheme to be discussed. On December 20th he drove forward a broader attack on the Ministers. He made many remember the lofty oratory they had admired in him when they had been his father's guests at Winchendon ten years before, and which had so impressed the Irish House of Lords. It was now arrogantly and wittily directed at them. With information from his wide range of anti-government acquaintances, from rich Earls in their London palaces like Lord Strafford to penniless poets in the "Spiller's Head" in Clare Market, he exposed and listed numerous corrupt dealings between the Directors of the South Sea Company and the Ministers. His speech attacked in particular the most guilty Minister, Sunderland. But it tried also to discredit Sunderland's colleagues, Walpole especially. On Philip's demand the books of the South Sea Company were ordered to be laid before the Lords, which annoyed the Commons, who also wanted them. The importance of Philip's two speeches is shown by the fact that they and the single one of Lord North and Grey's are the only speeches that the *Parliamentary History* bothers to report for the whole of this important short pre-Christmas sitting. When Parliament rose for the Christmas recess, it was clear that the Ministers would be hard pressed to remain in power and that the strongest opposition speaker in the House of Lords was Philip.

So with the prospect of political success in view he went down to Buckinghamshire for Christmas: not to Winchendon, but to Wooburn, because he wanted to be near Lord Cowper's seat at Panshanger in Hertfordshire, and also to be nearer to London. And here he was rejoined by Martha Duchess of Wharton, whom he had allowed to end her Northern exile at Christmas 1720. Perhaps he had been won by her affectionate letters, perhaps by the memory of her prettiness at barely twenty-one, or perhaps he may genuinely have missed their curious, coarse relationship with one another. And he certainly wanted to avoid the social stigma of being separated from his wife now that he was trying to become a respectable politician. With her near him again he roused the Buckinghamshire gentry to support him against the Ministers and to demand revenge for the wrongs of the South Sea Scheme, entertaining them in his usual regal manner: Wooburn House possessed all the paraphenalia required for rustic festivity, even tents for a fair in its grounds. He told Earl Cowper, "I have found my County neighbours entirely satisfied with my behaviour in Parliament." [5]

In his letters of the 2nd and 4th January he calls himself a disciple of Cowper and a follower, still, of the Prince of Wales. Whatever the world might say of him, and whatever the appearance of his alliance with the Tories — Lord North and Grey, Lord Bathurst, Lord Bingley, and Bishop Atterbury — Philip was not a Tory. He was of a different Whig school to Walpole and the Ministers, but he was still a Whig. He and his fellow "Grumbletonians" would say that they still stuck to the principles of the 1688 Revolution. He was a lover of liberty, a bit of an idealist, and no follower of monarchism, "arbitrary power", Popery or Jacobitism.

The Justices of the Peace asked him to chair the County Quarter-sessions. This would give him a chance of stirring up more county feeling with a Charge to the Grand Jury: such charges being political harangues rather than invitations to do justice to miscreants. But Cowper told him that it was no time to meddle in County business. He was to come straight back to London. Things there were rapidly coming to a head and he was needed.

CHAPTER SEVEN

The End of the Hell-Fire Club

"Lorenzo! This black brotherhood renounce;
Renounce St. Evremont, and read St. Paul."
Edward Young, *Night Thoughts*, 7.

Back in the Lords on January 9th 1721, Philip opened a new debate on the South Sea Scheme with becoming vehemence [1] in a House full with more Parliamentary peers than were seen at Westminster at any time except in a national emergency: nearly a hundred. He and Cowper were joined in the attack by the Tories, but they all fought with more gusto then cohesion. They put forward different reasons for the failure of the South Sea Scheme, and they blamed different people for it. Worse, they were soon deflected on to the question whether the Ministers had technically behaved illegally by appointing the Directors of the South Sea Company as their delegates to supervise the Scheme. The House divided on this point, and the opposition, after being told that they were wrong on it by the lawyers in the House, were outvoted by 63 votes to 23.

But the heat of this debate on January 9th 1721 welded the motley bands of Grumbletonians and Tories in the Lords into something like a party. Those who opposed Stanhope, Sunderland, Walpole and the South Sea Scheme, disagreeing with each other on everything except opposition, now rallied behind Lord Cowper and Philip. They included the Tories Lords Bingley, Bathurst, and the literary Lord Ossory; the Whigs Bishop Weston of Bath and Wells and Philip's cousin the debauched Earl of Lichfield; Scarsdale, Lord North and Grey and the ponderous Earl of Strafford, all of whom were so well-known as Jacobites as to be dangerous allies, and Francis Atterbury, Bishop of Rochester and Dean of Westminster.

Atterbury was the Tory champion of the lower clergy against the Whig Bishops. He was also the most important secret Jacobite in England. He was the natural follower of the Stuarts, a true descendant

The End of the Hell-Fire Club

of Archbishop Laud: impatient, gouty, high-church, a fine orator irritated by popularism and Whiggery and Democracy, a man of high principles but little tolerance. Swift called him a friend. Pope was to write him a sentimental epitaph. Philip considered him the most brilliant man in the Tory party.

Cowper became the leader of this unlikely alliance, and Philip, although otherwise he was by no means the most respected of the group, became their principal orator. They first met to discuss policy at 10.00 a.m., before the Parliamentary sitting began, on January 10th, the morning after the unsatisfactory South Sea debate. Then they decided that as well as attacking the Ministry in Parliament, they would appeal against them to the people at large. Their method would be to revive the old form of the "Protest", the formal complaint which was entered in the Journals of the House by any Lords of Parliament who dissented from a resolution of the majority there, and which (unlike most speeches) was allowed to be published outside the House. So when the sitting began and the Lords unsurprisingly rejected their demand that the previous day's vote be reopened, they entered a long Protest with reasons and quickly had it published throughout Westminster and London. The public, who were starved of accurate political information, received it with enthusiasm. It implied that the Ministers had stifled debate on the South Sea question, to conceal their guilt from the House of Lords.

Public faith in Stanhope and Sunderland's ministry sank still further when Robert Knight, the South Sea Company's cashier, fearing for his life after two days of questioning by Parliamentary Committee, disappeared on a yacht to Amsterdam with all the most incriminating evidence against himself and the Company. Everyone suspected Government complicity in the escape. When the news broke, Philip was busy in the House of Lords helping to cross-examine Sir John Blunt, the chief Director of the Company. Lord Stanhope himself was there. "Then a debate arose how to proceed in this unprecedented case," records Cobbett's *Parliamentary History:* [2]

> Severe reflections were made against those in power by the Duke of Wharton, who observed that the governments of the best Princes was oftentimes made intolerable to their

subjects by ill Ministers, which His Grace illustrated by the example of Sejanus, who made a division in the imperial family, and rendered the reign of the Emperor Claudius odious to the Romans.

An anonymous contemporary[3] continues:

> The Duke of Wharton says that in the time of Tiberius there was a favourite minister; the first step he took, was to alienate the Emperor's affections from his son; the next, to carry the Emperor abroad, and Rome was ruined. The Lord Sunderland was the person aimed at. To this Lord Stanhope answered: "That the Romans were a great people, and furnished great examples in their history, which ought to be carefully read, and which the noble peer that spoke last, he did not doubt, had lately done. The Romans were allowed to be a wise people, and showed it in nothing more than by debarring young noblemen speaking in their Senate till they understood good manners and propriety of language; and as there was an instance of a bad minister, he desired that noble lord would remember there was a great man called Brutus, a patriot of his country, who had a son so profligate, that he would have delivered up the properties of it, for which Brutus himself saw him whipped to death."

But as Stanhope finished his furious reply to Philip a searing pain shot through his head, and he sank fainting to the floor of the Chamber of the House. He was hastily carried to the nearby Cockpit. There his physicians, submitting him to the usual eighteenth century cure-all treatment, took some of his blood. In a few hours he recovered a little and was offered a clyster, an even more revolting remedy, a sort of anal douche. Turning to receive it, he fell heavily on to his face. When his head was lifted up he was dead.

It is said that King George I was so shocked by the death of Stanhope that he actually wept. Certainly he could not eat his supper that evening. The political world was stunned. And Philip's reputation as an orator was complete.

The End of the Hell-Fire Club

At the same time he was becoming well-known in the literary coffee-houses of London as a man of letters and a patron. His "high esteem for learning" had been praised by Mrs. Susanna Centilevre in her dedication of *A Bold Stroke for a Wife* to him in the previous year. Now he helped Edward Young to write his best play, *The Revenge*, which was naturally dedicated to him too. So was Gabriel Roussillon's *Revolutions of Portugal*, and a pamphlet against political corruption, signed *Britannicus*. He reciprocated public admiration with ostentatious display of wit and magnificence at his houses in London and in Buckinghamshire, and chiefly at Winchendon. Here he had brought from Wooburn his grandfather's unparallelled picture collection, to cover his walls with the finest Van Dycks ever assembled together. Once this year he entertained here one-twelfth of Britain's peerage: himself and the Dukes of Argyll and Dorset, the Earls of Stafford, Lichfield, Bute and Kinnoull, and Lord Bingley and Lord Bathurst, and a handful of other rakes, politicians and poets like Colley Cibber and Edward Young. The magnificence of it was unparalleled in England.

One freezing night in London early in 1721 he and Philip Dormer Stanhope, later the famous Lord Chesterfield, startled Lady Irwin with a "frolic":

> I must tell you a conceit of the Duke of Wharton's. Last night young Stanhope, His Grace and several other gay gentlemen hired a hearse and two or three mourning coaches and all the best music in the opera. They went in the coaches and put the music in the hearse and in this way serenaded the town. Their first serenade was here, where they bestowed a full half hour's music on us. the conceit was the burying of the South Sea.[4]

Soon afterwards he was introducing society to a man he said was a friend of his, Lord Rawlins. No-one had heard of him before, and underneath his embroidered clothes he was horribly crippled. But, as Philip's protégé, he was allowed the entrée to great London houses. At which Philip, inexplicably, hooted with laughter. Weeks passed before it turned out that Rawlins was no Lord at all, but of the obscurest origins, as undesirable socially as he was physically. Philip and his followers were delighted to have snubbed the fashionable world. But it is said that poor Lord Rawlins never recovered from the shock of being found out a commoner, and that he clung to his title when he subsequently became town crier of Tunbridge Wells, and that he died in a mad-house.

Horace Walpole, an admirer of Philip's wit, told Lady Ossory years later how Philip had woken up one of his mean guardians in the middle of the night to ask to borrow a pin. Such jocularity appeals little to modern taste.

Meanwhile at Westminster Lord Sunderland contrived to keep together his government after his prop, the Earl Stanhope, had died under Philip's onslaughts. It seemed that he would fail. The howl for the blood of those who were responsible for the South Sea disaster continued unquieted through February 1721. Aislabie, lately the Chancellor of the Exchequer, was sent to the Tower with his estates confiscated. James Craggs the elder, the Postmaster-General, committed suicide rather than face the Committee of Investigation a month later, by which time his son the Secretary of State James Craggs the younger had died of smallpox. Charles Stanhope, the Treasury Secretary, only escaped condemnation (to the fury of the populace) by three votes of the House of Commons because Lord Molesworth, a leader of his attackers in the Commons, was at home in bed with gout, and because Walpole used all his energies to save him.

Walpole's greatest feat was to save Sunderland himself. He disliked and envied Sunderland, but Sunderland was still the King's favourite adviser and leader of the Ministry, so he dared not let him fall lest he should fall too. And when on the 15th March 1721, at eight in the evening, the Commons acquitted Sunderland at his instigation, he showed Sunderland and the public that he was indispensable to the Government, and that Sunderland's star was waning as his own rose. Philip and Cowper were too pleased at Sunderland's embarrassment to pay enough attention to the danger from Walpole. Their party thought it unnecessary to publish any more protests during the Spring session. Philip turned to nursing his finances again.

In order to pay off his debts but allow himself a regular if small income, he conveyed the Winchendon, Wooburn, Aske and Wharton

Hall estates to Trustees, who were to raise £2,500 on them immediately, then pay him £2,500 a year, and save the rest of his income to redeem his debts. The trustees were the lawyer Alexander Denton and the bankers Thomas Gibson, John Jacob and Thomas Jacombe. But he kept one proviso in the Deed of Trust. They might sell no land to pay off any debts except with his permission.

Philip promptly spent £600 of his first £2,500 in defraying the expenses that Young had wasted trying to be elected his Member of Parliament for Cirencester at a by-election, and a further £350 as the first instalment of an annuity for young Lord Londonderry, who was in need of money because his father, Governor Pitt, was as mean as he was rich, and Londonderry presumably sold his vote in the Lords to Philip for the income. Philip's support in both Houses of Parliament had a tendency to drop away. Men in Parliament needed pensions and places which could only be given them by Ministers. It was worst for Philip in the Commons. His Member for Richmond, Richard Abell, had publicly quarrelled with him during the spring and had refused to go into opposition with him. Philip threatened to take the seat from him at the next election. But Abell knew, and Philip knew, that this would depend upon whether Wharton or the Ministers had stronger influence in Richmond when the next election came round. When in April Walpole was made Chancellor of the Exchequer and First Lord of the Treasury and Sunderland only kept abreast of him by preserving the Secret Service money for himself, most of the Wharton placemen in Parliament saw that following Philip against Walpole's growing forces was futile. There was no doubt that Walpole disliked Philip as much as Philip disliked Walpole; and the latter had enjoyed his new offices barely a fortnight before the Ministers aimed a heavy blow at Philip.

The Government knew that Philip led two lives. On the one hand he was a respectable Grumbletonian, friend of Lord Cowper, allied to the staidest Tories, and a serious man of letters. On the other hand he was a drunkard, a rioter, an infidel and a rake, whose marital unfaithfulness, gambling and debauchery were famous. So Sunderland and Walpole decided to break his power by dividing him and his Grumbletonian party from its moralistic Tory allies. They did so by impeaching the Hell-Fire Club, setting the high-church Tories, who hated immorality, at the throats of the liberal and dissipated Whartonian Whigs.

The King was accordingly persuaded to issue a general Proclamation against "horrid impieties", aimed specifically at the Hell-Fire Club. Next, the Ministers allowed the Bishops in the House of Lords to bring in an extraordinary harsh Bill, against dissenters and atheists and blasphemers, the sort of Bill which the Tories would support but which the Whigs naturally wouldn't. At the same time as the necessity of the Proclamation and the distastefulness of the Hell-Fire Club's activities were debated in the Lords, this Bill had its second reading:

> *The Lord Onslow* moved that it might be thrown out. He was seconded by
> *The Duke of Wharton*, who said he was not insensible of the common talk of the town concerning himself, and therefore he was glad of the opportunity to justify himself by declaring he was far from being a patron of blasphemy, or an enemy of religion. But, on the other hand, he could not be for this Bill, because he conceived it to be repugnant to the Holy Scripture. Then, taking an old family bible out of his pocket, he quoted and read several passages of the Epistles of St. Peter and St. Paul, concluding, that the Bill might be thrown out. He was supported by the Duke of Argyle and the Earls of Sunderland and Islay, the Lord Townshend, and Earl Cowper.
> *The Earl of Peterborough* said though he was for a Parliamentary King, yet he did not desire to have a Parliamentary God, or a Parliamentary religion; and, if the House were for such a one, he would go to Rome and endeavour to be chosen Cardinal, for he had rather sit in the Conclave than with their Lordships upon those terms...
> On the other hand, the *Earl of Nottingham*, the *Lord Bathurst*, the *Bishops of London, Winchester, Lichfield* and *Coventry* spoke for the Bill, as did likewise the *Lord Trevor*. One of these having said that he verily believed the present calamity, occasioned by the South Sea project was a

judgement of God on the blasphemy and profaneness the nation was guilty of..

The Lord Onslow replied, that noble peer must indeed have been a great sinner, for, he heard, he had lost considerably by the South Sea.[6]

The Bill was accordingly thrown out by 60 to 31. But the Hell-Fire Club was banned by the Proclamation. And, just as the Ministers had hoped, the debate showed the hollowness of Philip's alliance in the Lords. His Grumbletonians had been supported in the debate by Townshend and Sunderland themselves, and had been attacked by Lord Trevor, the Earl of Nottingham and Lord Bathurst, opposition Tories who had been shocked by the tales of Philip's filth and sacrilege. Clearly he had nothing at all in common with his Tory allies except a loathing for the Ministers. Together they were not a positive political force.

In the Proclamation against the Hell-Fire Club, the Officers of the Law were urged "To exert themselves in discovering any who are guilty of such impieties that they may be prosecuted and punished with the utmost severity." Luckily, not a single member of the London Club was traced, and not one witness was found to testify against Philip. But if the Proclamation failed to secure his prosecution or to discredit him in popular eyes, it ended his Club's meetings. The first Hell-Fire Club was closed quietly down, and left only its name for legend and awe. But before it died, it spawned some imitations of itself throughout Ireland, Scotland and the provinces, and these outlived it. Ironically, a hunting-lodge on his Rathfarnam estate was used, years after Philip's death, as the meeting place of the Hell-Fire Club of Dublin.

The Ministers' inability to convict anyone for membership of Philip's Hell-Fire Club was mocked by the popular press, which was passing through a phase of delightful scurrility. The most enterprising journalist in London was an acquaintance of Philip's called Nathaniel Mist, who wrote, and sometimes employed such as Daniel Defoe to write, a violent scandal-sheet called *Mist's Weekly Journal.* This year he published a letter in time for Oak-Apple Day, May 29th, the Anniversary of the occasion that Charles II had hidden from Roundheads up an oak tree at Boscobel in Shropshire:

> Shall we return thanks for a deliverance from rogues with swords in their hands, when we are ruined by footmen, pimps, pathics, parasites, whores, nay, what is more vexatious, old ugly whores! Such as would not find entertainment in the most hospitable hundred of old Drury? [7]

The Commons frantically censured this lewd reference to the King's two ugly mistresses as:

> A false, malicious, scandalous, infamous and traitorous libel, tending to alienate the affections of His Majesty's subjects and to excite the people to revolution and rebellion, with an intent to subvert the present happy Estabishment, and to introduce Popery and Arbitrary Power. [8]

Mist was packed off to Newgate and his press closed down, to Philip's indignation. But this did not silence him: a periodical soon appeared called *Fog's Weekly Journal.*

Philip was coming to Parliament less regularly as summer approached, preferring to drink with his political friends in the country. On Aril 27th, one of his Gargantuan bouts gave apoplexy to a Tory Member for the county of Oxford called James Herbert and toppled him into the River Thames where he drowned.

Meanwhile, Martha passed her days being agreeable to her county neighbours in Buckinghamshire, which was not hard, for at twenty-one she was at the peak of her beauty. Lady Fermanagh, one of the Tory Verneys who lived ten miles north of Winchendon at Claydon, had never before been on speaking terms with the Whig Whartons, but now that the Tories and the Grumbletonians were allies she was delighted to know the Duchess:

> *Claydon*   6 June 1721
> Yesterday we was at the judge's, where we met a vast deal of company [including] the Duchess of Wharton... The

Duke went yesterday to Malmesbury, but is to be at the House of Lords on Thursday. I told the Duchess I intended to wait on her; she was highly civil; shall I go before you come home or not?...[9]

Philip was at Malmesbury to quell an outbreak of dissent there. Although he had been High Steward of the Borough — which gave him the chairmanship of the council that controlled the Parliamentary elections for the borough — since 1717, he had always neglected to bribe or charm the corporation into supporting him wholeheartedly. They now threatened to allow an alderman who opposed his interest to be elected. His arrival stopped them, and before he left once more for Wooburn Manor he had seen a loyal alderman elected. But he had no cause to be complacent about the strength of his interest in other boroughs. Only a month later he was staving off a Government attack on his hold over Buckingham. His electoral influence now, rather too late, began to be a matter of concern to him. This was because in March 1722 there was to be the first general election for seven years.

CHAPTER EIGHT

The Election

> Though wondering Senates hung on all he spoke,
> The Club must hail him Master of the Joke"...
>   Pope on Wharton. *First Moral Essay,* 183-4.

Late in July 1721 his carriages and a cavalcade of outriders left Buckinghamshire for his estates and boroughs in Yorkshire, Westmorland and Cumberland, where he needed to whip up his support before the election in the spring.

The roads that he followed, though not deep in mud at this time of year, were rutted with caked earth and made dangerous by the stray boulders lying around on them. The air above them was soon heavy with the dust thrown up by the hooves and wheels of his horses and carriages. The upkeep of the roads of England had been the responsibility of the parishes which they crossed since Saxon times. The parishes seemed to compete with one another in neglecting them. Turnpike roads as yet barely existed. Even the Great North Road itself was so narrow, north of Grantham, that two teams of pack-horses could not pass one another on it. When herds of cattle and flocks of geese, bound for London, blocked the road and filled the air with noise and with filth, the Duke probably wished he had never left the South. On a hot afternoon he would ride ahead of his coach-and-six in search of air that was cleaner to breathe, and he would leave his servants to struggle along with the cavalcade as best they could.

He followed the Great North Road until branching off to York, where his party arrived in time for York Races, which were held (then as now) early in August. Heavy punting, paid for in the last resort with bills for £50 drawn on the Smailes's, his Yorkshire agents, and the composition of a *Song made at York Races,* (which is not his best literary work) wasted Philip's time here for a few days:

Ye powdered gallants who saunter at White's,

Attend and give ear to my ditty;
No longer dangle of Drawing-Room nights,
But mount, and repair to York City... [1]

He dined with the Archbishop, whose adultery he later remarked in another poem, and with his old guardian Lord Carlisle, who shared his passion for hunting. When the races were over he and Carlisle drove together to Castle Howard where Vanburgh's facades and lofty central hall, both newly completed, proclaimed Carlisle's ostentation and wealth. Such a palace, grander than any other English country house then finished, reminded Philip of Versailles or of the princely mansions he had seen in Germany. As he reported enthusiastically to Lord Cowper, "This is the finest seat in England and both nature and art have employed their utmost effort to embellish it. I believe it has cost an immense sum of money, but I must say that I think it is well laid out." [2]

He departed on August 10th for Gilling, near Richmond in North Yorkshire, the residence of his grasping, ingratiating agents the Smailes's. He reached them within a day and immediately borrowed from them enough money to make up his losses at York races, a sum which brought the total of what he owed them to nearly two thousand pounds. Then he provided a feast for his burgage tenants in Richmond to secure Wharton control over one of Richmond's two Parliamentary seats. Although the other was controlled by a rising local family called Yorke, he failed to enquire whether they were content with holding only one seat in the borough or wanted his seat as well. The loyalty his drunken tenants expressed for him too easily satisfied him that his electoral influence in Richmond was secure and after couple of days he set out again, now on horseback, along a bleak pack-horse track westwards across the Pennines towards Wharton Hall.

He left behind him his estates at Aske and Gilling, where the Smailes's lived, and rode up Swaledale, where new lead-mines were being opened on his land, to the head of the Swale between moorland masses called High Seat and Nine Standards Rigg. From there he could see Ravenstonedale and the rest of the Wharton Hall estate near Kirkby Stephen in Westmorland lying below him. From Richmond to the Hall his party covered thirty miles, almost entirely over his own land.

He had probably never seen Wharton Hall, the ancient home of his family, where he had lately housed his Duchess. Its original thick-walled tower which had defended the obscure fourteenth-century Whartons against Scottish raiders had been enlarged by the first Lord Wharton in the reigns of Henry VIII and Elizabeth as his own power grew, and over a gaunt new gatehouse he had inscribed his arms and the words "Pleasur in Acts d'Armys". He was a dreadful man, famous (and finally ennobled) for harrying the Scots, and as unpleasant to his neighbours as only a loyal servant of the Tudor monarchs could be. He demolished the village of Wharton and in its place enclosed for himself a huge deer-park within a high dry-stone wall. This made him so unpopular with his tenants that in later life he was actually in danger of being murdered, and he was obliged to retire to Healaugh in Yorkshire, where he died.

Philip has as little in common with the brazen uncouthness of his ancestor as Winchendon did with ugly old Wharton Hall. The starkness of the Westmorland countryside struck Philip as forcibly as it had struck poor Martha the year before. The early eighteenth century felt no enthusiasm for wild scenery. But after he had survived a sumptuous welcome from his servants and tenants, Philip wrote to Lord Cowper:

> I am now got to the old paternal seat of my family, where I enjoy the true simplicity of Old England, and am charmed with breathing my native air. I go into Cumberland tomorrow with Sir Christopher Musgrave....
> P.S. Your Lordship will forgive the paper, for I believe we have not yet seen any better in Westmorland.[3]

Philip and Sir "Kit" Musgrave, the Tory M.P. for Cumberland, as well as being cousins and neighbours in the North, were bound by a dislike of a new interest in Cumberland, that of the Lowther family. The Lowthers, who were Government Whigs, had built up a substantial coal and shipping trade at Whitehaven and at Cockermouth, which had once been a Wharton borough. So from Wharton Hall Philip and Kit Musgrave first directed their steps towards

Cockermouth.

Within three days their arrival had alarmed the agent of the Lowthers at Whitehaven, Mr. Spedding, who reported to Sir James Lowther his concern for the Lowther candidate, Sir Wilfred Lawson:

> Whitehaven Sep 1 1721
>
> Sir...
> The Duke of Wharton makes a mighty rout at Cockermouth and sticks not at saying anything he thinks will prejudice yours and Sir Wilfred's interest, but no doubt you have heard from all hands of the great pains he takes against you...[4]

Philip soon filled all the Cockermouth voters and their families and friends with ale. But this form of canvassing was not so persuasive as the threat of eviction or unemployment from the Lowthers. They were ever present in West Cumberland, to keep a close eye on their own interests. The presence of Philip, though flamboyant, was temporary. Drunkenness alone would not keep Cockermouth for the Duke. But Philip, noticing only how happy he made everyone, was oblivious of this.

For about a week he continued causing mild local inflation with the shower of borrowed gold which he lavished on the borough, and then submitted Workington and Whitehaven nearby to similar treatment, before retracing his route towards the decayed rustic town of Appleby forty miles away in Westmorland. Here the Westmorland county elections were to be held. The result had already been agreed between all parties concerned: one seat was for the Lowthers and the other for a Tory called Colonel James Graham, who (when he was not laying out a modern landscape around his old house at Levens Hall) practised old-fashioned extreme Toryism. He had been Privy Purse to James II. Philip supported him for lack of a Grumbletonian candidate, and gave a banquet for Appleby in his honour.

By now Philip and Sir Kit had been joined by more entertaining company — Phil Lloyd and the romantically-named young son of the Duke of Kent, Earl Harold, who was to meet a curious death the following year: he "choked to death on an ear of barley he inadvertently put in his mouth".[5] He was the son-in-law of the Earl of Thanet of Appleby Castle, the largest landowner in the neighbourhood. His carriages now accompanied those of Philip and his party towards Eden Hall, the mansion near Penrith that Sir Kit was engaged in restoring and enlarging, and which contained an ancient glass, called "The Luck of Eden Hall". It was said that if the glass broke, then so would break the good fortune of the house. For fun, Philip used to throw it up in the air and catch it again. Once, when he was drunk, he dropped it, but the glass was caught by an agile butler and saved.

They were all joined at Eden Hall by Mr. Bains, Philip's agent who had been locked in the Moot Hall at Appleby by the rebels in 1715. Philip and Sir Kit challenged the others to a drinking bout, which Philip celebrated in a ballad imitating the old border ballad of Chevy Chase:

>   A True and Lamentable Ballad
>   called
>   The Earl's Defeat
>   *(To the tune of Chevy-Chase)*
>
> "On both sides slaughter and gigantic deeds" — Milton.
>
> God proper long from being broke
> The Luck of Eden Hall;
> A doleful drinking-bout I sing,
> There lately did befall.
>
> To chase the spleen with cup and can
> Duke Philip took his way;
> Babes yet unborn shall never see
> The like of such a day...

Twenty-eight heroic verses tell how Earl Harold and then the Duke himself were drunk into unconsciousness, ending with a prayer for the Royal family and for George I's mistress:

> Thus did the dire contention end,

And each man of the slain
Were quickly carried off to bed,
Their senses to regain.

God Bless the King, the Duchess fat,
And keep the land in peace,
And grant that drunkenness henceforth
'Mong noblemen may cease.

And likewise bless our royal Prince,
The nation's other hope,
And give us grace for to defy
The devil, and the Pope. [6]

By now Philip was tired of electioneering, broad Northern accents and ruddy peasant complexions, and he wanted to be at Bicester for the racing at the end of the month. But in other boroughs and shires in other parts of England his rival politicians knew better. They were mastering any distaste they felt for the electorate. Sunderland and Walpole and their weak-willed colleague the Duke of Newcastle, who owned more boroughs than anyone, were not sober for weeks at a time. This was the period which was most crucial for the outcome of next year's election. Only Philip could not resist the attraction of Bicester races. His coach-and-six with its band of attendants arrived there in the middle of September.

At Bicester he found many who were as content to ignore political developments as he was: a £15 prize he donated was taken by Sir Ed O'Brien, whose "Squirrel" beat Lord Hillsborough's "Staghunter". A ball he gave for them and Lord Lichfield and low-reputed society at large, in the Long Room, an assembly room in the town, attracted ladies of ill fame all the way from London, including a certain "Martha from the Cocoa Tree Theatre".[7] Another Martha, the Duchess, was not present.

She was probably in London, where Philip's thoughts should have been, and where Robert Walpole and the Earl of Sunderland were still precariously sharing the rich benefits of office in between hectic canvassing visits to the provinces. Though notionally they were of the same party, these two principal ministers were still bitterly jealous of one another. The only reason why they were still balanced in power when parliament was recalled on October 19th was that they knew that if they divided against one another they might fall in the face of an attack by Cowper's alliance. But while Philip raced at Bicester and then at Newmarket during September and October, the Earl of Sunderland decided how to dispose of Walpole safely. He had not been married to a Churchill for twenty-one years without having learnt the elements of intrigue. He must create a party which was large enough to out-vote Walpole and all Walpole's huge Parliamentary faction. To do so he was prepared to negotiate with anyone: Grumbletonians, Tories or even Jacobites. He made overtures to Atterbury, and to Colonel James Hamilton the Tory Philip supported at Appleby, and to William Bromley, once Queen Anne's Secretary of State, who complained to his old leader Lord Harley that Sunderland was making "Promises... so extravagantly large,... That it was affronting me to imagine that I could think them sincere." [8]

Philip, back in London in October, was equally surprised by being approached by his old arch-enemy Sunderland. Would the whole Grumbletonian and Tory alliance agree to support Sunderland against Walpole? He did not know. As he remarked on it cryptically to Atterbury,

> The whole world has been for some time in suspense waiting for the event of unforeseen friendships. [9]

So political warfare in the House of Lords re-commenced on 2nd November 1721 in a mist of uncertainty. Philip and the opposition Lords stood their old ground, and were thrashed in each division by two to one, and published Protests on every possible occasion: on the 13th, the 15th and 20th November. Then Philip suddenly left them, and joined Sunderland.

Two events in November caused his change of heart. One was the arrival of a letter from Matthew Smailes complaining seriously of the huge sums he owed him, totalling altogether (including £1,400 sent to Newmarket) "£3,322 3s. 10½d. for which I, to serve your occasions, have drawn myself into upwards of £4,000 debts... [10]". The other was a display of personal hostility to him from some Tories who

The Election

were disgusted at his debauchery. As he complained to Cowper:

> December 2nd
> The manner in which some of the Tories have lately treated me is, I think, very ill return for the zeal with which I have acted in opposition to the present Ministers... When a man is sacrificing his fortune and his interest to a set of men, a decency in conversation is a small return. [11]

By breaking his alliance with these reactionary Tories (with whom he had nothing in common but self-interest) and by joining Sunderland, he hoped to sink Walpole, to save his own finances with a Ministerial pension, and yet not desert his "Old Whig" political sentiments.

So as a Government supporter he was received at Court (for the first time in years) and kissed the King's hand on the 5th December. The following day he went to the House of Lords. Cowper and his other late friends amongst the Grumbletonians there cynically assumed that he must have been induced to leave them by a vast sum out of Sunderland's Secret Service money. But as a correspondent of Lord Harley wrote a week later, he had not been bribed:

> Lord Wharton's return to the Court is no news to you. There is much talk of the terms which he made, but I am assured he sent the Ministry carte blanche. When he first appeared after his reconciliation in the House of Lords, he told everyone that he designed to make the Bishop of Rochester his confessor, and he did not doubt of satisfying the Bishop that what he had done was reasonable, and he went that very morning to the Bishop of Rochester. [12]

In truth Philip was unbribable. He was too high-principled, and he owed too much money. It was no more possible to bribe a man who was in debt as much as Philip was, than it was possible to bribe a man who was as rich as Philip had once been. And even though money would have been useful to him, he would not have taken it. He never accepted a bribe in his life. He was too proud.

Even if Atterbury condoned Philip's union with Sunderland,

most Grumbletonians and Tories did not. It looked as if he had deserted them for purely selfish reasons. When after Christmas he and Sunderland changed the procedure of the House of Lords so that opposition Protests could only be entered with inconvenience, their worst fears seemed justified; was he left with no anti-Government hankerings at all? Only possibly to his credit during December was the release from prison of the adventurous journalist Nathaniel Mist and his employment (aided by Daniel Defoe) by Sunderland to secretly pamphleteer against Walpole.

These grubby waters of political double-dealing rather depressed and shamed Philip. In his spare hours he turned back to mysticism. Perhaps a void had grown in his spiritual life since the Hell-Fire Club had closed in May. There now existed in London some mystics who would one day be more famous than the "Hell-Fires" had ever been. They called themselves the Order of Freemasons.

The Masons had probably once been a medieval stonemasons' guild whose members had been required by the nature of their craft to wander the country from building to building in search of work, and in order to recognise one another in remote places they had employed secret signs. When grand meetings of all the members of their craft were held, and young journeymen stonecutters initiated, the proceedings were necessarily secret too. In the seventeenth century, when other guilds were waning, some credulous antiquarians, interested by the secrecy of the masons and by their apparently ancient ceremonies, started to be admitted to the lodges on an honorary basis. These and a few increasingly out-of-place stonemasons in a dozen or so lodges scattered around Britain, with no head lodge, no leader and no central organisation, were what was left of the Freemasons at the turn of the eighteenth century. They might have yet died out but for the fact that the leaders of London intellectual society were growing tired of the scientific philosophy of Newton, Boyle, Locke and the rationalists, and pounced on the redundant artisan guild and declared it a fount of mystic wisdom. In 1717, the year that "druids" began once more to hold ceremonies at Stonehenge, just ten years after the Society of Antiquarians opened and a year before the Hell-Fire Club was founded, the rejuvenated Order of Masons organised the four existing London lodges into one Grand Lodge, and elected its first Grand

The Election

Master at the Goose and Gridiron tavern, St Paul's Churchyard. Then the whole brotherhood began searching for, and finding, or pretending to find, ancient "Gothic" documents which justified what they had done, and showed there had once been a Grand Lodge which had lapsed, and proved that the first Grand Master was King Solomon.

By the following year the Order had been swept up by the vogue for mysticism. Then, according to their first official history, The Constitutions of the Freemasons, "Some Noblemen were also made brothers, and more lodges were constituted."[13] Within three years, the Duke of Montagu was Grand Master. His elders, such as Dr William Stukely, the antiquary, who had joined masonry, "Suspecting it to be the remains of the Mysteries of the Ancients,"[14] were a little surprised at the quality of the new brothers. Those who flocked into Masonry later in the 1720's, the Dukes of Queensberry, St. Albans, and Richmond, Lord Waldegrave and Lord Paisley, Hogarth, Steele, Lord Kingston, the Earls of Rosse, Dalkeith and Chesterfield, and Elizabeth St. Leger, (admitted in spite of being a woman after having accidentally witnessed a ceremony) had little more in common with their humbler predecessors in the Order. Some of the new members were associated with the Hell-Fire Clubs or its satellites. The scurrilous Earl of Rosse founded the Dublin Hell-Fire Club, and became the first recorded Grand Master of the Irish Lodge of Masons in 1725. One side of Freemasonry was close to the serious aspect of the lately suppressed sacreligious society. It was never atheistical, but its creed was deist rather than Christian. It satisfied for members a desire for mystery which both atheism and Anglicanism did not.

Twenty-three year old Philip underwent the initiation rites one afternoon in the Spring of 1722 at the Stationers' Hall in the City which had been borrowed for the Lodge meeting. There he was half-undressed in a pseudo-religious ceremony which was intended to demonstrate his spiritual poverty, and by nightfall he was a Master Mason, eligible to be Master of one of the Lodges. But he aspired to being Grand Master, to rule over all the Masons in London and, as far as possible, over all other Masons as well.

But for the time being he had more important things on his mind. On March 10th the seven-year Parliament which had sat all George I's reign had been dissolved and the general election held. The

Duke's day of reckoning had arrived.

The election of 1722 was famous for its level of corruption and rowdiness. At the watershed between the days when Parliamentary elections had been quietly concerned with local matters, and the days when fierce contests became unnecessary because each borough was "owned" by a great magnate, the election days were bloody and expensive. After the result of the poll came the unfair election petitions. A successful candidate for a seat might discover that his election had been queried at Westminster by the losing candidate. His petition was heard, not on its merits, but on a party basis. If the unsuccessful candidate was a Ministry man, the majority of the House might uphold him; if he was not, they would reject him. The electorate had no say in the matter.

When the polling closed at the "Wharton" boroughs, it was clear that his change of party and his pusillanimous electioneering had yielded Philip as little as he deserved. He succeeded in having elected at least one of the two Members for Buckingham and Wycombe. In Malmesbury Lord Hillsborough and Sir John Rushout were elected though petitioned against. In Richmond, where he had resigned himself to losing one of the two seats to the local family of Yorke, Lord Holdernesse had put up his own brother Conyers Darcy to win the second seat in the Yorke's interest as well as the first. In Cockermouth Philip's candidate lost; in Appleby the Tory Colonel James Graham was not elected although his election had been agreed by all parties, and Graham retired to gardening at Levens. The story was the same throughout England. Philip was to be a man with little following in the House of Commons.

An even worse blow now struck him. On April 19th, before the election results were yet known, his leader and sole political ally, Sunderland, was struck down by the palsy and died. So when the election Petitions relating to his boroughs came to be heard, Philip lost the vote on them, and even Hillsborough was thrown out of the seat for Malmesbury.

He realised his political hopes were dashed. He decided to disappear into Horatian obscurity at the most favoured haven for eighteenth-century poets and political exiles. A contemporary reported, "The Duke of Wharton has restricted himself to £2,000 a year, and has taken a house at Twickenham for retirement for seven years." [15]

CHAPTER NINE

Twickenham

>   Twickenham, where frolic Wharton revelled,
>   Where Montagu, with locks dishevelled,
>   Conflict of dirt and warmth combined,
>   Invoked — and scandalised — the *Nine*.
>   Horace Walpole, *The Parish Register of Twickenham*.

At Twickenham in April 1722 Philip crammed his numerous servants and gentlemen followers into a residence which had stood empty since its last occupier, Secretary of State James Craggs the younger, had died early the previous year. Though not large it was comfortable, and stood back from the South side of the main street of the village just West of the lane to the Church, its wide gardens behind stretching almost to the river.

He had retired to Twickenham partly because it had become fashionable since Pope had settled in well-publicised seclusion to be visited by such Augustan wits as Swift, Elijah Fenton and George Berkeley here, partly because it was near the court of the Prince and Princess of Wales at Richmond, and partly because at Twickenham lived Lady Mary Wortley Montagu.

Lady Mary, the most remarkable Englishwoman of the eighteenth century, was the daughter of Philip's old guardian the Duke of Kingston. At thirty-one, eight years older than Philip, she was still very attractive. But her unpleasant bodily odour was famous even in this unwashed age; her vivacious face was marred by greasy black locks hanging uncurled and lank around it; and her lively figure was concealed by the odd-looking Turkish costume she had affected since returning from her husband's embassy to Constantinople. It was popularly believed that the Sultan of Turkey had fallen in love with her, and that she had been inside his harem, which added to her lurid reputation. Her conversation, though often indecent, was intelligent and thoughtful, and she was a better letter-writer than all the literati of the Augustan Age, with the possible exception of Vanbrugh. Her force of mind magnetised all who met her and dominated Twickenham. Poor crippled Alexander Pope (who also washed seldom) had been in love with her for years. But his visits to her house in the summer of 1722 were soon outnumbered by Philip's. Her intellect, vanity and humour echoed the latter's sharply; and within the year the literary lady and the young Duke were plunged into a tempestuous love affair which was to last several years, but the details of which are sadly almost entirely unknown.

With her Philip forgot his political setbacks. To ease his financial difficulties he had let all his own houses except Wharton Hall (which no one would want to rent) and Winchendon itself, where Martha was left with a hopelessly inadequate £500 a year. Wooburn had been mortgaged to Francis Charters who now took it over entirely, occupying it himself as a country seat. Philip's spare lands in Yorkshire were mortgaged for six thousand pounds. Rathfarnam Castle and its estate South of Dublin (whose sale in South Sea year had fallen through) were being sold. He gave his hosiers, Messrs. John Morris and Thomas Street of The Strand, a bond for £120 to cover their enormous bill, and because his promised annuity to Edward Young had never been paid, on July 12th he charged it on some of the land which he had previously assigned to his Trustees. But he never brooded on his desperate financial circumstances. He still buried himself in books and conversation, raced frequently to London to pursue richer pleasures, and continued planning to displace the Duke of Montagu as Grand Master of the Freemasons.

The annual election to this office (which had only been invented in 1717) was to be held on Midsummer's Day, June 24th. Montagu, a sober thirty-three year old with a serious interest in medicine, science and Freemasonry, was a popular Grand Master. The majority of Masons did not want to be rid of him, so had decided that no new election should be held this year. This did not suit Philip, who therefore called an election himself:

> Philip Duke of Wharton lately made a brother, though not a Master of a Lodge, being ambitious of the Chair, got a number of others to meet him at Stationers' Hall 24th June

1722, and having no Grand Officers, they put in the Chair the oldest Master Mason, and, without the usual decent ceremonials, the said old mason proclaimed aloud, "Philip Duke of Wharton, Grand Master of Mason."[1]

A generous dinner of haunches of venison baked in pastry and a lot of wine was provided by Philip in the Stationers' Hall after the ceremony and generated much goodwill. The important question of the validity of this election was laughed aside. The toasts were respectable and loyal to the Government, and when the orchestra struck up the Jacobite song,

> Let the King enjoy His Own again

it was asked to desist. Some of Philip's supporters, apprehensive about how his election to the leadership of their secret society would be taken by a Ministry who disliked him and who were liable to smell Jacobitism anywhere, had already visited Lord Townshend to assure him of the inoffensive nature of Freemasonry. According to the *London Journal* Townshend had cynically answered them that "they need not be apprehensive about any molestation from the Government... as... the secrets of the Society... must be of a very harmless nature, because, as much as mankind love mischief, nobody ever bothered to betray them."[2]

But by arranging his own dubious election, Philip understandably annoyed the many Masons who supported the Duke of Montagu or who missed the "decent ceremonials" of a proper investiture or who suspected that Philip would turn their unworldly Order into a tool for his own political ambition. Such refused to accept his election as valid. This did not deter Philip or his supporters from behaving as if he were the Grand Master. He had seized control. And his Grand Mastership was a great success, as even the *Constitutions of the Freemasons* admitted:

> Now Masonry flourished in harmony, reputation and numbers: many noblemen of the first rank desired to be admitted into the fraternity... The Grand Master was obliged to constitute more new lodges every week with his Deputy and

Wardens; and his worship was well pleased with their kind and respectful manner of receiving him, as they were with his affable and clever conversation.[3]

But during the autumn he canvassed Thomas Stukely, the Earl of Dalkeith, and other prominent Masons for support for his dubious title to the Grand Mastership. He won them round with flattery and charm, and then persuaded the Duke of Montagu the former Grand Master to call a Grand Lodge jointly with him, and there in January he was confirmed Grand Master in a proper fashion. So he continued next half year in office unquestioned in his authority, and did not pervert the Order from the path of inoffensive pseudo-mysticism.

The frontispiece to the *"Constitutions of the Freemasons"* by Dr. Desaguliers, the hand-book of Masonry, which was first published towards the end of Philip's year as Grand Master, shows the Duke of Montagu presenting a scroll to Philip who is standing in his Ducal robes, surounded by attendants. A piece of verse, called "The Warden's Song", which the book contains, concludes with the edifying lines:

...And with Geometry in skilful hand
Due homage pay
Without delay
To Wharton, noble Duke our Master Grand
He rules the Freeborn sons of Art
By love and friendship, hand and heart.

Philip and Lady Mary and the wits of Twickenham were used to better verse. Philip passed whole days in literary conversation with them, and read profusely in a multitude of languages, interspersing Cervantes, Shakespeare and Fénélon with Cicero and the Comte de Grammont. But of contemporary writers, Young was personally still his favourite. According to Pope, Philip had been so anxious to boost Young's tragedy *"The Revenge"*, that he had allowed himself to be persuaded into packing all the seats in the theatre with his supporters:

His wealth brave Timon gloriously confounds —

Asked for a groat, he gives a hundred pounds;
Or if three ladies like a luckless play
Takes the whole house upon the poet's day. [4]

Pope disliked the Whig Edward Young, preferring as company the Tory politicians Lord Orrery, Bishop Atterbury, Dr John Freind (the M.P. for Launceston and brother of the headmaster of Westminster School) and Lord Bathurst, who had all been Philip's allies in his Parliamentary opposition days. They were now in consternation at news from Whitehall. There Robert Walpole had annnounced that he had uncovered a monstrous Jacobite conspiracy threatening the King, the Government, the Protestant religion and the Hanoverian succession. Its leaders, he said, were the Tory opposition Lords.

The truth was that a small and impracticable plot for a rising indeed existed amongst the minor London Jacobites. It could never have been a threat to the Government. But Walpole knew the political value of a Jacobite scare to turn the eyes of Parliament away from the embers of the South Sea blaze, and to discredit the Tory opposition. So he pretended that the plot was very formidable. He marched all the Guards of the Household Division into Hyde Park to defend London, saw that several soldiers were flogged for showing Jacobite sympathies, and began to distil indictments for treason from the results of industrious search by his secret agents and decipherers of code at the Post Office, who had been opening letters to and from France and Rome for months.

The first to be arrested, two Irishmen called Kelly and Sample and an unbalanced barrister called Layer, after being threatened with torture, provided Walpole with the evidence he wanted. By autumn no chief of the opposition was safe. One by one the Tory politicians were imprisoned. And when Parliament sat in October 1722, the seats in Parliament which had formerly been filled by the leaders of the Tory party were vacant. Dr Freind, Francis Atterbury, Lord North and Grey who had lost a hand at Blenheim, and Lord Orrery who had been a General at Malplaquet, were all in the Tower. They were later joined by the inoffensive Duke of Norfolk, presumably because he was a Catholic.

Philip watched the arrests with dismay. The imprisoned men

who were charged with doing no more than what he himself had once been guilty of, had lately been his political allies. And, although he was still in theory a supporter of the Whig Government — Sunderland's death had not altered that — he was still a very close friend of Orrery, Dr Freind and Atterbury. Yet what could a discredited young Duke do for them?

Although his influence with the Whig Government was small because he was widely regarded with disgust as a man who had tried to change sides and betray his friends at strategic moments but had failed, still seven years of political and social restlessness had not entirely wasted his talents. Though exhaustion and decadence and drink and his bout of smallpox had worsened his once-fine features, he yet had a great name. He was still a Duke, an untarnishable leader of fashion and a dangerous orator. He kept close to Walpole whom he intensely disliked, to try to glean good for the imprisoned Lords. Public opinion, voiced by the London mob, soon showed that its sympathy lay more with the prisoners in the Tower than with the Ministers in Whitehall. In churches and chapels throughout London and Westminster on Sunday 16th September the curates and lesser clergy whose protector Atterbury had been, raised prayers publicly for the "deliverance" of the Bishop — ostensibly deliverance from an attack of gout. But when Parliament sat again three weeks later the Ministers were not perturbed. They kept up the myth of a great Jacobite conspiracy. The Habeus Corpus Act was suspended for a year; the prosecution of the Jacobites was voted; the remaining Opposition Lords, led by Cowper, protested in vain; and Philip coyly followed the court, speaking in the Ministers' favour when required to. In the commons Robert Walpole took an opportunity to direct anti-Jacobite feeling towards a useful end by proposing a tax on Catholics to raise £100,000, which he explained:

> Could not be thought either unjust or unreasonable, considering the ill use they made of the saving out of their incomes, which most of them laid out in maintaining the Pretender and his adherents abroad, and fomenting sedition and rebellion at home. [5]

By the end of the autumn session poor Christopher Layer had been tried and condemned to death. Dr Freind had been released from the Tower, where he had written a treatise on smallpox, but an election petition prevented him from taking his seat as Tory member for Launceston, so he was obliged to retire again from politics and write a "*History of Physic*". Kelly, Orrery, North and Grey and Atterbury were still closely confined in the Tower when the new year dawned. The Government were preparing a Bill of "Pains and Penalties" for them because no jury would convict them on the scanty evidence available against them.

Philip spent the winter at Twickenham watching for signs of a change in the political wind before seeking to alter his unhappy alliance with the Government, and rousing the slumbers of London with reckless pranks. One night in December the Whig M.P. Sir John Schaw and some friends were loose in Westminster foully drunk and intent on lewdly assaulting women. "We met the Duke of Wharton, as well refreshed as I," wrote Schaw subsequently. "He proposed to survey all the ladies in the galleries; I was for turning them all up; but he declined. He proposed to knock up Argyll; I proposed the King". Philip prevailed, and they called on the Duke of Argyll, who received them better than they deserved, and they all drank themselves insensible on Argyll's brandy.[6]

During the winter Philip, wanting to be a political force again and not just a famous rake, arranged for Philip Lloyd, the devoted gentleman follower of his from Swaledale, to be elected as his candidate in the by-election at the notoriously corrupt small borough of Saltash. The election cost Philip a large sum in promised bribes for the electors. Most of it was never paid. But Philip and Lloyd and the others of his scanty band of political followers could do little to oppose the impending prosecution of the Tories. Men of position throughout England watched events philosophically. At Button's, the London "wits" coffee-house, and at Twickenham, it was widely believed that Atterbury had been in treasonable correspondence with the Pretender, and that support for him against the will of the Ministers was hopeless. Neither of his friends Swift and Pope, the greatest writers of the age and both Tories, dared or bothered to publish anything to help him.

But Philip suffered painful remorse as he spent the wet Spring session of Parliament listening to Atterbury being accused, and to the other "Protesting Lords", not only Orrery and North and Grey, but also Kinnoul, Strafford, Craven, Scarsdale, Gower, Bingley, Bathurst and finally Lord Cowper being spoken against in connection with the Great Conspiracy. Cowper, a life-long Whig, was most justifiably indignant at being called a Jacobite, but his wife burnt half her diary in fright for his sake, fearing that innocence alone was no defence against Walpole's charges.

Philip supported the Government, and spoke on their behalf until North and Grey and Orrery had followed Dr Freind to freedom, but the Bill to inflict "Pains and Penalties" on Atterbury had passed the Commons and was before the Lords. It deprived Atterbury of his bishopric and all his offices, exiled him and declared that any Briton who corresponded or spoke with him was guilty of High Treason. Then, only ten days before the date fixed for the debate on it, May 15th 1723, Philip left the Government side and joined the opposition once more in its hour of danger.

His heart had always been with the opposition, although in the Commons the Tories and Grumbletonians could hardly be called a party at all, and in the Lords they were declining. And he rejoined them because they were his friends and he left the Government Whigs because he disliked them (especially the upstart Walpole) and because he thought them politically corrupt. He himself was still a political idealist in a very cynical age: he had never been bribed or bought. But idealism promised no relief to his apparently ruined fortunes.

On May 15th he was newly back amongst his old friends on the opposition benches of the House of Lords. Atterbury was already denying that certain letters were in his own handwriting, that any code could be deciphered in a way that implicated him, and that he knew other suspected Jacobites. He said that he had dined only once with Lord Strafford, that he had not seen Sir Harry Goring for over a year, and that he had never dined at Lord North and Grey's at all. His performance was magnificent:

> If by Your Lordships' judgements, springing from unknown motives, I shall be thought to be guilty; if for any reasons, or necessity of State, of the wisdom and justice of which I am

no competent judge, Your Lordships shall proceed to pass this Bill against me, God's will be done. "Naked came I out of my mother's womb, and naked shall I return; and whether he gives or takes away, blessed be the name of the Lord.[7]"

But for all their dignity and rhetoric, Atterbury's arguments did not have the ring of truth about them. They were not the defence of an innocent but of a politician, and the attack on him gained force. At this unpropitious moment, Philip rose to his defence. It was said that a few days earlier, when he was still a Government supporter, Philip had learnt from Walpole the whole of the case against the Bishop, which had provided him with all the information he now needed for his speech in the Bishop's defence:

My Lords, I shall take the liberty of considering the whole proofs that have been brought on this occasion, both by way of charge, defence, reply and rejoinder. And though I own myself very unequal to the task, yet, since no other Lord who could do it better has undertaken it, I think it my duty as a Peer and as an Englishman to lay it before your Lordships in the best manner I am able.[8]

It seemed to Philip's hearers in the Lords that his mind, long clouded by affectation, drink and doubts about his political stance, had suddenly cleared. His old rhetoric was still sound. Piece by piece he drily elucidated the evidence against the Bishop, and showed the weakness and discrepancy in its details. The speech was very long, it occupies over a hundred column-inches in Cobbett's *Parliamentary History*. He laboriously cited precedents and quoted judges. Not until late in the evening of a hot day — there was an unnatural heat-wave during the trial — did he at last finish:

I have now given your Lordships the reasons why I am against the Bill. I fear I have tired your patience; and shall therefore conclude with the words... in the case of the Earl of Clarendon: "We have an accusation upon hearsay, and if it is not made good, the blackest scandal Hell can invent lies at our doors." [9]

Philip's speech, being the only one in Atterbury's favour which covered every point in the Government's case, made a deep impression on the public as well as on the Lords. It was printed and dispersed widely. But in spite of it, and in spite of a thundering defence of the Bishop from Lord Cowper, the Government majority passed the Bill to exile Atterbury.

One month later the "late" Bishop of Rochester was at the Port of London, ready to board ship for France. Philip rode down to the water's edge near the Tower to see him depart, accompanied by huge crowds. It was one of his hey-days. It is said that before he took his leave of the Bishop on board the ship, he gave him a sword, inscribed on its two sides respectively,

Draw me not without reason

and

Put me not up without honour.

The City Tories saw and approved of his loyalty to Atterbury. Robert Walpole drily told Lord Townshend:

Whitehall   June 20th 1723
The late Bishop of Rochester went away on Tuesday. The crowd that attended him before his embarkation was not larger than was expected; but great numbers of boats attended him to the ship's side. Nothing very extraordinary but the Duke of Wharton's behaviour, who went on board the vessel with him. [10]

CHAPTER TEN

The True Briton

> The first beginning of the Calamities of Rome was the bribery that was introduced by ambitious men and practiced in all the Elections of Magistrates.
> Preface to *The True Briton* (1723)

> There is scarce such a living thing as a True Briton,
> *Tatler* 75 (Oct 1st 1709).

Inspired by his revived success as an opposition speaker, Philip began attacking Walpole's Government in print. His trivial poems about world-weariness, drink and love, like "The Duke of Wharton's Ballad", were already well known and sung to popular tunes. Most were too libellous or lewd to be published under his name during his lifetime, even if such publication were not socially inappropriate. His satire which circulated in manuscript most widely was called *On the Bishops and Judges,* or *The Duke of Wharton's WHENS:*

> When York to heaven shall lift a solemn eye
> And love his wife above adultery,
> When Godliness to Gain shall be preferred
> By more than two of the Right Reverend herd
> When Parker shall pronounce upright decrees
> And Hungerford refuse his double fees...

It concludes...

> Then I shall cease my charmer to adore
> And think of love and politics no more. [1]

Imitators of it mentioned Philip himself in the same couplet as a famous brothel-keeper:

The True Briton

> When Wharton's just, and learns to pay his debts
> And reputation lives at Mother Brett's... [2]

Now he published a more serious poem comparing the banishment of Atterbury to the banishment of Cicero:

> Thy wisdom was thy only guilt,
> Thy virtue thy offence;
> With Godlike zeal thou didst espouse
> Thy country's just defence:
> No sordid hopes could charm thy steady soul,
> Nor fears, nor guilty numbers could control... [3]

Probably dissatisfied with this pompous tone, he reverted to the ironic when associating "Robin" Walpole with Jonathan Wild, the famous dealer in stolen goods:

> *On Robbing the Exchequer*
> From sunset to daybreak, whilst folks are asleep,
> New watch are appointed th'Exchequer to keep
> New bolts and new bars fasten every door,
> And the chests are made three times as strong as before;
> Yet the thieves in the day-time the treasures may seize,
> For the same are entrusted with care of the keys;
> From the night till the morning 'tis true, all is right,
> But who will secure it from morning to night?
> Quoth Wild unto Walpole, 'Make me undertaker,
> I'll soon find the rogues that robbed the exchequer,
> I shan't look amongst those who are used to purloining,
> But shall, the first search in the Chapel adjoining.'
> Quoth Robin, 'That's right, for the cash you will find,
> Though I'm sure 'twas not they, for there's some left behind;
> But if it were they, you could not well complain
> For what they have emptied, they'll soon fill again. [4]

More important, before Atterbury's departure he had also started a political journal to broadcast his views on the Government to a wider public than could hear his poems and conversation in his Twickenham drawing-room or attend Parliament or grand debauches to listen to his speeches.

The True Briton was published twice weekly from 3rd June 1723. It was printed for Philip on a press in Salisbury Court off Fleet Street by Samuel Richardson who, in his novel *Clarissa Harlowe* written years later, is said to have depicted Philip as his fickle but romantic hero "Lovelace". Philip was assisted as editor by a middle-aged Tory pamphleteer he rescued from poverty called William Oldisworthy, a veteran of Preston and of literary battles against Addison's *Tatler*. He and Philip attacked the Whigs with gentle satire. On Walpole's heavy and unfair new tax on the Catholics, *The True Briton* mused

> I am certain the tax laid upon the Papists must be warranted by the laws of God and Man, because a majority of the Bishops voted for it, and our Glorious Parliament assented to it. [5]

It was the first proper political journal that had ever appeared in England. Although on the one hand isolated political pamphlets had been common in England since the Civil War, and on the other hand no less than sixteen regular news-sheets such as *Mist's Weekly Journal*, dealing with miscellaneous bits of society rumour and gossip, existed in London at this time, a regular purely political paper was something new. *The True Briton* was soon supplying unprecedentedly up-to-date and well-informed news of the recent trial of Atterbury and the imminent election of the City Sheriffs on Midsummer's Day. And it tirelessly sniped and sniggered at the Ministers. They soon guessed who wrote it. The Duke of Newcastle tried to impede its publication after he had seen seven issues, as he told his fellow Secretary of State Lord Townshend, who was with the King at Pyrmont, the watering-place in Prussia:

> Claremont   June 28 1723
> ...You have heard of His Grace of Wharton, who has appeared in the City at the head of the Jacobites, and whose

whole discourse is nothing but infamous scandal against the Government. If you have the paper called The True Briton you will see what a fine part that young man is acting. We have ordered the printer to be prosecuted, and by this shall put the Duke of Wharton to some expense.[6]

A printer of *The True Briton* — not Richardson, but a certain Payne — was duly indicted before the King's Bench, fined £400, and sentenced to one year's imprisonment, which confirmed Philip's view of the partiality of the judges.

He was now attacking the Government barely six weeks after he had left its ranks during Atterbury's trial. His hatred of it spread to every corner of his life, and even soured the newly fashionable meetings of the Freemasons in the Stationers' Hall over which he presided as Grand Master. On midsummer's day the election of his successor to the Chair was held. At the meeting (which was before dinner, during the afternoon), he did not propose the candidate he actually supported — the Earl of Dalkeith — because Dalkeith was a Whig, and to have proposed him might have been misunderstood by the Tories. The Lodge proposed and elected Dalkeith themselves, and Dalkeith (although himself absent) duly became the Mason's new Grand Master. He had previously told his agent and proxy, one Robinson, that in this eventuality he proposed as his deputy the eccentric Dr. Desaguliers, author of the recently-published *Constitutions of the Freemasons*. But because Philip greatly disliked Desaguliers' Whiggery, the latter was only approved by the meeting as the new deputy by a margin of one vote. After a benign dinner Philip suggested that the vote be tried again, as there was an irregularity, he said, in the first vote. Robinson understandably objected to such a course of action, and stalled Philip by producing a written authority from the Earl, appointing Desaguliers his deputy, as a Grand Master had power to do. Philip abruptly departed, missing the "decent ceremonials" appropriate to mark the end of his term of office, just as he had missed them on the occasion of his original election.

But his hurried disappearance was excusable, for tonight was also election-night for the sheriffs of London. The power and importance of these sheriffs was great, for they not only chose jurors (corruptly when necessary), but also commanded the train-bands, the city's militia, a force of many tens of thousands. The City itself was relatively self-governing and democratic, and more independent than any other part of Britain. And its political opinion was crucial to any Government. Its disfavour had cost Charles I his capital, and thus England, and his head, only eighty years before. Forty years later under Charles II its favour had saved Lord Shaftesbury from the block which a Tory Government had prepared for him. Since 1716 the London mob (ever anti-Government) had itself turned Tory and taken to calling itself the "Ormonde" mob, after the Jacobite General the Duke of Ormonde. Although the aldermen and greater merchant families were mostly Whig, the common liverymen of the city were mostly Tory or Jacobite. And it was the common liverymen who elected the sheriffs.

The better to direct their discontent to a useful end, Philip himself had joined a livery-company. It was something no other nobleman or political leader had dreamt of doing. He and his henchman, Walter Pryse, when they were admitted to the Wax-Chandlers Company in April, were the first gentlemen ever to have joined the livery. In the books of the Company Philip's "trade" is listed as "Duke", and his address is stated mockingly as "Leicester Fields".[7] He had probably chosen to join the Wax-Chandlers, one of the smaller Companies, because it was run by an energetically Jacobite brewer from Aldgate, called Humphrey Parsons, who had the distinction of having earned a monopoly of exporting beer to France by impressing the French King with his skill out hunting.

Parsons and Francis Child the banker, another Jacobite, had enjoyed office as sheriffs of London for the last year, and now they were responsible for organising the election of their successors. They had duly called a meeting of the liverymen in Common Hall, which Philip missed because he was still dining at the Grand Lodge of the Freemasons. But he had lavishly entertained and harangued the City for several weeks before, and his absence now did not matter. The proceedings were exactly as expected. After some rowdiness the two old sheriffs, Parsons and Child, declared that Williams and Lockwood, the Tory candidates, were elected. The Whigs then exercised their right to demand a poll. It was held for the next three days. But Whig and

Tory writers give contradictory accounts of its result. According to *The True Briton* of 1st and 5th July, the Tories won in spite of the Government deceitfully sending soldiers disguised as liverymen to vote for the Whigs; but the Duke of Newcastle told Lord Townshend on June 28th that the Whigs earned a fair majority.[8] Whatever was the real result, the Tory out-going sheriffs predictably declared again that the Tory candidates were elected. But Sir Gerard Conyers, the Whig Lord Mayor, said the result was false. The Common Council of the City, (being Tory) indignantly protested that the decision of the outgoing sheriffs was final, and that the Mayor had no say in the matter. But the court of aldermen, the body that actually summoned the sheriffs to office, had a Whig majority, and so in spite of the Common Council summoned to office the two Whigs. Philip's party was, therefore, finally defeated.

An Aldermanic election for Cripplegate Ward followed the election of the sheriffs, and there the Tory Sir John Williams, one of the unlucky candidates for sheriff, unquestionably defeated the Whig, Mr. Feast. The mob who supported him, incited by Philip and a lot of ale, celebrated his election on the evening of July 25th by smashing the windows of Mr. Feast and of all the Whigs in Cripplegate who had supported him. But this was small revenge for the liverymen for losing the election of their sheriffs. *The True Briton* complained on July 28th that the liberties of London had been poisoned by Whig corruption. It said that thugs hired by the Whigs could attack Philip's Tory supporters without being arrested, but that Tories could not defend themselves without being dispersed by the Guards:

> When Sir John Williams came at length to receive his right, and be sworn Alderman of Cripplegate Ward, those who assembled to express their joy on that occasion, and who innocently were drinking his health round a bonfire, found themselves attacked in the most violent manner, without their having given the least provocation. And such was the barbarity of the faction, that some men fired down in the midst of them, out of the Crown Tavern; and yet the constables were there, tamely permitting these barbarous attempts.

When the mob, thus irritated, began to defend themselves, the Proclamation was immediately read, and before they could possibly separate, several of them were apprehended, sent to prison, and even threatened with the loss of their lives.

The True Briton's moans were heeded by many, for in these early days of political journalism it was easy to give a rough Government a bad name; and the Whigs were already unpopular, not only in the City but also in the country at large. In the shires many felt that the prosecution of Atterbury had been unnecessary or unfair. London was still angry that the culprits for the South Sea disaster had been sheltered; they nicknamed Walpole "The Skreen". It was said that the Prince of Wales was once more considering breaking his unhappy truce with his father and going into active Opposition again. The muttering of a discontented people rose from dusty London during the long, hot summer of 1723, an indignant murmur against the clampdown of the new oligarchic system of government.

This year saw the fall of two of the greatest opposition fires: Atterbury had been exiled, and next Cowper, whose health had been worn down by gout in recent years, died on October 10th. His thirty-five years of public service were trumpeted by *The True Briton:*

> There is no speaking in his due praise, no way for any single man's expressing sufficient sorrow for so general a loss; for, when he grew silent, oratory was struck dumb...[9]

His death spurred the opposition on. A cluster of Philip's coaches were often seen hurrying between Twickenham and Westminster or the City or Lord Hillsborough's in Hanover Square or the Earl of Strafford's. He was still hopelessly extravagant. Opposition life had always been expensive, and Philip still led the life of a rake as well: brandy, faro, brothels and elections, the usual luxuries of an eighteenth-century aristocrat, steadily devoured his remaining guineas. He sold the advowson of Croglin to Matthew Smailes, his unpleasant Yorkshire agent. He found a new buyer for the estate and Elizabethan castle at Rathfarnham, accepting only £62,000 for it, from

William Conolly, the rich and wily old Speaker of the Irish House of Commons. Then in August, when a certain Benjamin Haskins Stiles petitioned the Court of Chancery to order that the estates that the trustees held — Over Winchendon, Westcot, Wooburn, Aske, Catterton and Wharton — should be sold to pay the £42,000 he owed him, Philip was forced to convey the last of his patrimony, (a few farms in Ireland, at Malmesbury and at Westport in Wiltshire, and the lead-mines in Swaledale) to the trustees as further security for his borrowings. The lead-mines, however, were extremely valuable, and gave a large yield in cash.

But his financial misfortune and Lady Mary's company were both forgotten during the late summer, when he left Twickenham for the North, to revisit the house for which he perhaps retained a romantic affection, "The old paternal seat of my family", Wharton Hall, and to rouse opposition sentiment in Yorkshire, Westmorland and Cumberland with robust speeches, helped by a crowd of noisy revellers, led by Sir Kit Musgrave. They hunted in the deer park at Wharton on Sundays, which disgusted the low-church yeomanry of the County. They roused Philip's tenants with inordinate amounts of drink. But their generosity did not stop their rollicking Jacobitism shocking the natives of Westmorland who, from Sir James Lowther in Lowther Hall to the humblest "statesman" farmer in Ravenstonedale, had been taught by the earlier Whartons to be Whigs almost to a man. In the middle of September when Philip's party was staying near Richmond, perhaps at Matthew Smailes's house at Gilling, he so exceeded himself that the Lowthers fifty miles away hoped they might get a charge of treason up against him:

> Lowther Sep 26 '23
>
> The Duke of Wharton went about ten days ago to his estate in Swaledale near Richmond, and Sir C. Musgrave alone with him. When they were there the Duke took an occasion of treating about three score of the country people, and after they had drank a good deal, the Duke and Sir C. Musgrave pulled off their coats and waistcoats, fell down upon their knees, and drank the Pretender's health by the name of James III of England and VIIIth of Scotland, and obliged all the

people who were with them to do the same. The noise of this was quickly spread, and the wives and daughters of the people who were in company came immediately, crying to fetch their husbands away. Some of the company being frightened, themselves went to make information of this to a Justice of the Peace, but the Justice, in all probability not caring to meddle with so great a man, told the people who came to him, that if they would bring the offenders before him, he would do as the law directed, but he would grant no warrant. Whether any part of the story be true or not, I can't pretend to say... [10]

But Philip was soon obliged to return from the North to attend duty as the editor and author of *The True Briton*, because in August the Whigs had become so alarmed by its success that they started publishing a rival to it called *The Briton*. During his absence Richardson and Oldisworthy had filled *The True Briton* with letters — some genuine, most bogus — written under pseudonyms like "Athaliah Dormant", "Orthodox" or "Old Honesty". But in its thirty-fifth issue, on September 30th, [11] the *True Briton* contains purely editorial matter, no letters, so we can guess that Philip was back at work.

He soon received, or more probably composed, and printed, a delightful letter, signed "A.Z.", declaring affection for all English laws, and especially for

> His Majesty's Worshipful *Justices of the Peace*. There is not, in my opinion, so solemn, so venerable a creature under the sun, as a Justice. Mark him! With what deliberation he smokes his pipe, or drinks his coffee! With what composure of countenance he receives the Homage of the Vulgar! With which promptness and knowledge he interprets an obscure point of law! Such is a single country justice. But when they are in sessions, when a whole bench of them are assembled, their united awefulness is inexpressible. Nay, though a man be in himself contemptible, a fellow of no mark nor likelihood, yet as soon as he is in the Commission for the Peace, in my eyes he becomes considerable. Thus a round piece of

copper, in diameter an inch, is worthless, only fit to mend a kettle; but let the Sovereign's head be stamped on it, it straight grows current coin through the land, will purchase Half-a-penny loaf of bread, or get your honour's shoes double-Japanned. [12]

Similarly ironical is a letter signed "Violette" purporting to condemn vice and promiscuity caused by the prevalence of masked balls, "masquerades", which perhaps Lady Mary wrote for Philip. He introduced it with a few pious words of his own: [13]

THE TRUE BRITON
Number LXXVI
Monday February 3 1723-4

We shall present our Readers with the following Letter from a Lady, who seems to have but too much reason to exclaim against a Diversion that may be of the most pernicious consequence to Youth, and especially of the Fair Sex, as it seems to have a natural tendency to poison and debauch the Morals of the British Gentry, and throws down and levels all Orders and Distinctions; coupling the Nobleman with the Peasant, the Duchess with the Groom, the fine Ladies with the most abandoned and profligate Rakes, and subjects the greatest to the attacks of the meanest ruffian... The practices of the Generality of Mankind shew the world to be but ONE GREAT MASQUERADE, and when we are so depraved in General, we have little need of introducing Arts to help forward and propagate the Mischief to individuals, especially of that Sex whose only Ornaments and Defence are Inviolable Modesty and Strict Virtue...

To the TRUE BRITON
SIR
'Tis with Pleasure I find many of our Reverend Clergy, and the *whole bench* of Bishops, join to descry the *Masquerades*, and interpose their Authority to prevent the Ladies of *Great Britain* being exposed to the attacks of their footmen... The

unseasonable hours; the promiscuous company; the unbounded freedom of the place; the inspiring liquors, and tempting viands, and the unbridled liberties of converse, are strange temptations, and fit for very few who are not abandoned to the luxuries of a most degenerate age, and cannot act a part in the blackest and most criminal parts of corrupted life...

The sex had so many Vanities and Foibles before, that *Celibacy* was never so common, nor *Matrimony* more despised; and in a while, the sober Part of Mankind will disclaim the Tie that gives them a chance so unequal to their merits, and exposes their Beds to the Intrigues and Pollutions of abandoned rakes and jilting coquettes; and then the sex may thank themselves for becoming a prey, both Persons and Fortunes, for want of better offers, to the hardened attempts of *Irish* impudence, whose natural talent is *masquerading* in every Part of Life. You will excuse me this Warmth of Expression, which is owing to the utter ruin of a dear Kinswoman, whose ample Fortunes and blooming beauties are destroyed and blasted by successful villainy and corroding Diseases, the consequence of an intrigue that began *last Masquerading time*...

Your humble servant
VIOLETTE

Lady Mary herself, who was still Philip's mistress, had complained of the decline in marriage only a few months earlier, in a letter to her sister the wife of King James's Minister Lord Mar, and had added:

> I am very sorry for the forlorn state of matrimony... You may imagine, we married women look very silly; we have nothing to excuse ourselves, but that it was done a great while ago, and we were very young when we did it. [14]

During the London spring of 1724 she had been doing worse things with Philip than mere "masquerading". In March, she described a club which he and Hillsborough had founded to encourage sexual infidelity:

> Never was gallantry in so elevated a figure as it is at present. Twenty very pretty fellows (The Duke of Wharton being President and their chief director) have formed themselves into a committee of gallantry. They call themselves Schemers, and meet regularly three times a week to consult on Gallant Schemes for the advancement of that branch of happiness which the vulgar call Whoring. Viscount Hillsborough... has turned his house, one of the handsomest in Hanover Square, into an edifice appropriated to this use. He opened on Ash Wednesday by the best contrived entertainment in the world, and the only remedy against spleen and vapours occasioned by the formality of that day, which still subsists amongst other rage of Popery not yet rooted out.
>
> The Schemers were all sworn to several articles absolutely necessary for the promotion of public good and the conservation of peace in private families:
>
> 1. That every member should come in at the hour of six masked in a dominie, leading in the then predominant lady of his affections masked likewise.
>
> 2. That no member should presume, by peeping, squeaking, staring or any other impertinence, to discover his brother's incognita, who should remain wholly and solely his, without any molestation soever, to his use for that night being.
>
> 3. No member should dare to introduce any Lady who did not appear barefaced at the Drawing Room, Lady Stafford's etc.
>
> 4. And lastly, that if by accident or the lady's indiscretion her name should by chance be discovered by one or more of the Schemers, that name should remain sacred and unspeakable as the name of the Deity among the Jews.
>
> You may imagine that such wholesome laws brought all the best company to this polite assembly; and to these the in-

ducement of good music, fine liquors, a splendid supper and the best punch ever tasted. But you'll ask, how could they sup without showing their faces? You must know the very garrets were cleaned and lighted out at this solemnity. The whole company viewed the supper, which was large enough to suffer every fair one to point to what she thought most delightful, to be conveyed to her respective apartment. Those who were yet in a state of probation, and scrupled too much happiness in this world for fear of its being deducted in the next, had screens set round little public tables, which were as inviolate (but by the partners) as walls of adamant. You may imagine there were few of this latter class, and 'tis to be hoped that good examples and the indefatigable endeavours of the Schemers (who spare no pains in carrying on the good cause) will lessen them daily. These gallantries are continued every Wednesday during Lent... The whole generation of fathers, mothers and husbands raise as great a clamour against this new institution as the pagan priests did of old against the light of the Gospel, and for the same reasons, since it sticks at the very foundation of their authority, which authority is built on a gross imposition upon mankind. [15]

Although Philip was never wholly constant to anything or anybody, Lady Mary continued to hold the highest place in his affections. He responded happily to her combative wit. She shared his well-known taste for practical jokes, one of which he now aimed at the Masons. His reign over the Freemasons, though making them fashionable, had lowered their repute amongst sober folk. In the blunt words of William Stukeley, the Order "took a run and ran itself out of breath through the folly of its members." [16] And now that he was no longer Grand Master, many of his wilder followers left its ranks. So Philip himself resigned also. But he pretended to turn his back on its mystical principles. He then joined, or founded, a club called The Gormogans, which met at the Castle Tavern in Fleet Street, and whose object was to ridicule the Masons. A mock advertisement appeared in the Daily Post in September 1724, declaring that it had a mystical history which parodied the Freemasons' improbable legends:—

> The truly Antient Noble Order of the Gormogans instituted by Chin-Quaw Ky-Po, the first Emperor of China, many thousands of years before Adam and of which the great Confucius was Oecumenical Volgee, has lately been brought into England by a Mandarin... This is to inform the public that there will be no drawn sword at the door, nor ladder in a dark room, nor will any Mason be received as a member till he has renounced his novel Order and been properly degraded. [17]

Nothing more is known about the Gormogans, though in the *Merry Thought*, a periodical published late in the 1720s, the Gormogans are listed with the Royal Society itself as a "learned society". [18]

Having tired of the Masons, Philip now lost his enthusiasm for *The True Briton* also. Although after five or six dozen enormously popular issues [19] it had reached wide high-church Tory readership without suffering the implications of scandal and irresponsibility that plagued the Jacobite *Mist's Weekly Journal*, yet perhaps because its sale no longer grew or because *The Briton* was successfully discrediting it, he pretended that it was being no particular help to the opposition. Certainly publishing it twice a week and bailing out printers who were imprisoned for libelling the Government was very expensive. So in February 1724, just after its best articles had been published, he decided abruptly to close it down. Its last issue fired a broadside of backhanded abuse at the Whigs and their system of Government. *The Briton*, the Whig's periodical, closed down a week later.

But Philip was wrong if he thought that freedom from journalistic pressures would allow him to become more effective in Parliament, where confidence in the opposition, which now lacked both Atterbury and Cowper, was waning. Although on March 16th he attacked the Mutiny Bill in one of his great orations, haranguing the Ministry Lords with the sweeping eloquence that reminded his enemies of how dangerous he could be, his speech achieved no purpose, and succeeded in raising only 22 votes against the Government's 77. It is quoted in full in the Parliamentary History [20] and in Hazlitt's

Eloquence of the British Senate, [21] and was printed contemporaneously by Philip himself in an unmodest way, together with his now famous speech in defence of Atterbury, probably on Richardson's presses which lay idle after *The True Briton* had ceased publication.

When Parliament rose for six months on April 26th, he was resigned to the Government being impregnable. "Politics are no more", wrote Lady Mary. The country, she said, enjoyed "all the joys of arbitrary power." [22] Dean Swift took to pitying Philip, a sure sign he though him a failure:

> I sometimes think Duke Wharton intends to take my advice of fancying to have virtue. I remember Mrs. Bracegirdle got more by acting that part than any of the more abandoned playhouse females, there is a sort of contrast in it. I saw a long printed speech of his, and intend to know it when I can. [23]

In London a pamphlet addressed to "The Earl of P— and M—" by "D.F.R." appeared in Philip's favour, defending him from the moral indignation that the old Hugenot theologian J.A.Dubourdieu, now the Chaplain of the Savoy, had vented in a sermon calling him Mephiboseth which he had preached in January and printed with a pointed dedication to:

> Duc de ——, Macon libre, Breton de faux aloy, Ecrivain Hebdomadaire, Bourgeouise de la ville de Londres, Maitre cirier & c...

Philip spent the summer devoted to Lady Mary, poetry and the noisy celebration of Phil Lloyd's marriage in June:

> The Duke of Wharton's Mr. Floyd [sic] has run away with a Miss 'Cade: she has £5,000 and he nothing, but they have set up a coach and chariot and make a great flutter, have given favours with a little purple in the middle of them, which they say is a badge of the extravagant society they are of, for they are both gallant schemers. [24]

Philip's idle hours were spent at Twickenham dallying with Edward Young and Elijah Fenton, snarling at Pope, exchanging obscene verse satires with Lady Mary, and starting to write a blank-verse tragedy on Mary Queen of Scots, for which Lady Mary wrote an epilogue, but which is otherwise wholly lost except for four rather indifferent lines:

> Sure were I free, and Norfolk were a prisoner,
> I'd fly with more patience to his arms,
> Than the poor Israelite gaz'd on the serpent
> When life was the reward of every look. [25]

When Lady Mary wrote a short poem on the death of a young bride called Mrs. Bowes, his answer to it implies that having been exposed to her company so exhaustively this summer, he was beginning to find her a too demanding mistress; "Wortley" in line 15 is Lady Mary, and "Montagu" in line 14 is her estranged husband:

> Hail Poetess! for thou art truly blest,
> Of wit, of beauty and of love possessed:
> Your muse does seem to bless poor Bowes's fate,
> But far 'tis from you to desire her state.
> In every line your wanton soul appears,
> Your verse though smooth, scare fit for modest ears;
> No pangs of jealous fondness doth thou show,
> And bitter dregs of love thou ne'er didst know;
> The coldness, that your husband oft hath mourned,
> Does vanish quite often when warmed on Turkish ground;
> For fame does say, if fame don't lying prove,
> You paid obedience to the Sultan's love;
> Who, fair one, was your imperious lord?
> Not Montagu's but Mahomet's, the sword:
> Great as your wit, just so is Wortley's love,
> Your next attempt will be on thundering Jove;
> The little angels you on Bowes bestow,
> But gods themselves are only fit for you. [26]

While their public flirtation carried on, poor crippled Alexander

Pope, who had always loved her, grew more jealous. He had written pages of poetry, which is not his best, about her and to her. Now he evidently quarrelled with her, and for the rest of his life lost no opportunity to lash her in his published verse. The reasons he had given for their well-publicised quarrel were various; she laughed at him when he declared his passion for her, or she wrote a satire, said it was his, and distributed it, (a common Twickenham joke) so that he received the blame. But, according to the Countess of Pomfret, who as Lady of the Bedchamber to the Princess of Wales was constantly at nearby Richmond Palace, Lady Mary "Got much acquainted with the Duke of Wharton, that Mr. Pope grew jealous, and that occasioned the breach." [27] Philip himself, who only made enemies by accident, never sought a quarrel with Pope; but it is a sad reflection on the failure of Philip's name that he is best remembered for the magnificent jealous lines on him Pope published in his First Moral Essay, and which but for the publisher's remonstrance [28] would have been yet more bitter:

> *Wharton*, the scorn and wonder of our days
> Whose ruling passion was the lust of praise;
> Born with whate'er could win it from the wise,
> Women and fools must like him or he dies;
> Though wondering senates hung on all he spoke,
> The club must hail him master of the joke;
> Shall parts so various aim at nothing new?
> He'll shine a Tully and a Wilmot too;
> Then turn repentant, and his God adores
> With the same spirit that he drinks and whores;
> Enough if all around him but admire,
> And now the punk applaud, and now the friar.
> Thus with each gift of nature and of art
> And wanting nothing but an honest heart
> Grown all to all — from no one vice exempt —
> And most contemptible to shun contempt,
> His passion still, to covet general praise,
> His life, to forfeit it a thousand ways;
> A constant bounty, which no friend has made,

An angel tongue which no man can persuade,
A fool with more of wit than half mankind,
Too rash for thought, for action too refined,
A tyrant to the wife his heart approves,
A rebel to the very king he loves,
He dies, sad outcast of each church and state,
And, harder still, flagitious, yet not great. [29]

Of his old Tory political friends Philip now saw more of those most inclined to Jacobitism, Orrery, North and Grey, Lichfield, Brooke, Scarsdale and Lord Strafford, rather than those of Pope's circle, Lord Bathurst and Sir William Wyndham and their fellow admirers of the turncoat Harry Bolingbroke who had returned to England with a Government pardon at the time of Atterbury's exile. Most important for Philip this autumn was the ending of his friendship for Edward Young. Young had never left the Whig party. Nor had he found it easy to live on an annuity from the Duke which was never paid. In exasperation he returned to Oxford to take Holy Orders and earn a living of his own. He considered he had been badly treated, as he told Thomas Tickell the publisher:

> I therefore earnestly beg you to contribute your friendship to me... because the very great injury I at present suffer from the Duke might recommend me to the kind offices even of a stranger. [30]

Perhaps Young was jealous of Lady Mary's place in Philip's affection. But he need not have been. Philip and she were both so demanding, outspoken and fickle in love, that their friendship, which was founded on mutual respect, was now developing into mutual rivalry. From being partners they became competitors. Often during 1724 they quarrelled about trivia. He found her too close a friend to "Molly" Skerrett, who had lately become mistress to Robert Walpole. So he wrote a satire on another of her friends and distributed it as hers. Lady Mary was justifiably angry. This started their final quarrel. On February 5th 1725 she wrote about him in the pretence-

Jacobite code she used to her sister Lady Mar, which required her (curiously) to call him "Sophia":

> Sophia and I have been quite reconciled and are now quite broke, and I believe not likely to piece up again. [31]

So their lurid romance ended. Sadly most details of it have been lost. Almost none of her letters from this period survive, because after her death Edward Young sorted through them and burnt most of them for their obscenity.

Not only Philip's love for Lady Mary but also his love for Twickenham and Augustan literature waned during the winter of 1724/5. Nursing a bruised heart, he sought his wife, who was living quietly in Holland Street, in Soho. Her beauty and her devotion to him soon earned her the position of his confidante, which she had never been before. He returned to her rather motherly affection as a reaction to the wild flightiness of Lady Mary, who cattily remarked:

> The Duke of Wharton has brought his Duchess to town, and is fond of her to distraction, in order to break the hearts of all other women that have any claim on him... As well as the usual attentions which he pretends to perform o'nights, he has public devotions twice a day, and assists at them in person with exemplary devotion. And there is nothing pleasanter than the remarks of some pious ladies on the conversation of such a sinner. [32]

Although the innuendo behind Lady Mary's words "pretends to perform" implies that Philip's excesses were making him impotent, his revived affection for his wife was soon fruitful. On his twenty-sixth birthday, near Christmas time in 1724, Martha Duchess of Wharton found herself pregnant again.

This piece of news was the only light in Philip's dark prospects ahead. The next six months saw his English fortunes sink to their lowest ebb. But he now laid foundations for a new life. Exasperated by Parliamentary politics he turned to something shadier. He wrote to Rome, to John Hay, the Pretender's Secretary of State, and asked for a position of authority over the Jacobites in England, and for a small salary. His pressing debts, he said deceitfully, were only a few hundred pounds.

Hay sent him £25 and stiffly replied that if the Duke's debts were so small, then surely his friends amongst the Tory lords would pay them; and if the Jacobites wanted him to have any authority over them, they could appoint him themselves. Philip took the hint. When he wrote again with the London political news he did not mention his insolvency or his ambitions. Martha, on his instructions, wrote to James's wife, Queen Clementina, who was also expecting a child:

> Madam   Feb 24 1725
> ...I should think myself most happy if your majesty would at any time honour me with your commands here which I shall punctually obey with the greatest cheerfulness and be ready constantly to do all the service in my poor power for the common cause by encouraging my husband to pursue with steadiness and resolution the noble part which I hope providence will enable him to act... [33]

But Martha's own pregnancy was not going well. In spite of the attention of expensive doctors, Dr. Meade and Dr. Beauclerk, she continued ill throughout the Spring. Philip, rather unconcernedly, wrote during February to suggest that James should be godfather to his child if it were a boy — Lord Lichfield standing as Royal proxy — or, if it were a girl, that the Queen might be godmother. James agreed, and because his second son, Prince Henry was born early in March, he could add rather touchingly,

> Pray make many kind compliments from your lady to me, I wish she may soon follow my wife's example. [34]

Philip's debts were the roots of his despondency. Although his estate was mortgaged and in trust for his creditors, the management of it was still in his own irresponsible hands. On February 5th he calculated he owed £70,000. So he conveyed all his remaining assets, and assigned all his existing rights under the trusts, to Walter Pryse, and gave power of attorney to Nathaniel Piggott the lawyer, acting with Lord Orrery and Sir Kit Musgrave, to pay off everything and to save what remained of his property for him. He himself set aside a borrowed £10,500 for his own use, sending £6,500 of this to a Jacobite banker called Benjamin Gascoigne in Rotterdam and the rest to Walters, the Jacobite banker at Paris. He was thinking of going abroad.

This resolution in him hardened as life in London became more ignoble for him. In February he was dining with Sir William Stapleton in company which included Sir William's younger brother, a hot-headed and very patriotic Whig ensign in the Guards. To liven up the evening Philip drank to the Pretender's health, and said he "wondered the French did not send ten thousand men with the Pretender, that now was the only time, for there was nothing but boys in the army".[35] At this Ensign Stapleton told him he was a coward and a famous one: words which, of course, demanded that Philip should challenge him. But Philip did nothing; as usual he refused to fight. He always paled to see a drawn sword, which was strange, as his father had been a great duellist, but perhaps lucky, or he might long ago have been run through by any irate Whig Guards Officer who had a quarrel with him. But the rest of the company at dinner sneered, and Ensign Stapleton fumed as Philip was taken away in sedan chair surrounded with bodyguards.

He himself made light of his feebleness. He once wrote about how he had once been arrested by the Royal Guard for singing Jacobite songs while he was drunk in St. James's Park, and had allowed himself to be disarmed:

> The Duke he drew out half his sword,
> The Guard drew out the rest...

On another occasion he had gone to visit Colonel Charters at Wooburn, and when Charters was trying to explain a conversational point by waving his sword around, the Duke fainted away. But as he was well aware, his cowardice brought him into public scorn. Dr. King, a contemporary, noted that

He wanted personal courage. The last, however, would probably have been concealed, if he had been a sober man. But he drank immoderately, and was very abusive and sometimes very mischievous in his wine, so that he drew on himself frequent challenges, which he would never honour.[36]

In June after he and his Tory friend Lord Scarsdale had insulted the Government and the Crown by drinking the Pretender's health at a dinner which his sometime leader the Prince of Wales attended, the Whig Lord Scarborough sent a second to challenge Lord Scarsdale, but the latter refused to accept it on the grounds it had never been his idea to drink to the Pretender, but that Wharton, with drawn sword, had forced him to. Lord Scarborough's second blandly replied to this that he would tell his principal it was not worth his while waiting in the park with a sword and pistol for such a poltroon as could be frightened by as great a coward as Wharton, but that he would cut a piece out of his nose when they next met.

In politics during the early part of 1725, Philip was faring no better. The session that began on January 11th saw matters debated which would have brought down a Government in the old days of a strong opposition. The Lord Chancellor, Lord Macclesfield, was shown guilty of corruption; the democratic constitution of the City of London was to be "reframed" so that it would be less Tory; Lord Bolingbroke was to be allowed his estates once more; and the Highlanders of Scotland were to be forcibly stripped of their arms. But even in the face of such provocative measures, Philip and the opposition Lords failed to regain any potency. Walpole's "management" of Parliament had been utterly successful. A pathetic five names signed their protests against the Highland Bill. But the effect of Bolingbroke's Bill was saddest. Some of the opposition, including Philip, knew how Bolingbroke had betrayed the Pretender, and hated him as a traitor. Others, like Lord Bathurst, Sir William Wyndham, Swift and Pope, remembered only his glories as a leader of the Tories with Lord Oxford under Queen Anne, and they supported him. So the Bolingbroke Bill divided even the ranks of the opposition party. And this trivial split had large repercussions. Those who now voted for Bolingbroke were declaring themselves against the Pretender; they were the first Hanoverian or anti-Jacobite Tories, the ancestors of the Tories of George III and the nineteenth century. Philip's little force, on the other hand, the last Parliamentary Jacobites, who opposed Bolingbroke, were henceforth political outcasts, to be hounded from the fields of political respectability into wastes of intrigue and treason.

By the summer of 1725, Philip and the world had both realised the hopelessness of his position. A contemporary remarked, "The Court don't much mind what the Duke of Wharton says or does, they give him rope supposing he'll at last hang himself, when they get a hank over him they'll go near to stop for good and all his future proceedings." [37] In Parliament, he had actually been elected to chair two committees, one of them the committee considering Lord Macclesfield's impeachment, which showed that the House regarded him as harmless. Bankrupt and politically redundant, his wife, who was temporarily his best friend, was ill; Lady Mary and he were "broke to an irredeemable degree", [38] and Whig society at large no longer tolerated him. But he had already decided on his next move. What he could do for the Jacobites had dawned upon him during the last dismal months. He would leave England, and would not return until he had engaged an invasion force for the support of James.

In late June he set out and sailed for the continent. He gave word only to his most trusted Tory friends as to where he was going and for what reason: Charles Cesar, the leader of the Jacobites in the Commons, Lord Orrery, Strafford and Dr. Friend. He kept the secret even from his two young sisters, Lucy and Jane, and Lady Mary thought he had gone to Paris. He told them and others that he was going abroad to economise and live quietly until his debts were paid off. In England he left only a desolate Duchess and a bitter song, an imitation of that *Sung at the opera by Mrs.... on her leaving the English stage to return to Italy:*

> Puppies! whom I now am leaving,
> Sometimes merry, always mad,
> Who lavish most when debts are craving
> On fool, and farce, and masquerade;
> Oh who would from such bubbles run

The True Briton

Or leave such blessings, for the sun?

* * *

Happy soil! and simple crew,
Let old sharpers yield to new,
Cullies all, adieu! adieu! [39]

CHAPTER ELEVEN

Vienna

> His passion still, to covet general praise,
> His life, to forfeit it a thousand ways...
> > Pope on Wharton, *First Moral Essay*, 196-7

In late June 1725 Philip sailed for Rotterdam, en route for Vienna and the Court of the Holy Roman Emperor, Charles VI of Austria.

Of all the monarchs in Europe, Charles was the most cautious, conventional and (probably) reliable. His manners were formal and his mind was slow. Communication with his brother monarchs was impeded because he refused to allow them the title of "Majesty", which he claimed was solely an Imperial title, and most refused to be addressed as anything else. Philip thought (as we know from his letters of this period which were preserved in abundance at the Jacobite Court, and which now survive in the Royal Archives at Windsor) that a man such as the Emperor would approve of King James's sound hereditary right to the throne of Britain, and that if he was secured as a friend, he could be relied upon as the cornerstone of an alliance to drive the Hanoverians and Walpoleites out of England. He was already angry with the British. They had let him down by making a separate peace with France at the Treaty of Utrecht and so depriving him of the advantages of the great victories at Blenheim and afterwards, which his own general, Prince Eugen, had won in conjunction with the Duke of Marlborough. And now their jealousy opposed his plans to set up a trading company at Ostend, in his own Austrian Netherlands. Because George I, being a Prince of the Holy Roman Empire as well as the King of Great Britain, was theoretically a vassal of his, he regarded this disagreeable attitude as slightly impertinent.

So Philip drove hopefully towards Vienna. His carriages carried with him a handful of servants including his two valets-de-chambre, Scipio and Harry, two gentlemen hangers-on called Quinn and Michael Stecho, and a Jacobite agent called James Hamilton. But compared to the foreign representatives of the great European powers, each backed by a network of secret agents, whose world of intrigue he was entering, he lacked any experience or reliable staff. He was terribly ignorant of the details of European foreign affairs. He had no knowledge of diplomacy. But he held a few good cards in the diplomatic game. He purported to be the representative of the Jacobites of Britain. And all the Ministers of Europe, from Walpole in Whitehall to the humblest Jesuit in the Vatican, were ignorant, to a man, of the strength or weakness of the Jacobite cause. No one knew whether the English Tory squires who surreptitiously drank to "the little gentleman in black velvet" and "the King over the water" would turn out as dragoons for the Stuarts as their grandfathers had done for King Charles. All that was certain was that the English were accustomed to deposing Kings at internals of approximately forty years, and by that reckoning it was time for a fresh coup d'état.

Philip had to persuade the Emperor of two things: that Britain was ripe for rebellion, and that an invasion of England on behalf of the Pretender was militarily possible. He was confident in the first; there was enough evidence that the British loathed George I and Walpole's Government. But could he show that a Restoration from abroad was practicable in the face of Whig defiance? This depended on the strength of the invasion, which depended on the European alliances which supported it. And on this he heard good news at Rotterdam. The Emperor, he gathered, had lately signed two treaties with Spain.

The eccentric monarchs of Spain, feeble-minded Philip V and his formidable Queen Elizabeth Farnese, disliked Britain as much as the Emperor did, principally for capturing Gibraltar and Minorca in the name of a contender in the War of Spanish Succession twenty years before and not giving them back; and because their Catholic Majesties were as fanatically Catholic as any of their Catholic predecessors had been, they naturally supported the Catholic claimant to the thrones of England and Scotland. In 1719 they had actually sent a new Armada to invade Britain on behalf of the Pretender. It had not arrived. But only their isolation, bankruptcy and inefficiency kept them from launching another one now.

In truth, however, the Jacobites were not quite ready for a Restoration. Since John Hay, Lord Kinnoul's brother, had replaced as their Secretary of State the incompetent Lord Mar who had so fumbled the 'Fifteen, he had grown suspicious of Lord Mar's loyalty, and told James he suspected him of selling their secrets to the Whigs. So when Bishop Atterbury arrived in Paris in 1723 he was commissioned by James to search Mar's private papers, and having done so he declared that what he found was incriminating. Mar, although protesting he had always acted with James's approval, was dismissed from all his Jacobite offices, and was replaced at Paris by Atterbury himself. He retired to sulk outside Paris with a few friends. The Whig secret service spread rumours amongst the Jacobites that he had been maligned. John Hay, the Secretary of State at Rome, was given the title Earl of Inverness for his part in the exposure of Mar. The Jacobites as a whole had been made to seem slightly ridiculous by the affair.

Philip was determined to be a credit to them. He knew his faults; that he was a drunkard, hopelessly extravagant and too talkative. He resolved now to be sober and to spend little and to be discreet. So he arranged for at least one close Jacobite friend to accompany him on every stage of his journey, to keep an eye on him and provide him with someone to unburden himself to. From London to Rotterdam the polished and learned agent of the English Jacobites, James Hamilton, served this purpose perhaps too well, for he seems to have fallen in love with Philip and afterwards wrote to him in terms of doting affection. But he was left at Rotterdam to co-ordinate Jacobite affairs there, and particularly to keep open Philip's supply of money from Waters the banker there and from London if necessary. From Rotterdam to Frankfurt his place in Philip's coach was taken by Captain Butler, who held a commission in an Irish regiment in the Spanish service and was a bastard son of the pleasant old Duke of Ormonde. His semi-literate bluffness contrasted sharply with the manners of gentle James Hamilton, and although (according to Philip) he was good company when drunk, he was an inefficient assistant for the difficult cyphering and decyphering of the correspondence that Philip exchanged with Rome. But he could hold his tongue. Shortly before leaving England Philip had been rebuked for slackness in the use of code for his letters to Rome, and he was determined not to be corrected for indiscreetness again. So he reported to Lord Mar a

Jacobite doctor whom he met on the road and who talked too much about the court at Rome. And he trusted few with even the secret of their destination, though he could absolutely depend on Scipio and Harry, his valets-de-chambre, who had been with him when he had visited James at Avignon nine years before. Lord North and Grey, who arrived at Rotterdam with his Dutch wife shortly after Philip had left, was ignorant of their purpose. Philip knew his garrulous drinking habits too well to be able to trust him. Nor did he even correspond with Atterbury in Paris, although the Bishop badly wanted to see him, and wrote advice and poems in Latin telling him so. Philip guessed that the French, who were allied to Britain, opened all the Bishop's letters and passed everything of interest in them to London.

So when Philip's outriders clattered into the outskirts of Vienna, the Whigs in England and their agents throughout Europe had no inkling that his journey had a serious purpose. They thought he was on an idle Grand Tour, and were happy to forget him. But the affection his friends felt for him show in the shower of letters that followed him to Vienna. Lord Orrery and Walter Pryse told him they were making headway with his financial affairs. Over sixty thousand pounds had been offered by the Duchess of Marlborough for the Winchendon estate, and an offer of £20,000 was expected for the manor of Aske in Yorkshire. When he returned to England, they said, then he might return to enjoy a fortune once more. But James Hamilton, writing as soon as he had reached London on his return from Rotterdam, reported the bad news that the Duchess had lost her child:

> London   July 27th (O.S.) 1725
> My Lord Duke,
> I was thirteen days rolling between Rotterdam and this, in squalls and very bad weather and in a fair way of feeding the fish, but the Gods will take care of Cato. On my arrival I waited on my Lady Duchess who I found in a sad state of health, it seems Her Grace has a false conception. The physicians gave forcing medicines which on Saturday last had the desired effect, Her Grace is yet in a weak condition. As my Lord Orrery hath been daily with Her Grace at the

physician's house and is to write fully on this subject to Your Grace, I need not say any more than that His Lordship acts for Your Grace as if you were his son...

My Beckie earnestly desires that her duty and best wishes may be acceptable to Your Grace, and she longs to lead the same sort of life with Your Grace as she had the honour of doing when you was here.[1]

The loss of his second child was a terrible blow to Philip; but the loss was greater for Martha. The hope of an heir had been one of the few links between herself and her whimsical husband. Now her health continued to deteriorate.

Philip and his party took an unfashionable house in a quiet suburb of Vienna on Monday 23rd July. He noticed it was a cosmopolitan, Asiatic city, still part medieval and part oriental. In the manners of its people and in the style of its architecture it kept an eastern sleepiness that was both romantic and pompous. The great buildings of the Imperial city, the Stephansdom and the Hofburg, were vast in dimensions and solid in style. The manners of the Imperial Court seemed to a foreigner to be similarly laborious, old-fashioned and dreary. The perambulations of the Emperor from the Hofburg to the summer palace at Schönbrunn, from Schöbrunn to his hunting-lodge at Mayerlin, and thence back to the Hofburg, were as monotonous as the predictable working of his Ministers. The leisure hours of the nobility were usually spent in playing sedate billiards in grand public billiard-halls, an dallying with elderly mistresses. To have a youthful mistress was quite out of fashion. Vienna seemed to be a city of the antique.

Lady Mary, who had stayed in the town nine years earlier, had been struck by the disharmony of grandeur and squalor in the great houses of the city:

> The appartments of the greatest ladies and even of the Ministers of State are divided but by a partition from that of a tailor or a shoe-maker, and I know nobody that has above two floors in any house, one for their own use and one higher for their servants. Those that have houses of their own let out the rest of them to whoever will take 'em: thus

the great stairs (which are all of stone) are as common and as dirty as the street.[2]

Philip found the Jacobite Resident at Vienna was a clever and charming Irishman called Thomas Sheridan, who lived so far away in the outskirts of the city that Philip had difficulty in finding him. He set up his own household deliberately near his so that he could see him secretly, and so that even if Sheridan had been smelt out by the Whig secret service, nothing of his malodour would attach to himself. Philip was happy, too, to escape appearing at Court for the present, so as to seem uninterested by Governments and Ministers. He wanted to be thought a mere idle tourist. All of which he reported to James, who approved it as much as he approved Philip's report of Sheridan, the almost perfect secret agent: charming, discreet, witty and brave. He was one of many Irishmen who served the Jacobites loyally for little reward. They were often badly treated by James, who preferred the dour competence of his Scottish subjects to the erratic brilliance of the Irish.

Sheridan was soon Philip's guide, instructor, secretary and friend. He taught Philip the ways of the Imperial Court, and provided the intelligent audience that was needed to receive Philip's ever-flowing stream of plans and ideas. Captain Butler, feeling that he was being squeezed out of the Duke's favour by Sheridan, soon left the two to their own company and departed for Paris.

Only when Philip had discussed the whole of his mission with Sheridan did he begin to appreciate the difficulty of his task. First, he had arrived at a very formal Court with no credentials, seemingly no ambassador but a mere travelling nobleman. Next, he had to propose to the Austrians a plan to overturn his own Government, with whom they were still theoretically on friendly terms. If he succeeded even in obtaining an audience with one of the Emperor's ministers, which was itself unlikely, he might be rewarded for his impertinent proposals by prompt expulsion from Austria and a treason charge in Britain. The dangers of his task were appalling. But greater, to Philip, were the hopes of success. If he arranged a Restoration he could demand from James III honours so fantastic that they would make the Whigs' gift of Blenheim Palace to the Duke of Marlborough seem mean by comparison.

On the day after he met Philip, Sheridan introduced him to Baron de Saint-Saphorin, the British Government's consul (then called a "Minister" or "Resident") at Vienna. According to Philip he was "a Swiss by birth, a most cunning inveterate fellow".[3] But Sheridan and Philip's admirable discreetness prevented him from knowing that either of them were Jacobites. He was therefore pleased and honoured to meet an English Duke, and came to call on Philip at the first possible opportunity after he was introduced. Sheridan witnessed this visit with glee. Philip told Saint-Saphorin that he had given up politics and had come to Vienna only in pursuit of pleasure, but that he would like Saint-Saphorin to introduce him to the Court. The "Minister" naturally swallowed this, and thereby, as Sheridan later said, he "gave the Duke of Wharton a great deal of secret pleasure."[4] He promised to introduce Philip to the principal Ministers of Austria, but lamented that Hanoverian Britain was not in favour there. The new friendship between Spain and the Emperor, he said, had been concluded without his knowledge; indeed, he had flatly been told that no proposal for such a thing existed. The arrogance of Spain, he added, was most alarming and the man he hated most in the world was Ripperda, the bombastic Spanish Ambassador at Vienna.

Jan Willem Ripperda had been born a Catholic Dutchman, but being ambitious he had turned Protestant to enter the Dutch government service, and had been sent to Spain. There he turned Catholic once more, joined the Spanish, and was employed by Elizabeth Farnese, the Queen, as an adviser and agent. Through her he became one of the most powerful men in Spain, and after being created Duke of Ripperda, to the disgust of the Grandees, he had been sent as ambassador to Vienna. Here his flamboyant and energetic style of diplomacy was proving successful. He was a war-monger; he believed in turning the eyes of the Spaniards towards an Austrian alliance and hostilities with the French and Hanoverians. The British representative in Madrid, the Whig William Stanhope, described him as "An infamous character".[5]

Philip realised from the gullible Saint-Saphorin how important Ripperda could be to the Jacobites. He immediately wrote to Rome to say that Ripperda was a man for the King to befriend.

Next Sheridan introduced Philip to the Pope's Nuncio at Vienna, Grimaldi, in whose unsearchable mail-bags the Jacobite despatches were sent to Rome. He told Philip that the Emperor's foreign policy had been run for many years by Prince Eugen, probably the greatest general alive in spite of his unprepossessing looks — he was small and pointed-faced. But his credit with the Emperor was waning, because the Emperor rightly suspected Eugen of Anglophilia. He was not actually in disgrace; the Emperor owed him too much for past services for that; but the proud, ponderous Great Chancellor, the Count Zindendorff, who seemed the incarnation of the characteristics of the Imperial city, was now replacing him as the Emperor's First Minister in foreign affairs as he was already in every other field of policy.

The Papal Nuncio advised Philip strongly not to be direct with Zindendorff, who was as yet no Jacobite supporter. Philip suggested that he should approach the Emperor personally, and not through Zindendorff. The Nuncio said that this would be disastrous; Zindendorff would discover and resent it. He advised that Zindendorff himself must be approached, but that he should be approached with guile, and if possible with Ripperda's support. So as soon as Philip was alone again he sent another carefully encoded express despatch to Rome, with two requests: first that he should be accorded formal credentials as James's Ambassador to the Court of Vienna, so that the Emperor would be able to receive him, and secondly that Spain be persuaded to support his mission. If Ripperda was ordered to support the Jacobite cause, he said, the Zindendorff might do the same.

August 1725 came to Vienna and found Philip spending his leisure hours in the best drawing-rooms and learning a lot about billiards. Saint-Saphorin had kept his promise and had given Philip the entrée to the Court by introducing him to everyone important there whom he knew. Perhaps the Duke's reputation as a man of fashion had preceded him to Vienna; anyway, his impudent wit opened all doors before him. He had dined with Prince Eugen at his new Belvedere palace and had met all the important Ministers and foreign ambassadors before he had even organised enough liveried servants to constitute an "equipage" grand enough for a Duke's appearance at the Emperor's court. His arrival was the best society news to penetrate the hot, dull state-rooms of the city that summer.

Philip Duke of Wharton. Rosalba Cariera. Royal Collection.

Thomas Marquis of Wharton. Sir Godfrey Kneller. Private Collection.

Ice-Fair. The Frozen Thames early in 1716.

Philip in his Ducal robes after taking his seat in the House of Lords. December 1719. Charles Jervas. Private Collection.

Frontispiece to the Constitutions of the Freemasons, Philip is presented with the book by the Duke of Montagu.

Gateway of Wharton Hall, Westmoreland.

Maria-Theresa, second Duchess of Wharton. Unknown Artist. Private Collection.

*Philip's last portrait. The neck-tie bears a quotation from Horace which translates "with love and jests".
Unknown Artist. Private Collection.*

As he drank and dawdled in billiard-halls and at faro-tables, the Ministers of the Whigs sat late at their conferences and their Cabinet meetings in Whitehall. Through their telegraph system of agents, ambassadors and spies, they had detected that the Jacobites throughout Europe were once more up to something. Lord Townshend, who was at Pyrmont, near Hanover, with King George, had first detected the source of their danger. As early as the time of Ripperda's first negotiations in Vienna he had written,

> I know not by what fatality things are come to pass, that there is as much curiosity to hear what is said and as much stress laid upon what is doing at Vienna, as there was to know what was said and done at Versailles in the height of the late King of France's glory... [6]

Robert Walpole's brother Horatio, who had reached Paris as British ambassador on July 22nd, now reported that the Jacobites were muttering of another invasion plan for England, boasting that they had Austrian support. Alderman Humphrey Parsons, Philip's friend the London Jacobite, was in Paris, and had been seen talking earnestly to Atterbury there. Something, the Whigs knew, was up. But they had no reason to suspect that Philip was trying to play any part in it.

But after Philip had been a week in Vienna, Saint-Saphorin wrote to Townshend to complain about him. Not because he yet believed him to be a Jacobite — he had no inkling of such a thing — but because Philip in the course of his meteroric social success at the Imperial Court had failed (not surprisingly) to say a good word for Saint-Saphorin. The latter wailed that he found himself and Britain as unpopular as ever. But fortunately for Philip this did not bother Townshend very much, partly because he did not guess that anyone would have employed the disreputable Philip for any serious intrigue, but more because he was now very busy. He was concerned with what Ripperda was doing, and with what Horatio Walpole had reported from France, and what was to be done about the Maltsters of Edinburgh and Glasgow who had organised a strike of all bakers and brewers as a protest against the Whig malt tax.

So Philip's true purpose in Vienna remained unknown both to his

Vienna

enemies and to the Ministers he was befriending at Vienna. And because he could do nothing for James until his credentials arrived from Rome, he simply waited, continuing to dine with Zindendorff and Prince Eugen in their palaces, charming them with his company, but breathing no word to them of "business", and attracting the eyes of the Emperor to himself by frequent appearances at Court and on the hunting-field. He did not worry about being spied on because he was discreet and because Sheridan kept a careful watch on all known Whig spies who came to Vienna and who seemed to take an interest in him. Saint-Saphorin continued to decline in the Emperor's favour; after a quarrel with the Sardinian Resident it seemed that he would have to retire from Court altogether. As Sheridan wrote to Rome on August 4th:

> ...I have often seen the Duke of Wharton. The Emperor and everybody else has received him very civilly, and many of them endeavour to divert and entertain him, and some also to pump him, for few people will be persuaded that he is come only out of curiosity... St. Saphorin goes this day and it is believed he will hardly return. [7]

Philip plunged into a love-affair with a young Countess, whose charms had been overlooked by the Austrian noblemen, probably because she was too young for them, and with her and plenty of drink and a certain amount of gambling he had soon forgotten that he had resolved to give up debauchery. But Thomas Sheridan, whom he liked greatly, stopped him becoming too single-mindedly sensual. He stopped him from leading the life of pure vice which he had sometimes led in London. Philip was lucky to have him there.

Such luck, in Philip's life did not usually last. Accordingly, early in August, they received orders from James III that Sheridan should return to Rome immediately. He was to be appointed under-tutor to the small, ill-fated boy Charles Edward, "Bonnie Prince Charlie", last Stuart Prince of Wales.

CHAPTER TWELVE

The Invasion of England

> In foreign realms, (for thou has travelled far),
> How curious to contemplate two state-rooks,
> Studious their nests to feather in a trice
> With all the necromantics of their art,
> Playing the game of *faces* at each other;
> Making court sweet-meats of their latent gall
> In foolish hope to steal each others' trust;
> Both cheating, both exulting, both deceived;
> And sometimes, both (let earth rejoice), undone!
>   Edward Young, *Night Thoughts,* Book 8.

Prince Charles Edward Stuart was now five. He was James's eldest son by Clementina Sobieska, the silly, rather sentimental and very pious Polish princess whom James had married in 1719. James doted on the boy, and maintained that he was advanced for his years. So early in 1725 he had ordered him to be taken prematurely out of the nursery and put in the care of two tutors, Sheridan and James Murray, a brother-in-law of Lord Inverness the Secretary of State. Murray was currently assisting Atterbury in Paris, but his recall to Rome was harmless to the Jacobites there. By contrast, Sheridan was being invaluable in Vienna. He was keeping Philip from vice, and Philip was beginning one of the most crucial and hopeful negotiations of James's life. James was a Stuart and not a subtle man, and he did not understand that Sheridan's present occupation was more honourable to Sheridan and a great deal more useful to the Cause than waiting daily on one of the Persons of His Majesty's Royal Family.

It was out of the question for Sheridan to refuse his new post. But he and the Duke both wrote to Rome to say how untimely this appointment was. Sheridan, referring to himself in the third person as the Jacobite code required, wrote and complained loudly about his proposed removal:

> Now, Sir, give me leave to tell you that I cannot but think (my) stay at Vienna more necessary than ever for the King's service, and the Duke of Wharton is of the same opinion...
>
> I cannot but think he stands very much in want of such assistance, and if you consider how melancholy a thing it is for a person of his character in the circumstances to be left in the hands of common servants and without any one person about him that he can confide in or converse freely with, you will be apt to think so too. [1]

But James wanted Sheridan to help Murray tutor his son because, unlike many Jacobites, both were Protestants, and he rightly thought that although Prince Charles was to be brought up a Catholic, the more Protestants that were stationed around the Prince the more acceptable he would be to Britain. So Thomas Sheridan sadly started to shut up his Viennese lodgings.

Meanwhile Philip kicked his heels in the spacious corridors and marble halls of the Hofburg and the Belvedere palaces. At the end of August, he had still not begun "business". His official credentials as Ambassador had not arrived from Rome. The best he could do was to ingratiate himself socially with Zindendorff, the Emperor's solemn Great Chancellor, and see him often without mentioning politics or "business" to him. They met at billiards, at Court and at dinner in Zinderdorff's own palace. Philip found this rather pleasant. He found that Viennese life rather suited him. But Atterbury and James Hamilton complained of his slackness as a correspondent, and suggested he was wasting his time. Each demanded to know what he was up to in Austria. He told them nothing. To Atterbury he sent only an account of affairs in England as he had left them. To James Hamilton he replied tetchily:

> You still could not forbear casting reflections upon me as if the love of a Bewitching Bottle and a precipitate manner of transacting business were two vices inseparable from me...
>
> I hope to hear no more suspicions of that kind... The King and Lord Inverness are, I think, satisfied with my behaviour and I thank God I have had Mr. Sheridan with me who has

been an eye-witness of all my actions.[2]

In his spare hours he composed a "Memorandum" to Zindendorff and the Emperor outlining the state of Britain and the Jacobite case, and making a dignified request for help from the Austrian Empire to liberate England from Whiggery:

> The People of England who labour under the greatest calamities and oppressions from the tyranny of the House of Hanover supported by a corrupt majority in Parliament, most humbly implore His Imperial and Catholic Majesty's protection to redeem them from slavery and to free them from an intolerable foreign yoke by restoring their native and lawful prince to the Throne of his ancestors...[3]

It described all the measures that the Walpoleites had taken to secure their own power, and all the constitutional changes and the infringements of liberty from which the Opposition felt that they had suffered. It complained of the bribery at Parliamentary and City elections; of the use of election Petitions to throw opposition MPs out of Parliament; of the use of public money by governments to buy votes from MPs; and of the new-modelling of the City of London constitution. It complained of the many new Whig peerages, and that the Riot Act branded political meetings as insurrections, and of the suspension of Habeus Corpus, and of the use of the army to over-awe London. It stated that the Whigs and the Hanoverians and their whole system of government were generally hated, and that King George was unpopular for being a recluse, as Robert Walpole was for being an upstart. It was a great essay in the political principles of the Grumbletonians who felt that the Bill of Rights and the English seventeenth-century political settlement had been sold wholesale and replaced by oligarchy and corruption, and it articulated the murmurs of the many opposition Britons, exiled Jacobites, Irish Catholics and disenfranchised London liverymen whose voices, in the early eighteenth-century, were being suppressed. The Memorandum explained how easy it would be to overthrow the Hanoverians. All that would be needed would be a small force of men to be shipped from Ostend to England. When these landed near London, it said, the City train-bands and liverymen would rise in James's favour. They would be supported by risings in Scotland and Ireland, and the wheel of political fortune would swing in favour of the Stuarts again as easily as it had turned in their favour at the Restoration of 1660. The Memorandum concluded:

> It was in order to lay those affairs before His Imperial and Catholic Majesty that I was desired by persons of great interest and credit at home to undertake a journey to Vienna, and I have received directions from the King my Master to enter into a negotiation on his behalf, and to express the great desire he has to obtain the Emperor's friendship. The affair may be managed with the utmost secrecy, and I am thoroughly persuaded that I shall give entire satisfaction as to every part of this Memorial whenever I can be assured it will be agreeable to the Emperor to receive it.
> Aug 23rd 1725   Wharton[4]

What would old Thomas Wharton, the Whig pillar, who (it is said) had drafted the letter inviting William of Orange to take the Throne from James II in 1688, have said of Philip's invitation to the Emperor to restore James II's son? Probably he would have called it treason and an insult to the cause of Parliament and Protestantism. But perhaps he and the other apostles of the Glorious Revolution, including Lord Cowper the last and one of the most upright of them, would have approved of it. Philip believed he was still a follower of theirs, and that they would have agreed that their Good Old Cause had not been pressed through the revolutions of the seventeenth century to establish a Norfolk squire as despot of England.

While composing his Memorandum Philip refused to let Sheridan leave for Rome, justifying this on the ground that he needed him as an adviser and secretary to help in its preparation. The truth was that he knew he would miss Sheridan, his only true friend in Vienna. So even when the Memorandum was ready Philip did not release Sheridan, but told Rome that he first wanted him to see how its presentation to the Court was received. And the presentation could not take place until his ambassadorial credentials had arrived; and still he heard no news of them, either because they had been delayed in the Alps, or because James's Ministers at Rome were uncertain as to their correct form, or perhaps because the Papal Nuncio, under whose seal they travelled, had slowed their delivery for some mysterious reason of his own.

So Philip, who liked doing business at breakneck speed, felt frustrated. At length his patience ran out, and he decided to declare his position to Zindendorff whether his credentials had arrived or not. So at a quiet moment over a billiard-table in proper Viennese form, he whispered to Zindendorff that he wanted a private audience. It was naturally granted. On Thursday 23rd August he and Sheridan discussed state business with an Austrian Minister for the first time.

They delivered the Memorial and explained the purpose of their mission. Zindendorff was neither surprised nor displeased. By now he had already investigated Philip's English political record. He assured them of his goodwill, accepted their Memorandum, and because it was far too long to read while they waited, he dismissed them.

Philip well knew the danger of their situation. If the Memorial was taken amiss, they might be arrested or denounced to Walpole's Government as traitors. They passed a disquieting weekend, and on Monday August 27th, returned to Zindendorff's audience-chamber with a sense of apprehension that can be imagined.

But Zindendorff was all smiles. He had delivered the Memorial to the Emperor, he said (which was more than Philip had dared hope, for the Emperor was not accustomed to receiving submissions from persons who held no official status) and the Emperor had accepted it graciously. The truth was that Zindendorff, and probably also the Emperor, was extremely glad to find that Philip was a Jacobite representative. Ripperda had spoken to Zindendorff, (though Philip did not know this) about how useful the Jacobites could be in a war against Hanoverian Britain. So a Jacobite Ambassador at Vienna was exactly what Zindendorff wanted.

To Philip this seemed almost too good to be true. Though his credentials still had not arrived, a path to the Emperor had opened before him. But when he asked Zindendorff if the Emperor would lend James any troops, Zindendorff hedged. A few days must pass he said before a reply would be forthcoming on that. The Duke must wait.

But when Sheridan finally departed from Rome on August 29th, six days after the Duke had delivered the Memorial, they had still been given no formal reply. And delay was becoming dangerous. Every day that passed increased the chances that the French or the British secret service detected, or merely suspected, the purpose of Philip's visit. The city, he knew, was full of spies. Zindendorff warned him of them. Early in September an English Catholic padre called Abbé Strickland, who (after an adventurous career) was a secret agent of King George, arrived nonchalantly in the city, which alarmed Philip enough for him to write to Lord Inverness asking for the help of the Pope against him. Lord Inverness told the Vatican, and the Pope duly sent a letter to the Emperor, "giving Strickland" in Philip's words, "the character he deserves."[5] Strickland was accordingly discredited at the Viennese Court, at least temporarily.

Now Zindendorff summoned the Duke frequently to dinner; he engaged him in long discussions; he questioned him for hours about how Britain could be invaded. But he promised no certain loan of Austrian regiments. All that King James's Ambassador was given was rich entertainment. It made him miserable. At length, in mid-September, he actually took a few days off, reporting to Lord North and Grey (who was still ignorant of his true purpose in Austria), that:

> "I have been two days paying my court at Newstadt, where His Imperial Majesty is taking the diversion of hunting whilst the Empress is bathing in order to present Europe with an Archduke. I am retired from the world and never intend to meddle in public business again."[6]

Whilst he was chasing the Emperor's deer, his long-awaited ambassadorial appointment at last reached Vienna. They were brought by John Graeme, who had been sent by the King to replace Sheridan as his secretary and assistant. The news elated Philip again, and he hurried back to the city.

He found Graeme a very different man to Sheridan. He was a Scot, the other an Irishman. Sheridan was carefree, imaginative and charming; Graeme was careful, meticulous and dour. Philip cautiously told Lord Inverness that Graeme was "A very pretty gentleman, and I believe will be of great service to me here."[7] Graeme in turn told Rome "Duke Wharton is the heartiest person in the King's interest I ever conversed with, and he is mighty civil to me."[8] But Graeme was not a man of pleasure, as Sheridan had been. So he could not restrain the Duke from plunging deep into debauchery, because he himself never put his toe in it. He was therefore not half as useful as Sheridan. But this did not immediately matter, because back in the city again Philip, armed with his new credentials, could start "business" and neglect vice.

First he formally introduced himself as James's ambassador to the Duc de Ripperda, the tempestuous ambassador from Spain. He was pleased with what he found. Ripperda was an energetic if slightly self-deluded optimist, who shouted his opinions and banged the table to emphasise them. Details were nothing to him; with gusto, he felt, anything could be done. Philip shared this erroneous belief, and they were soon friends. As Philip's encoded despatches soon reported to Rome:

> That Minister is so violent in his expressions that he even outdoes Wharton when he used to harangue one of the city clubs, with two bottles of port in my head. He is for exculpating the Hanover family root and branch...[9]

Ripperda was soon actively supporting Philip at Court, demanding in the King of Spain's name that Austria take measures to support James, which (as Ripperda told Philip) surprised the Emperor but apparently did not displease him, for he appreciated that supporting the Jacobites would certainly be an easy, and cheap, method of undermining Britain. Zindendorff had already mentioned this to him. But because the Emperor never decided anything if a decision could possibly be avoided, he did not actually commit himself to supporting an invasion of England. He had merely listened sympathetically to Ripperda, who reported to Philip that he had "Met with better success upon a first overture than he expected from so cautious and phlegmatic a Prince."[10]

The Duke followed up Ripperda's advance himself. He went to

see Zindendorff again. Now that he had detailed orders from Rome as to the extent of his powers as Jacobite ambassador, he could negotiate more formally with the Great Chancellor. He spoke to Zindendorff of the terms that James was prepared to offer the Emperor. These had been detailed to him in the instructions Graeme brought from Rome.

In England Philip's personal affairs which had been so chaotic when he had tried to run them himself were looking better now he was out of the way. In the North, Sir Kit Musgrave had organised the Swaledale lead-mines into producing a clear three thousand a year, and John Jacob was preparing to sack Mr. Smailes, his Yorkshire agent. Smailes had at last gone too far. On a demand for some accounts for the rents of the manor of Aske, he provided nothing at all. So John Jacob, the banker, sent a surveyor, who had lately surveyed Winchendon, to value Aske in preparation for its sale. They prepared to cut out permanently the odious Smailes family from any power over the Duke's land. In Buckinghamshire, the great house at Winchendon and its large estate (including the manor of Waddesdon) were now nearly sold. Such was the pressure of creditors on the property that it was almost lost to one of them, the economical Duchess of Marlborough, for £53,000, which Nathaniel Piggott regarded as a paltry sum. A sale at this price was only averted with the help of Francis Charters, who was still living at Wooburn, as Nathaniel Piggott told Philip and begged him:

> Not to make Col. Charters your enemy. Your Grace wrote an obliging letter to me in his behalf which made him in a good humour, and ready to serve Your Grace, and indeed he was very considerable in preventing Her Grace having the estate at her own rate. But His Grace the Duke of Argyll had let fall some words which were repeated to Colonel Charters by Colonel Earle, that Your Grace had wrote word that he had sharp'd and cheated Your Grace; which put him in such a passion that he swore he would move the Court to stop Your Grace's 2500 a year. I had much pains to pacify him.[11]

Winchendon was sold before the Colonel's "passion' had done any harm. It cost the Duchess of Marlborough £62,000. At the same time his grandfather's Van Dyck collection was sold. The best of it was (ironically) bought by Sir Robert Walpole, Philip's worst enemy. Eleven full-length portraits, including those of Charles I, Charles II as Prince of Wales, Queen Henrietta Maria, Prince Rupert, several members of the Wharton family and a half-length study of Archbishop Laud, travelled to Norfolk to grace Walpole's ostentatious new palace at Houghton. They cost him about £100 each. But they remained there barely half a century; then they were sold by a spendthrift grandson of Sir Robert Walpole to Catherine the Great of Russia, and became the cornerstone of the collection in the Hermitage Palace.

Most of Philip's friends in England thought that he was in Vienna to economise and to pursue pleasure, if both were possible. When Phil Lloyd wrote with news of Lord Hillsborough and Ned Thompson, he said what they thought was detaining Philip in Vienna:

> A woman must certainly be the case; for I can't apprehend the Emperor's Ministers have alone charms enough to keep you at that Court... [12]

He was partly right, for Philip's Viennese Countess, the maid of honour, consoled him in his frustration. Lord Inverness, whom he had told of her in a private letter, remarked coarsely, "I'll engage you won't hurt her in unmaidening her." [13] Philip also told Martha about her. Since her miscarriage, Martha had been surrounded by expensive doctors, supervised by Walter Pryse and Lord Orrery, but in spite of them all her health steadily improved throughout the autumn, and soon she could complain of his infidelity in long, lewd, affectionate unpunctuated letters written in a huge childish scrawl:

> London Oct 15th
>
> My Dear Lord,
> I have the pleasure of yours...; but for the Lady Countess I envy her prodigiously that is so happy to gain your affection, but hope that your passion there will have no long date, being in hopes of seeing you soon in England. Lord Orrery presents his service to Your Grace, and wonders he has not heard from you; he leaves this on Saturday to go for France,

which is a very great concern to me, tho' he leaves me in Mr. Pryse's care till his return. There is nothing done in your affairs as yet and the blaime is laid on Jacobs, Sir Christopher has wrote word the mines proves very well, for they bring in clear £10 a day... All your friends begs their humble service...

My dearest dear,
Your affectionate and dutiful wife. [14]

Other letters from England were concerned with the election of the Mayor at High Wycombe. Philip's agents (having received no orders to the contrary) still tried to keep up his electoral interest against (amongst others) Dr. Edward Young, who was actively supporting Walpole's candidate there. Dr. Paterson, a staunch Whig who disliked both Philip's extravagance and his politics, wrote lamenting that money formerly wasted on annuities to the Duke's old mistresses was now being wasted on the borough corporation:

Oct 25 1725

If you happen to receive this in the morning, and are sober, you have sense enough to know that by this I wish Your Grace well with all my soul, and have ever done so but when you have been an author or a politician...

(The Duchess) has mightily recovered to what she had been, and I believe pays due obedience to your commands by spending her time amongst those that are most agreeable to you. She certainly loves you, and I hope you will deserve it...

The pension you gave Madame Vanhutyt ceases by her death, the maid at Highgate has been so terrified that she does not demand hers, Dr. Young has taken Holy Orders, so that he will not want his. The £500 a year given for superstitious uses to Piggott should be recalled. Your old servants have made a great stand at the election of a mayor at Wickham... so that the Mayor... has lost about £1600 at a time when Your Grace might have employed it much better... [15]

Letters in a more congenial tone arrived often from Atterbury, but they were arriving late. Philip rightly guessed that they were being intercepted by the French secret service, which was alarming since some of them indiscreetly said that the British Jacobites were ready for rebellion, and especially that, "The harvest is, I think, plainly ripe in Scotland." [16] James Hamilton in London was equally optimistic about English sentiment: He urged Philip to find a force to land in the mouth of the Thames to rally to itself the army and the city train-bands in support of James III:

> The sea-ports of England and wherever ships of war lay would take their instructions from whoever was in possession of Whitehall, so would the militia and all the corporations and officers in the kingdom... [17]

By early September Horatio Walpole, the British Ambassador to France, had learnt that Philip was in Vienna, and thought he was there to receive from Ripperda a certain politically dangerous letter which King George had sent secretly to the King of Spain in May 1721, promising to return Gibraltar to Spain. If its existence was revealed to Parliament or to the public, the Ministry might be forced to resign. Actually, Philip either knew nothing of this letter or (more probably) thought it not worth bothering about.

He was still passing his time in Vienna loitering at Court, dining with Zinderdorff, being fed with promises, and discussing with Ripperda the details of the proposed invasion of England and the Jacobite rising. Philip was no soldier, but he was sensible enough to know that the military strategy which was adopted in 1689, in the 'Fifteen, and which would again be adopted in the 'Forty-five, was useless: a rebellion begun in Scotland or Ireland could not hope to subdue London. By the time that a rebel army from so far away had arrived in central England, the English Government would have raised or borrowed a strong enough army to quell it. But Britain could be taken with comparative ease by capturing the capital. He proposed James Hamilton's plan to Ripperda: that King James should bring an army over from Austrian Flanders to the mouth of the Thames. Upon the appearance of the old royalist banner of the Stuarts, he said, the liverymen, watermen, the "Ormonde mob" and the common soldiers of London would rise. And at the same moment a smaller force from Spain could land in Ireland, with arms for 50,000 native Catholics there. In Scotland the clans and many lowlanders would rise without any outside help. Philip reckoned King George would then retire to his preferred Hanover, and James III could enter London in bloodless triumph in 1725 as his uncle Charles II had done in 1660.

To this excellent plan Ripperda had an objection: to launch a flotilla from Flanders would be imposible if the British fleet opposed it. He therefore suggested that the fleet should be burnt at anchor in Chatham harbour by the many Londoners whom Philip said were loyal to King James. But Philip was naturally appalled at the idea. So were Graeme and Lord Inverness, when in due course he mentioned it to them. To burn the British fleet was unthinkable. Philip ingeniously pointed out that in fact sinking the fleet was unnecessary because any invasion from Flanders would be borne on an easterly wind which would bottle up the British fleet in the mouth of the Thames or the Medway, where it would not be any threat. Ripperda did not ask him what would happen if it was at sea already, sailing the Channel, when the flotilla was launched. These were all matters of detail, they agreed. The crucial question was whether any foreign troops were available to the Jacobites at all. Ripperda reassured Philip on this. The number of troops needed were so few, he said, that he could provide them all from Spain if necessary. Philip told Rome:

> ...He says the King our master's affairs were never in so flourishing a condition, and that he will always have reason to remember the year 1725. [18]

James's ministers of state in his gloomy palace in Rome were delighted, and Inverness told Graeme on October 20th:

> Wharton's conduct proves the great character the world has given him, and King James is charmed with it; I hope to see him one day the first subject in England. [19]

But if they were happy with Spanish promises, he was not. The lack of any solid progress towards a "Twenty-five" Jacobite invasion made him worry. Always he was told to wait. In late October at the end of his third month in Vienna he even allowed himself to suspect that he was being tricked in all his negotiations, and that neither Spain nor Austria had ever intended to help him at all. He voiced his fears to Ripperda, and hinted them to Zindendorff. Both men laughed, but sympathised with his view. Each told him that diplomacy was necessarily a slow business, and that his own demands must wait until details of a new treaty between Spain, Austria and Russia were agreed. Further, Ripperda said he intended to dispute precedence with the Duc de Richelieu, the notoriously proud ambassador from France whose formal entry into Vienna was later in the year. That might be made an excuse for the outbreak of the war between France and Spain, he said, and in a general European war King James would be restored.

More damaging to Philip than his own doubts were those of his secretary Graeme, who now began secretly telling Rome how he suspected the efficacy of Philip's skill as a diplomat and how Philip spent huge sums of money on entertainment, gambling, servants, brandy and the Countess. Although Philip had been receiving periodic sums from John Jacob in London, he was indeed once more short of cash. Graeme was obliged to send to Rome for funds, which annoyed him, for to a Scotsman extravagance is the grossest of vices. And when he noticed the wildness and incompetence which went with the Duke's political enthusiasm, he was exasperated. He saw no value in Philip's energy and wit, which had opened all the diplomatic doors in Vienna. In early November he wrote:

> I wish heartily he were more exact and pointed in his audiences, and that he recollected before he gets to them the several different points he is to speak upon, for he, having a great facility of language, runs out so far upon the first things started that he often forgets to inform himself of what is more material... [20]

Philip never knew that Graeme was criticising him. But he knew that Graeme was dull company. So he spent more time with Quinn and Michael Stecho, who had accompanied him from England, and whom Graeme disapproved of.

The Invasion of England

Then, in early November, at the time of Richelieu's magnificent entry to Vienna, the tide of affairs turned. Ripperda suddenly took Philip aside and told him that he was exasperated with Zindendorff, whom he called "a poltroon" [21] for prevaricating with Philip so long. He said that Philip must go directly to Prince Eugen to ask for troops. The time was ripe, he said, because Spain, Austria and Russia had at last agreed an alliance, and it was a secret term of the alliance — the treaty of Vienna, as it was called — that the Pretender should be assisted.

Before Philip could recover from his surprise at these developments Ripperda disappeared from Vienna. One day after the formal arrival of the French Ambassador, and before his promised quarrel with him over precedence, Ripperda set out for Madrid accompanied only by a valet and a footman, and leaving his twenty-year-old son Baron Ripperda as ambassador in his place. The Viennese Court believed he had been recalled to be chief minister at Madrid; but to Philip his rapid departure smelt strongly of a desire to avoid a dispute with France.

Whilst deliberating his next move Philip paid a call upon Richelieu himself, and unexpectedly found him very congenial. He was a mystic, a snob, a friend of Voltaire, a drunkard and an outstanding debauchee. His most harmless hobby was to gloat over his hoard of love-letters from all the French ladies he had seduced; but later in his life he was to find himself in serious trouble for allegedly dabbling in witchcraft at Vienna: he was accused of trying to improve his considerable sexual virility by sacrificing a black lamb in mysterious circumstances. Understandably Philip and he liked each other, though secretly both knew the other was his enemy. On first meeting they spent an hour exchanging compliments with one another, which both enjoyed.

In spite of Ripperda's exasperation with Zindendorff and his disappearance, Philip found himself more trusted by Zindendorff than ever. At his next meeting with him, which he secured in the usual manner by whispering in his ear over a billiard table, he satisfied him that his invasion plan was feasible in all its details. At least it was flexible: if the movement of 6,000 Austrian troops in Flanders might risk provoking an invasion of Flanders by France, then the chief Jacobite invasion force might have to be supplied by Catherine I in Russia. 20,000 men of Catherine I's troops could be embarked at Archangel without Europe being aware of their existence, they agreed. Graeme cheerfully reported that:

> Nov 10th
> Count Zindendorff heard all this with pleasure, then told Duke Wharton he must now speak to the Emperor himself, but first communicate the affairs to Prince Eugen...
> Zindendorff does not relish Ripperda's opinion of burning the fleet or anything that looks like conquering England, but only to help his own loyal subjects to restore him. [22]

Zindendorff now promised Philip the troops he needed if only his plan could be given the stamp of military approval. That meant being approved by Prince Eugen, a man who although he liked Philip dining with him, was not an easy man to persuade. He was a proud, cold pro-Hanoverian who lived chiefly for his art collection, the greatest in the Empire, housed in the two great Viennese palaces the Upper and Lower Belvedere. Philip, through a number of intermediaries, in a manner suited to his Ambassadorial status, boldly arranged a private audience with him.

Philip's enthusiasm warmed the flinty soldier. With the aid of a map he persuaded him how an invasion force could embark at Archangel without being detected, how a smaller one could sail from Ostend to capture the naval stores at Chatham, and how easily London could be seized. Then they discussed a Commander for the force. Eugen did not approve of either Ormonde or North and Grey. He considered that Cadogan, Orrery or Lord Strafford was better than either of them. But he thought that Orrery and Strafford were statesmen rather than soldiers, though both had been with him at Blenheim. Why not appoint Lord Cadogan, asked Eugen? Philip prevaricated, saying he could not be relied upon. This was certainly true; in Graeme's phrase, Cadogan was "a very notorious Whig".[23] There was one leader, however, in the minds of both men. That was Eugen himself whose leadership would virtually ensure the success of a "Twenty-five". But Philip knew that he could not ask him to be the

The Invasion of England

leader of an invasion army without direct authority from Rome.

As his audience progressed, Philip saw his difficulties fade. Because of the soundness of the strategy, and because of the effect of Philip's enthusiastic eloquence on him, the Prince approved the plan. As Philip told Rome in a self-congratulatory tone:

> I this morning had an audience of Prince Eugen. I found him as I could wish. He enquired much into the situation of our affairs and seemed of an opinion that an attempt upon England would certainly succeed, notwithstanding the Government's heat, provided it were well concerted.[24]

So in November 1725, it seemed that Philip's Viennese mission had reached a satisfactory conclusion. He had won Ripperda over to his cause, and then Zindendorff, and now Eugen. A few months hence Bishop Atterbury at Paris heard that Prince Eugen had said of Philip, "Young as he was, he might be ventured against *le plus habile Ministre d'Europe.*"[25]

CHAPTER THIRTEEN

Rome

> A fool, with more of wit than half mankind,
> Too rash for thought, for action too refined...
>   Pope on Wharton, *First Moral Essay,* 199-200

The first threat to the success of Philip's invasion plan came from the Stuart family itself. The work he had done was half spoilt, and chances of James being restored were badly reduced, by a rather ludicrous incident in the Royal household at the Palazzo Muti in Rome.

When James had selected Sheridan and Murray (now Earl of Dunbar) to be Prince Charles's tutors, he had not consulted Queen Clementina. Long ago he had found out that she was not an intelligent person, and he consulted her seldom. Now she decided to assert herself. She announced that she objected to the choice of these two Protestants as tutors for her Catholic boy. And when James told her to mind her own business, she declared that she could no longer bear living with him, and on November 15th 1725 she retired to the convent of St. Cecilia outside the City. From there she sent vituperative squibs at her husband in the form of sharp notes delivered by her ladies' maid.

Nor did she confine her quarrel with her startled husband and sovereign to the question of the Protestant tutors. She said she disliked Lord Inverness, the Secretary of State, and that he was unpopular amongst the British Jacobites, and that he ought to be removed. Then she hinted that Lord Inverness's wife was James's mistress, which was very unfair, for although James never paid much attention to his Queen, he never paid much attention to any other woman either. Next she said that James, as a true Catholic, should not allow the service of the Church of England to be held daily in the Palazzo Muti. And she publicised her views upon all these matters as widely as possible, particularly in letters to Their Catholic Majesties the King and Queen of Spain and to His Holiness the Pope.

Faced by this difficult crisis at a difficult time, James behaved surprisingly well. He sent a few sparse luxuries to the convent so that she could not complain of ill-treatment:

2 doz's of Silver plates
6 complete covers, knives, forks and spoons
1 soup spoon
1 mustard pot
1 sugar box [1]

Next, he flatly told her that his arrangement of the Royal household was no concern of anyone except himself, and that it was her duty to obey him. Then he employed Thomas Sheridan, who by now had arrived from Vienna, to write a circular letter to the principal Jacobites throughout Europe recounting and explaining his actions, so that no false rumours of his maltreatement of the Queen would be believed. He himself wrote such a letter to the Pope.

But Lord Mar, out of jealousy for Lord and Lady Inverness, and his friend General Dillon who was living near him in retirement in France and who was the brother-in-law of Prince Charles's late governess, both said that the Queen was being maligned and maltreated. Soon stories of her suffering and how James's present advisers were incompetent or disloyal reached England. The Whig secret service, with its usual efficiency, picked them up and spread them. Philip's old friend Lord North and Grey, who was in Flanders, believed them. But the most important reactions to the news were those of the Pope, and the monarchs of Spain (whose finances, but not their consciences, were now controlled by Ripperda): they were concerned with the credit of Roman Catholicism, and were appalled at the prospect of two Protestants being the Prince of Wales's tutors, and of a Protestant service being heard in the Palazzo Muti. So while Queen Clementina remained stubbornly in her convent, and James refused to bend to any of her demands, relations between James and his Catholic patrons worsened. This mattered a great deal; for Ripperda's Spain was the country which most enthusiastically supported James's cause, and James's chief source of income was his pension from the Pope.

Although Philip satisfied Zindendorff and the Emperor that James had behaved properly, James's fall from Papal and Spanish favour greatly weakened Philip's position in Vienna. And news of it came at a time when Richelieu and Saint-Saphorin were beginning a concerted effort to budge him from his influence at Court. James Hamilton from London confirmed that the Whigs (and therefore, presumably, the French) were now sure he was the Jacobite agent in Vienna. In the last weeks he had become carelessly indiscreet: if there was to be a Stuart Restoration, he thought, what did it matter what the Whigs thought of Wharton? He had refused to feign friendship for Saint-Saphorin when he reappeared at Court after a few weeks' disgrace, as he told Lord Inverness:

> I will not make any court to him, which I should think would be unbecoming hypocrisy in one, since both Saint-Saphorin and everybody else knows the errand that brought me hither. [2]

So neither he nor Graeme were surprised when early in December the Sardinian envoy, acting as an agent for the Whigs, offered him a huge bribe to disclose what he was up to. Graeme wrote rhetorically to Rome to say how nobly Philip turned it down. But Graeme need not have been so impressed. The Duke, though loaded with vices, had one shining virtue: he was quite uncorruptible. Almost alone amongst statesmen of his age, he was never bought.

Having failed to bribe him, the agents of Richelieu and Saint-Saphorin stepped up their watch on him. The number of spies who watched him in the billiard-hall, at court, and with the Countess, increased. Early in the new year, Philip received his congé from both Saint-Saphorin and the French Ambassador; that is, they told him that they could not receive him or be entertained by him any more. Richelieu personally regretted this, but Saint-Saphorin did not, and gleefully trumpeted around the City the news that he had been told to insult the Duke. Philip, angry at impertinence from the Swiss who represented Britain, snubbed Saint-Saphorin back:

> I modestly assured him that I did not believe he had any such orders from his master who could not forget that my father

had placed him on the Throne.[3]

The Whigs in England were hoping that Philip's unsavoury habits and reputation would eventually discredit him at the staid Viennese Court. Their hopes were justified. The Duke of Newcastle was told how:

> ...at an entertainment one day... his whole conversation turned upon the most scandalous raillery of His Majesty and the Treaty of Hanover, accompanied with personal injuries against the French King and Monsieur le Duc which were raised to such a degree with the large quantity of wine that he drank as made his own company ashamed of the conversation...
>
> The Duke of Wharton proposed play, being pleased to deal himself at Pharaon, and having amongst other sums lost particularly to the Duc de Richelieu 500 ducats, he sent the money the next morning to the French Ambassador, in Spanish Pistoles coined in the year 1725 at Madrid.[4]

Walpole's cabinet believed this payment in Spanish coins meant that Philip was being paid a pension from Ripperda, which made them hate him all the more.

But Graeme was appalled at his wild gambling, and complained bitterly to Rome of having to raise 500 ducats to pay one debt. Philip protested to Lord Inverness that such extravagence had only been necessary, "Whilst I kept company with the French Ambassador and his crew."[5] In February he was borrowing heavily from an English friend at Vienna called Mr. Sorrel. By then he had already written by express to England to ask his agents for a thousand pounds. James Hamilton, who had told him before that he could expect nothing above his allowance until his estates were cleared of debt, replied with elegant sarcasm:

> I had your short and pithy letter of Dec 5th in due course, and as it was for raising a huge sum of money, I concluded you had a mind to be merry with your poor friend... I durst

not mention your demand to your man in the City, for fear he should stop your allowance.[6]

His English financial position had not improved since the autumn. Some more of his money had been wasted on bribing the Wycombe corporation, to very little effect. Sir Kit Musgrave had not been able to discharge any mortgages on his estates in the North, because the deed of attorney he had sent Philip to sign and seal had never returned from Vienna. The Duchess of Wharton was so short of money that she had to dismiss one of her servants, called Forster, for his extravagance, and to pledge to Gibson, the banker, everything of Philip's that she still had except the silver she used, but she expected even this to be removed by bailiffs or creditors soon.

Under the strain she began to suffer fits of paralysis. But she exaggerated their seriousness. Shortly after Christmas she ordered a caller, George Chardin, to write to Philip for her because she said she was too feeble to write herself. He obediently wrote that she said she was dying, but privately added a footnote to say that she was better than she said she was:

31 Dec
Holland Street

My Dearest...
Mr. Gibson having asked where I would be buried I said at St. Anne's to save charges, but if it please God that I recover I shall immediately set out for Paris where it would be the greatest joy to me to meet you...
I am my dearest dear entirely yours,

M

My Lady Duchess could not write her name, 'twas with great difficulty her Grace made the M.
P.S. I beg leave to tell Your Grace I don't apprehend my Lady Duchess to be in any danger, and hope she will soon be able to undertake a journey.[7]

He evidently sent her a short, thin letter in reply to this, for Captain Butler, who had reached England from Paris and was living in

Chelsea, gave her bawdy answer to it in a letter he wrote Philip a month later:

> My Lord Scarsdale showed me a letter he received from your Grace and one enclosed to Martha, and as to Martha's she gives her duty to your Grace and desired me let you know unless your tarce be stiffer than the one you sent her she says you may keep it for the Jermyn hores at Vienna. [8]

Such a vulgar remark as this shows the strangely coarse relationship which existed between Philip and Martha.

He needed lewd jests at this time, to prevent himself from getting too bored. Graeme was dull company. Only prevarication came from the Imperial Ministers. He no longer had Ripperda to encourage him, although they had agreed on a cypher in which they could correspond with each other. At Vienna, early in the year 1726, nothing seemed to progress.

So she was right to suggest that lechery was now his chief interest in Austria, for "business" seemed at a standstill. When Zindendorff said he would send an agent to England to check the accuracy of all that Philip had said, Philip was not even worried (as he ought to have been) that his account of Jacobite feeling should be found to be exaggerated. He just took it to be another excuse for delay by Zindendorff.

By the end of January 1726 he had had enough. If the Emperor did not want to reap for himself the enormous political advantages that would be his if he restored James III, he thought, then Russia or Spain alone could do so. So he told Zindendorff that he was leaving for Madrid or St. Petersburg; at which, he reported, Zindendorff "appeared very uneasy, and made me promise to remain." [9]

For Zindendorff, although at times he found Philip's flamboyance a political as well as a social embarrassment because it provoked demands from Richelieu and Saint-Saphorin for his expulsion, badly needed a Jacobite ambassador at Vienna, because the Jacobites were going to play an important part in the forthcoming war against France and Britain. Further, he personally wanted to remain on good terms with Philip, who had lately hinted to him that a Cardinal's hat might be available for Abbé Zindendorff, his son, when James took his turn as a Catholic monarch to exercise the right to nominate a Cardinal. Philip himself knew that he must not leave Vienna if his departure would look like a diplomatic success for the Whigs and French. So he decided to compromise by leaving Vienna for only a month. He would visit Rome and his Royal master whom he had not seen in ten years. This would give the Whigs no cause for self-congratulation, he thought, but it would give him a holiday, it might worry Zindendorff, and it would make little or no difference to his diplomatic work at Vienna because things there moved so extraordinarily slowly.

Because he only expected to be absent for a few weeks he took no formal leave of the Emperor's Court, but introduced Graeme (whose insidious remarks about him to James he was still unaware of) to Zindendorff and gave him power to continue his correspondence during his absence. Then, keeping his destination secret, he disappeared. His creditors found this rather unnerving, for he left debts of over five thousand pounds.

When they heard that he was preparing to leave Vienna, the Whigs were delighted. They treated his departure as a great victory for their diplomacy. Historians have tended to agree with them, and to state that Philip was driven from Vienna by the Imperial Ministers as a result of his debauchery and his political disreputableness.

After he had decided to visit Rome, he told the King of it, and set out almost immediately. All his papers, most of his possessions, his carriage, and his followers and servants, even his two faithful valets Harry and the blackamoor Scipio who had accompanied him on all his travels since his boyhood, remained in Vienna. He only bid farewell to the Countess and Mr. Quinn and Mr. Sorrel from whom he had borrowed so much money. Then, on February 11th, in the depths of the Austrian winter, he set out with only one companion, Michael Stecho, for Salzburg.

They travelled post; that is, with no vehicle of their own, but hiring a light travelling-sleigh, a "traineau", at each inn. At first the cold was worse than anything Philip had known; but at least the heavy snow lessened the chances of them being attacked by robbers for their furs and gold.

In milder weather after Salzburg they pressed on up to Innsbruck, where six years before Queen Clementina, then a Polish princess, had been imprisoned by the Emperor as she had travelled through Austria to marry James. Philip and Stecho spent two nights without sleep on the road because avalanches brought down by the sudden thaw blocked the passes, and they reached the town very tired, at nine in the morning. Philip bore it better than Stecho, as he wrote to Graeme:

> About three posts from hence, in the middle of the night, the postmaster, not having a traineau that would hold two, gave us two single ones in the room of it. A postillion conducted mine, but the Valiant Stecho, full of the Spirit of Knight Errantry, undertook like Phaeton to direct his courser in person, and humbly beseeched me that I would permit him to undertake this great and perilous task. I, like my renowned predecessor Don Quixote... graciously condescended to indulge my companion's ambition.
> But as great attempts often prove fatal to the undertakers, so fared it with our hero... [Stecho was] fast asleep in the middle of the highway with his palfrey as quiet as himself, and to his eternal dishonour Stecho had lost his hat and periwig, which, by reason of the light, could not be found... He looks upon this unheard of misfortune as a judgement of Providence inflicted upon him for his wicked life and conversation... He desires me to request it of you that his clothes and all other his estate real and personal may be converted into specie and delivered to the Franciscan Convent at Vienna to say masses for the repose of his soul in case of accident.[10]

They surmounted the snow-bound Alps at break-neck speed, and were soon descending into Italy in Venetian territory near Lake Garda, where Philip practised for the first time the Italian that he had learnt as a boy, and where they abandoned sledges in favour of carriages. Only five days after they had left Innsbruck they had crossed northern Italy and driven down the Adriatic coast, entered Papal territory, and were over the great bridge of Tiberius at Rimini. On the night of February

22nd they were within two posts of Rome. On the morning of the next day they had arrived at the Palazzo Muti.

This rather nondescript palace which King James III of England and VIII of Scotland had been lent by the Pope, graced a small piazza off the Via del Corso, and was convenient for the church of Santi Apostoli, where James used to hear Mass. Standing around a small central court-yard entered by an archway from the street, it was four stories high, and contained a great many small rooms. Even if dark, smelly and old-fashioned, it was perfectly comfortable, conveniently placed and not half as dingy as the Whigs in England pretended it was. It well housed numerous Jacobites clustered around the King who were honoured with his peerages and titles and great offices of State.

Philip, refreshed by the invigorating journey, arrived in high spirits. They were raised higher by the welcome that Thomas Sheridan and the other courtiers gave him. Lord Inverness and King James, who believed as frankly as Philip did all the promises that Zindendorff and Ripperda and Prince Eugen had made him, hailed him as the only successful diplomat that they had ever found. He drank heavily with Lord Inverness and he talked long with James and all three were as happy as if they were already back at Whitehall or in Windsor. James said:

> I cannot on this occasion sufficiently express to you how much I am satisfied with the Duke of Wharton; his great talents, his zeal and his sincere attachement to me are every day more manifest to me... [11]

Philip himself could now safely write to Atterbury, apologising that his security precautions had prevented him from writing from Vienna, and also to James Hamilton, Sir Christopher Musgrave and Alderman Parsons, telling them that the King looked like Charles II, that he was standing up manfully to the Pope, and that Prince Charles was a fine boy. "If it is my fate to perish in His Majesty's service", he told Parsons, "It will be the glory of my family hereafter that I fell in defending the King's right and asserting the ancient independency of Old England." [12] He reported to Graeme:

155

> Rome February 23rd
> There is no news here but that the Pope is run mad, and Jemmy Edgar is clap't and has desired me to give his distempered humble service to your pox. Pray deliver the enclosed to the Chancellor, be a good boy and mind your business.
>
> Wharton [13]

James had decided, probably rightly, that only Spain and not Austria or Russia was belligerent enough to start the war for his Restoration. Ripperda had promised Philip that Spain alone would restore James if no other country would. But the monarchs of Spain supported Clementina and the Pope against James on the question of his orthodoxy, and would not lend him an army, whatever Ripperda said, unless his behaviour on this was justified to them. It was therefore crucial that James's interest were promptly and efficiently represented at Madrid. Rather dazzled by Philip, James now decided he was the best person to send. So before Philip had been in Rome a week he had accepted James's commission to present a letter to the King and Queen of Spain explaining the Clementina affair and asking for their immediate armed support, and he had contentedly written an apologetic letter to the ever-indecisive Zindendorff to say that his return to the Austrian court would unfortunately but unavoidably be delayed. Lord Inverness told all the Jacobite agents throughout Europe who might be in any way concerned in diplomatic negotiation about the appointment, in order that they would concert their efforts towards seeing that Philip succeeded. Then Philip prepared to depart.

Unfortunately, the King and Lord Inverness had overlooked one detail. There were already two Jacobite Dukes in Spain. One of them, the lazy and amiable old Duke of Ormonde, once the darling of the London mob, never quarrelled with James's appointments and would help Philip. But the other, the Duke of Liria, the son of the Duke of Berwick, and so an illegitimate nephew of James, was different. He had an extraordinary belief in his own rank and abilities and importance. As he wrote to Atterbury in March 11 of this year:

> None, I dare say, have the occasions of speaking and acting

for His Majesty's service that I have. I am the Ministers' friend and besides my character and employments give me facilities that none else of your nation can have. [14]

James and Lord Inverness by thoughtlessness or cowardice failed to tell Philip or Liria what their relative status was to be. But reasonably enough Philip expected that as James's accredited ambassador he would take charge of all Jacobite business in Madrid.

The confidence that the King and Court at Rome had in Philip was confirmed when at a small ceremony on March 4th 1726 James invested him with a Knighthood of the Order of the Garter, the highest order of chivalry. Philip had once asked him for it ten years before, just before James had made him a Duke. Now James had exhausted his honours on him.

Philip set out post for Madrid early in March 1726 without a thought that his success might cause jealousy amongst the other Jacobites who had served James for rather longer than he had. He was more carefree than he had been for years. Even his money troubles seemed far behind, for he was now being financed by James from Rome. He travelled the road to Genoa with a light heart and at enormous speed, averaging seventy miles a day.

At Genoa he paused. The only transport available for the sea-journey round the hostile coast of France was a derelict Spanish paquet with no cabin, crowded with deserters from the French, Sardinian and German armies. So he stripped himself of the splendid appearance which he had readopted in Rome, disguised himself, and according to a slightly unreliable account [15], assumed the alias "Philibert", the Christian name of the Count de Grammont, whose published salacious Memoirs of the Court of Charles II were popular in England. Once abroad, Philip spent nine nights in the hold of the ship, with (according to his own account), "52 persons, amongst whom I had the honour to have for my companions 17 deserters from the French and Piedmontese service, with 2 trulls that followed them, three lousy galley slaves that had been redeemed in Turkey, one Carmelite brother that had fled from his convent, and a number of beggars." [16]

Unfortunately, his Quixotic dress and alias did not deceive three Spanish officers of the emperor of Austria's army, who remembered him from his Viennese days. But when he studiously ignored and avoided them they guessed that he wanted to be anonymous and tactfully pretended not to know him. He had another fright when the ship passed Marseilles and the captain, seeing another ship approaching, declared it was an Algerian pirate vessel, so they must take refuge. The prospect of facing pirates in open water was not so bad for Philip as that of seeking haven in a French port, where an inquisitive official might discover and even arrest him. But when they harboured in the fishing village of La Ciotat no Frenchman chose to come aboard their uninviting vessel to investigate its seedy passengers, so he was undisturbed. The pirate, if pirate she was, passed on. After a few hours delay they sailed once more and reached Barcelona after a journey of three or four hundred miles on March 23rd 1726.

CHAPTER FOURTEEN

Madrid

> A constant bounty, which no friend has made;
> An angel tongue which no man can persuade...
> > Pope on Wharton, *First Moral Essay,* 197-8.

On a Thursday in late March 1726, at nine in the morning, unshaven and filthy, he stepped on to the quay at Barcelona. It was not a prepossessing town, but he was obliged to stay there briefly while he resumed his ambassadorial identity, so he sought out some lodgings for himself, and there he was shaved and dressed. Then he rode through the busy markets and alleys out of the sea-port to the villa of its Governor, the Marquis of Risbourg. He gave his credentials to the footman who admitted him, and waited.

The Governor was with him in a trice. Philip bowed, and paid him formal compliments in Spanish, a tongue he had learnt in his idle literary days at Winchendon. The Marquis was delighted to see him. Perhaps he was even more surprised than delighted; it cannot have been often than an accredited Ambassador arrived unannounced at Barcelona. Over dinner he told him all the political information about Spain that he knew. Unfortunately not much of what he said was useful. Philip told Rome, "He is not troubled with an elasticity of genius." [1] But he was forced to accept more hospitality from him than he had planned because a fall from his horse as he returned to his lodgings in Barcelona gave him a badly bruised and sprained ankle, and the Marquis insisted on putting him up until it healed. This delay irked Philip, but it was recompensed when the Marquis, overwhelmed by his wit and importance, ordered one of the Spanish Royal Extraordinary Couriers to attend him when he finally left for Madrid.

So he rode down the Mediterranean coast in late March decently escorted, though a little weak in one leg. He told Lord Inverness that he was hastening towards Ripperda, "With more impatience than Lord Dunbar ever did to a mistress, or Tom Forster to a bottle." [2] But at Lérida, afer a hundred miles of riding and several nights on the road, his leg became unbearably painful. They slowed the pace, and at Saragossa stopped for a few days to rest. Here, by a delightful chance, they found the Duke of Ormonde, whom Philip had not seen since Avignon in 1716. As soon as Philip's bruised leg had rested, they rode on towards Madrid together. Buried in talk, the rest of their journey passed easily.

At Madrid Philip went to call upon the Secretary of State Ripperda at once, but found him busy, because the whole hopelessly inefficient official administration of Spain was now his responsibility. He told Philip with regret that he could not deal with him immediately, because of the pressure of work, but would make an appointment with him shortly. Philip did not want it to be thought that Ripperda was refusing to see him, so as soon as he had called upon the principal Spanish Jacobites he retired to the walled hillside town of S. Ildefonso, twenty-five miles north of Madrid, pretending to rest. As he went Ormonde's Irish secretary, Major Zeck Hamilton, who acted as the general Jacobite agent, scribbled his praises to Lord Inverness:

> So great vivacity and sprightliness of wit, mixed with so clear and sound a judgement, is very rarely to be met with. His talents are entirely dedicated to the service of the King. He does on all occasions justice to you... [3]

At S. Ildefonso Philip heard bad news from home. The Dutch Gazette, which served as the international newspaper for Europe, told him that his candidate Captain Collier had won the Wycombe Parliamentary election but had been challenged on an election petition for electoral malpractices by Waller, the unsuccessful Whig candidate. The House of Commons had voted predictably, by 264 to 94, that Collier was guilty, and declared that Waller elected in his place. The Mayor of Wycombe was soon afterwards imprisoned for what he did for Philip during the election: his malpractices had been iniquitous by any standards, and particularly by the standards of Philip, who often complained piously about the corrupt practices of the Whigs. But, however illogically, the Wycombe decision angered Philip.

He also received letters which had been despatched from England to him at Vienna as long ago as February. Some news they brought was predictable: the Whig government was building more ships, the Earl of Strafford had gout, his own financial affairs were still in chaos. James Hamilton wrote jocularly:

> 16th Feb.
> ...By your silence I ought to conclude that you are in some remote part of the world that hath no communication with the rest of mankind; but Fame, whose trumpet is universally heard, sounds aloud some of your Bacchanalian achievements... [4]

Hamilton also sent the more serious news that the British Government might issue an Order under the Privy Seal requiring Philip to return to England immediately. Disobeying such an order would be tantamount to an admission of treason.

Pondering this and his present position in Spain as he returned to Madrid a week later, two courses of action presented themselves. The first, which he soon rejected, was to keep the purpose of his embassy secret from the Whigs so that if anything went wrong he could prevent himself from being convicted as a Jacobite traitor if ever he returned to England. The other was to proclaim publicly his true purpose and by showing the world that he cared no longer what the Whigs or French thought of him, give the impression that the success of a Restoration plan seemed to him to be certain; thus by burning his boats he would help the Cause.

Within the next few days William Stanhope, the British Resident in Madrid, heard the startling news that the Duke of Wharton, whom he thought was still in Vienna, was now in Madrid proclaiming himself James's Ambassador, that he had openly been granted an audience by Ripperda, and that at a public ceremony in the city he had been invested with the robes and insignia of the Garter in a theatrical manner by the Duke of Ormonde. Stanhope's couriers hurried the news across Europe. King George's ministers were soon aghast. Whitehall had already been filled with rumours of an impending Jacobite invasion; indeed the Government suspected that Russian or Spanish weapons might already have been landed in Scotland and

Ireland. Their secret service reported that Lord Orrery and Humphrey Parsons were both in Paris talking of nothing but war, that Lord Craven had given James £3,000, and that the young Duke of Beaufort and the Marquis of Blandford, Marlborough's heir, both in Paris on the Grand Tour, were now Jacobites. The Duke of Atholl had been heard to say that "There was more than thirty thousand sturdy fellows that would rise tomorrow, would the Chevalier but give his order."[5] Walpole even knew one of the Parisian Jacobites' invasion plans. The Earl Marischal of Scotland and Lord Seaforth were to land with James in the North; Ormonde and Prince Charles Edward would land in England; and the main foreign invasion force would sail from Flanders, provided with fifty ships by a Scottish émigré wine merchant from Bordeaux named Gordon.

The news of Philip flaunting his Jacobite star and garter confirmed the Whig's worst fears, just as he had hoped. The Duke of Newcastle glumly wrote:

> It is not to be imagined that Wharton, how so mad and indiscreet soever he may be thought to be, would at this time stigmatise himself in so public a manner if he did not think himself well assured of the support both of the Empire and Spain, and that by their means some attempt would be forthwith made.[6]

Philip's friends in Paris were full of optimism. Atterbury boasted of Philip's worth in Parliament years before, and declared him to have been "of more use than all the Protesting Lords."[7] Nor did they think Britain in a settled enough state to withstand a Jacobite invasion and rising. In England the administration was not popular; in Scotland, the Malt Tax had made it hated. In Ireland the matter of Wood's half-pence had actually united the English and Irish and the Protestants and the Catholics against it. And everyone doubted that France would fight the Jacobites for Britain if a war was to break out. The Stuarts were the only consistently loyal allies in England that the French had ever had. The Whigs and Hanoverians, therefore, could only survive by encouraging disunity and weakness amongst James's supporters and allies.

Here they had some hope. Walpole rightly thought that neither Russia nor Austria would make a move against England without Spanish support. And William Stanhope said that although during the course of the summer the Spanish treasure-fleet from South America was due to arrive, the Spanish treasury was at present empty. The revenue of Spain, he said, totalled three and a half million pounds sterling, less than half the British revenue, and two thirds of it was spent on keeping up a peace-time army of sixty-seven thousand men. There was no money left over to pay for the further seventy thousand men which Spain had promised her allies that she would provide to fight Britain and France on behalf of the Jacobites.

And the Jacobites were still squabbling amongst themselves. The English, who were few, generally sneered at the Scots. The Scots, as usual, detested the Irish. The Irish were jealous of the King's preference for Scotsmen, and they generally sympathised with General Dillon and Lord Mar who had been supplanted by Lords Inverness and Dunbar in Royal favour. The Duke of Ormonde tended to agree with them in their dislike for Inverness and Dunbar, but he preferred Atterbury to either Dillon or Mar controlling affairs at Paris. Atterbury was growing disillusioned with them all; the Duke of Liria never admired anyone but himself; and the Duke of Wharton tried to remain aloof from party squabbles.

But he had failed to avoid making enemies. John Graeme, whom he had innocently left as his representative in Austria, had begun to detest him warmly. He disliked his debauched manners, his witty letters, his debts left at Vienna, his local servants there who had to be discharged, and his valets, Scipio and Harry, who had to be paid. Most he disliked working in the shadow of Philip's successful diplomacy. This feeling was sharpened when he tried to carry on the Duke's negotiating by arguing with Zindendorff about some details in the invasion plan. Zindendorff told him that his proposals were, "As impractical as to sail up to the top of St. Stephen's tower,"[8] and said that he should ask Philip to request Ripperda to put pressure on the Emperor from Madrid. Graeme, very peeved, wrote to Inverness in his usual priggish tone to say that he would not negotiate any more until Philip's return, because, "As His Grace is naturally of a jealous temper, I must avoid as much as possible giving him any reason to think me his rival."[9]

Lord Inverness curtly told Graeme not to be so lengthy in his despatches, and replied:

> March 16th
> I could not perceive in Wharton the least mark of jealousy he had ever entertained for you. On the contrary, I found that you had acted in everything very much to his satisfaction. [10]

But Lord Inverness knew that Graeme had some good reasons for disapproving of Wharton. They were all embarrassed, too, when Zindendorff told Saint-Saphorin that he had asked Philip to leave Vienna because of his debauchery.

In Madrid Philip now appeared in public and in conference with Ripperda wearing the Garter Star on his coat and the pale blue ribbon across his breast. (The Jacobites never adopted the dark blue ribbon of the Garter which the Hanoverians introduced.) He established himself with Ambassadorial splendour in lodgings in Bernard Street, a quarter full of Jacobite emigré Irishmen. They were important in the city, for they had three regiments in the Spanish army, and both the King's physician and his Ambassador to Versailles were Irish. Although many of them disliked Lord Inverness and were sympathetic to Queen Clementina which annoyed Philip, he was soon popular with them and a favourite in the drawing-rooms of their wives. Even the difficult Duke of Liria liked him, and they often drank together. Once they called together on Benjamin Keene, a man very conscious of his position as Secretary to William Stanhope the British Ambassador, and they spent an evening drinking his brandy and filling his ears with falsehoods about King James. He reported in disgust of Philip that:

> ...He has not been sober, or scarce had a pipe out of his mouth since he came back from his expedition to St. Ildefonse... On Tuesday last, I had some company with me that the Dukes of Liria and Wharton wanted to speak with; upon which they came directly into the room. Wharton made his compliments and placed himself by me. I did not think myself obliged to turn out his star and garter; because, as he is an everlasting talker and tippler, in all probability he

would lavish out something that might be of use to know...

He declared himself the Pretender's Prime Minister, and Duke of Wharton and Northumberland. 'Hitherto', (says he) 'my master's interest has been managed by the Duchess of Perth and three or four other old women who meet under the portal of S. Germains; he wanted a Whig, and a brisk one, and I am the man; you may now look upon me as Sir Philip Wharton, Knight of the Garter, and Sir Robert Walpole, Knight of the Bath, running a course, and, by God, he shall be hard pressed; he bought my family pictues, but they will not be long in his possession...

I used him very cavalierment; upon which he was affronted; sword and pistol next day; but before I slept a gentleman was sent to desire everything might be forgot: what a pleasure must it have been to have killed a Prime Minister?...

I think you will see our new Knight strip himself of his new honours before twelve months are passed, if he be thought worth the receiving... [11]

Meanwhile, when sober, Philip was still negotiating with Ripperda and trying to see the half-mad, highly Catholic King of Spain or the ruthless, vulgar and insatiably ambitious Queen. He was soon on excellent terms again with Ripperda, but found him not the boisterous, optimistic man he had known in Vienna. His protectress, the Queen, who had induced her weak-willed husband to give him supreme power mainly because Ripperda had always been prepared to offer anything she wanted, had noticed that both the ludicrously proud grandees of Spain and the bankers and merchants who fished in the troubled waters of Spanish finance hated him for his expensive and bellicose schemes. They hinted that the expected South American treasure-fleet did not contain gold enough to pay the huge pension he had promised the Emperor of Austria in exchange for his armed alliance. And the Queen began considering blaming Ripperda for the rashness of her own ambitions.

Ripperda did not mention this to Philip at any of the three audiences he granted him the first week that Philip was back in Madrid,

Madrid

but told him that Spain would certainly fight for James and that the Emperor, if paid enough, would support them. He delivered to his Monarchs the vital letters which Philip brought from James. But to Philip's disappointment and indignation he could not persuade them to see Philip, because they were still angry with James. Ripperda urged Philip to satisfy them with a compromise solution to the problems at the court of Rome. Could not James appoint Ormonde, who was acceptable at Madrid although a Protestant, to be tutor to Prince Charles Edward? And could not Lord Inverness retire, and Philip himself take over as Secretary of State? Philip told Rome:

> April 13th
> I answered that though I should always be proud of serving the King in any situation, yet I would never consent to accept of any employment from which I should be liable to be removed by the caprice of the Queen or the malice of one of her maids. [12]

Ripperda accepted the point. He knew the dangers of royal whims. He agreed that Philip should wait another ten days or so at court to see if he could winkle his way into the Royal presence, and then return to Rome or Vienna.

As Philip complained in disgust, the next week was Holy Week, and "being employed in Devotion, no business could be done," [13] so he spent it writing letters. Prompted by Zeck Hamilton, Ormonde's secretary, whose services and loyalty he had borrowed, he wrote to John Sterne, Laurence Sterne's great-uncle, the Bishop of Clogher in Ireland, surrendering his salary as a Privy Counsellor of Ireland (which had not been paid for six years) to be held in trust for a clergyman to preach annually on the subject of the Divine Right of Episcopacy. This was intended to resurrect the question of the power of the Bishops, which the Whigs had quenched. Unfortunately, it probably never reached Bishop Sterne, for Philip's salary was certainly never devoted to the purpose he wanted it to be, though the letter was a thousand words long with a touching postcript:

> Pray inform me whether the House and Gardens of Rathfarnham are kept in good repair and order. [14]

Madrid

Then Philip drafted a "Memorial" for the Court of Spain upon the same lines as the one he had given the Emperor almost a year before. If the monarchs would not see him personally, he thought, then he would present his own opinions to them in writing, and at length. When it was finished he gave it to Ripperda to present to them, and spent several more afternoons discussing the Jacobite position with him, and with Count Königsegg, the Austrian ambassador, and planning the start of his journey back to Rome by coach, since his sprained leg was again too weak for him to ride post. Then on about May 13th, he set out on the first stage of the journey. But meanwhile, disaster was in the air. The Spanish Queen had realised that Ripperda was not going to be able to provide enough money for a great war against France and Hanoverian England, and goaded by complaints from Königsegg that the vast sums of money promised to his Imperial master were not being paid, she abruptly dismissed Ripperda from all his offices. He, however, had foreseen this, and did not lose his head. He was at the embassy of his old countrymen the Dutch, in floods of tears, begging for help, before the news of his fall was generally known. The Dutch Ambassador, sympathetic but alarmed, took him in his coach to the house of William Stanhope, the English resident, who he thought might help. Stanhope, arriving back at his house rather late on May 14th after a visit to Aranjuez, was astounded to find there the man he thought was Secretary of State of Spain. Ripperda sadly explained he was a Minister no longer, and asked for sanctuary. In return he offered to tell Stanhope all the Spanish and Jacobite secrets. Stanhope immediately agreed. So Wharton was betrayed.

An express messenger, sent by the Madrid Jacobites overtook Philip's coach, and told him this terrible news. By chance, he had just met on the road the Earl Marischal, the Scottish Jacobite leader of the attempted 1719 Spanish invasion of Scotland, riding towards Madrid, flaunting his Jacobite ribbon of the Order of St. Andrew in rather a Whartonian way. Equally flabbergasted by Ripperda's treachery, they hastened back towards Madrid together.

The news was even worse for Philip than it was for the Jacobite cause as a whole. Ripperda knew so much about him that the Whigs could probably convict him of treason on Ripperda's evidence alone.

And his was the Jacobite plan for the invasion of England which Ripperda knew in detail and had betrayed. So if the Monarchs of Spain accepted any Jacobite invasion plan, which was still possible, clearly that plan could not be his. Worse, the all-powerful Queen was naturally furious at Ripperda's flight to the English whom she hated; and Philip, whom she had always disliked for his stance against Queen Clementina and the Pope, had openly been Ripperda's friend. From having been the most important Jacobite in Madrid, Philip now became the most useless.

But he did not re-enter the city with a heavy heart. For instead of wanting to leave the dull Spanish Court for the levity of Rome once more, he had been sad to go. At this crucial and dangerous moment he had once more fallen in love.

CHAPTER FIFTEEN

Love and the Fall

> Such a meteor having never before appeared in this horizon, it attracted the eyes and raised the astonishment of all mankind...
> He is a living scarecrow against Love... [1]
> Zeck Hamilton on the Duke of Wharton.

Maria-Theresa O'Neill O'Beirne was the daughter of the Colonel O'Beirne who had introduced to the Spanish Army the regiment of Irish exiles called the *Hibernia*. At his death her mother had been granted a pension by the King of Spain, but this pension, although (unlike many Spanish pensions) it was occasionally paid, could not support Maria-Theresa and her two sisters, her brother and her grandmother. Maria-Theresa was therefore obliged to earn her keep by serving at the most dreary and formal court in Europe as a "Camarista" in waiting on the Queen.

But the gloom of the Escorial palace itself could not dull her vivacity or her large dark eyes. She was:

> Not only very handsome, but a woman of lively wit, extreme good sense, and mistress of everything that could form the agreeable; nor was her virtue inferior to her charm. [2]

As soon as Philip saw her, early in May, he was struck. And she in turn was soon overwhelmed by the attentions of the flamboyant young Duke, King James's most favoured follower. Within days of meeting, each was in love. But their relationship, if passionate, was necessarily chaste. Morality in Madrid was stricter than morality in Vienna or London.

By a coincidence the month which brought his love for Maria-Theresa also brought him the news that Martha, his Duchess, worn out by sickness and distress, had died at the house in Holland Street, on April 14th. She had been buried eight days later as she had asked, in St. Anne's Church, Soho, and no monument was ever raised to her memory. At the news Philip wept.

He received another despatch from London that week. Crew, a Royal Messenger of King George, brought the Order that James Hamilton had warned him of: a Privy Seal demanding his immediate return to England. As he reported to Lord Inverness, it arrived unexpectedly:

> I send you here enclosed a copy of a Pretended Privy Seal which was served upon me on the 3rd instant by a messenger offering it to me in my coach. I took it at first, not knowing what it might be, but when I felt the tin-box in which it was enclosed I threw it at his head but he threw it into the coach again and I returned it with the same civility. It was left in the street and taken up by the next person that passed by.
>
> You see now that I am banished England, (which is an obligation I owe to the Duke of Ripperda). I set out infallibly on Tuesday next and hope to be with you in three weeks, wind, weather, moors and Whigs permitting. I am told by good hands that I am to be intercepted by the enemy in my passage...
>
> I wish that the King would recall his Irish subjects from this country, for they have really infected the King and Queen of Spain.[3]

In answer to the Privy Seal, Zeck Hamilton, writing as Philip's valet de chambre because it was beneath a Duke's dignity to reply personally, protested to Lord Trevor the Lord Privy Seal in London. Then he persuaded Liria to protest to the Spanish court about it in the name of King James III, on the grounds that its delivery was a breach of the law of nations, being an act of sovereign power within a foreign realm, and an insult to Their Majesties, coming from a usurper to the British throne. The King of Spain accordingly sent a stiff complaint about it to William Stanhope. Such a complaint confirmed Stanhope's view that Philip's influence was still powerful at court. So he tried to

Love and the Fall

neutralise him — in the well-worn Whig way — by offering him a pardon and a fortune at home if he would turn his coat. He sent his secretary to negotiate the terms. At an all-night drinking-bout Philip was told that a lead-mine had been discovered on his Swaledale estate which could yield a huge income, and that the Privy Seal might be suspended and a pardon granted if only he sold what he knew to Stanhope.

Philip naturally laughed at the offers. When the Madrid Jacobites, who were never sure what he would do next, heard of this, they were delighted by his disinterestedness. The Duke of Liria wrote rather naively:

> His conduct and resolution are heroical. Many proposals have been made to him by the Duke of Hanover's emissaries... He... despises most gloriously all the offers.
>
> Some of the foolish subjects that the King has in this country (who are in a pretty good number) have done all they could to discredit the Duke in this court.[4]

Now his feelings for Maria-Theresa drove other matters from his mind. He even wrote of his love in his despatches to Rome. Within a month of meeting, they agreed to marry. On May 28th, less than a fortnight after Ripperda's fall, he settled on her as a marriage settlement not only the £500 a year which had been Martha's pin-money, but also half of the £2,500 that his trustees in England allowed him. The deed of settlement was witnessed by the Duke of Liria and three others including Scipio, who was not there, but Philip forged his signature because he prudently wanted at least one subject of King George as a witness. Scipio, though black, was a good Englishman and had a wife in London and could write, though his spelling was dreadful.

Greater problems than the perennial one of money still lay in the path of Philip and Maria-Theresa. They needed the Queen's consent to their match, since all Maria-Theresa's family depended upon the Court for a livelihood. And, which was worse, they needed the Pope's consent for her to marry a Protestant. But the Pope detested Philip because of the side he had taken against Queen Clementina. So Philip

Love and the Fall

evaded this difficulty in a manner which was a little surprising. He formally abjured the Anglican faith on July 4th, entered a Capuchin convent a few hundred yards outside the walls of Madrid, wore a cowl (much to the disgust of his debauched acquaintances), and after about a fortnight convinced his confessors of his religious conversion and was accepted into the Roman Church. Did he do it just in order to marry Maria-Theresa? Everyone in Madrid thought so, and decided that he was a rascal accordingly.

The truth is less certain. He had other reasons for his conversion. He had realised that his political task at Madrid was now (since Ripperda's fall) quite hopeless. But he was still an object of jealousy to the many Jacobites who had served James for ten times as long as he had and for less reward. He realised that he must find support — form a party, as it were — amongst the Jacobites in Madrid; he must no longer be a lone Minister of James, but a true leader of Jacobites, supported by his own faction, as Walpole was in England. Most of the Jacobites in Spain, being Irishmen, considered their leader to be the popular Irish Viceroy, the Duke of Ormonde. But Ormonde was a Church of England man, a Protestant. The bulk of the Irish in Spain were Catholics. And not all of them were happy to make Spain their home for ever, leaving Ireland to the Whigs. These, the militant and the violently Catholic Irish exiles, had no leader. Philip saw that he could secure a permanent place amongst the Jacobites by setting himself at the head of them if he turned Catholic.

And there was undoubtedly some sincerity in his change of faith. He had always been something of a mystic. Perhaps the great Easter celebrations at Madrid touched a chord in the Duke which sang to him of the more serious purposes of the Hell-Fire Club and the Freemasons. Here was ceremony; here was mystery; here, perhaps, was God.

His letters show that he pondered the matter. In three letters written between June 7th and June 29th, before his conversion, he protested unecessarily that he would always remain a member of the Church of England. But to turn Catholic was to utterly reject his old political creed. For until now he had always regarded himself as an Old Whig, who had joined the Tories and Jacobites merely in order to press the principles of the 1688 Revolution, the Bill of Rights and his father's Good Old Cause, against the corruption and despotism of the new Walpoleian and Hanoverian Whigs. Catholicism was associated with the opposite: with Royalism, Toryism, autocracy and "arbitrary power". If he became a Catholic, he was in danger of having no political creed at all.

But love or self-interest drove him on, and by late July he had startled Madrid with the announcement that he was now a Catholic. But if he no longer needed Papal consent to his marriage, he still needed the Spanish Queen's. Predictably, it was at first refused. According to the Marquis d'Argens, a rather fanciful writer, this made Philip so ill with grief, he seemed likely to die. The Queen sent to tell him that she would be happier if he lived, and when he had recovered his health he was to see her. He collected all his friends, went to Court, and there threw himself at the Queen's feet:

> From Your Majesty's Lips, (says he) I expect the determination of my Fate; Life or Death, (there is no medium) depends upon your words. If you continue inflexible, I have a ministering hand, which shall assist in conveying me to that unknown shore from whose bourne no traveller returns.
>
> You have my consent to marry the lady, (answered the Queen) but it is much against my inclination; and I have reason to fear you will, one day, repent of the rashness of the action.

Zeck Hamilton continues:

> The Bride had begged in the morning that the King and Queen of Spain would allow Duke Wharton to kiss their hands. They were married between three and four in the afternoon, and as their majesties passed through the apartments to go to the Bull Feast, the new pair were introduced by the Curate of the Palace who married them, and they kissed H.M.'s hands: King of Spain said nothing to them, or so little and in so low a voice that they who stood behind heard nothing, and Queen of Spain said only to Wharton,

"Je vous recommends cette pauvre fille", and thus the audience ended.[6]

His second marriage was almost as unpopular as his first had been, because none of his friends in Madrid, most of whom were Catholics, believed that his conversion was sincere, and all were shocked by this apparent cynicism. Zeck Hamilton, who had so lately been devoted to him, now vented an indignation born of disillusionment in a despatch of prodigious length to Lord Inverness. He began it in the baking heat of the Madrid July three days before the marriage, continued it a week later with a description of the wedding, and only finished it after third and fourth instalments at weekly intervals thereafter:

> He is surely the most wild, giddy and unaccountable man that has appeared in the world for some ages past...His chief point of view at present is to be Governor to the Prince of Wales, and to get a recommendation from this court to that purpose, for he says that this court would be satisfied with the choice of him since his change of religion for that employment, and that his friends in England would be also pleased with him because they will still believe he is a Protestant... I am sure there is not any honest man in England but would rather wish that the Prince were under the care of a heathen or a Mahomedan who was a moral man than entrusted to the Duke of Wharton even before he changed his religion, for his character is well known in that country not only since the rise of the Hellfire Club of which he was an illustrious member, but before the setting up of that diabolical society; God preserve the Prince from such a Governor, for he would change if possible the mild and merciful temper of the Stuarts into that of a Nero or a Caligula...
>
> The Emperor's Minister told Duke Wharton plainly that the King of Spain wished Duke Wharton was gone out of Spain and his staying so long after the King of Spain had refused to see him was a grief to all the King's subjects, because it was a triumph to all Duke Hanover's traitors and

was a daily slight put upon one who had the honour to be sent hither by the King. Whether the motives of his stay were love, or his design to change his religion (if he ever had any) or both is hard to determine...

Even Duke Ripperda thought Duke Wharton was madder than himself, and since his disgrace has spoke of him with contempt and by the distinguishing epithets of étourdi and le Jeun Fol. So that I suspect some of Duke Wharton's pompous accounts of his conversations with Duke Ripperda were apocryphal, and that to magnify himself he added considerably to them. For Duke Wharton has no sort of regard for truth. He learned of that noble quality when he was a professed Whig, and he was bred under an excellent master of the art of lying...

The King should send him to Muscovy or keep him in Rome... Duke Wharton will give little disturbance at the King's Court for he is a very pacific man, remarkable of a long time for being a coward, and fear of being beaten would keep him quiet if a sense of duty wouldn't restrain him...[7]

Duke Wharton has a good store of what they call an humble, condescending pride, and a strong ambition to be considered in a party, and therefore when his love, the cause of his follies, is abated, and that he finds to how low a degree of contempt he is fallen in England and elsewhere, he will take, I fear, some desperate course and either hang himself or make his peace by endeavouring to hang others.[8]

On August 3rd:

I was exceedingly deceived by him. His narratives of his Parliamentary battles, of the good dispositions of London and of the sentiments of England in general both amused and pleased me, I liked his vivacity, I loved his zeal...His failings...I was not a witness to...he once so far dissembled with me as to profess a great concern for his habitual drunkeness.[9]

On August 10th:

> It can't be conceived with what horror and contempt all orders and degrees of man speak of him, particularly the Ministers, as the Marquis Castelar, Marquis de la Paz and Confessor... [10]

The Duke of Liria, trying to forget that he had been Philip's most constant companion, wrote in his Journal a few months later:

> He was the most worthless individual I have ever known in my life, being without faith, law, honour or religion. He lied every time that he opened his mouth. He was a poltroon, a gasbag and a drunkard; in effect, he had every vice, and his single virtue was that he was a perfect flatterer... he asked me to be present at the wedding. I replied acidly that I would do no such thing, that I did not wish to have any more to do with him, and that I would be glad if he would take up his residence elsewhere than at my home... [11]

Such an outburst against Philip could not have been caused only by his tactless religious "conversion" and socially unsuitable marriage, though Madrid opinion was easily offended by such things. What shocked his old friends most was that Philip evidently wanted an important new role as a leader of their party, and that he refused to acknowledge either to himself or to them that his aspirations threatened their positions and those of Inverness and Dunbar at Rome. When they had discovered this they closed ranks against him, declared that his explanation for his unconventional behaviour was not self-delusion but deliberate deceit, and reckoned that when he disappeared from their midst because he was chasing "love", he was really betraying them. From having doted on him, they turned to hating him, and hated him the more because they despised themselves for previously believing in him.

Philip could do nothing to abate the flood of enmity which now flowed against him, but tried to carry on his work as James's representative and as a Jacobite. He wrote to the University of

Oxford, the Tory stronghold, justifying Toryism and Jacobitism as a continuation of Old Whig principles, of the "Truly Good Old Cause for which I have willingly ventured my estate, and for which I will cheerfully hazard my life." [12] Then he wrote a semi-public letter to his sister Jane (who had lately married a man of whom Lady Mary Wortley Montagu disapproved called John Holt), justifying his own political position and warning her of the treason trial, which, even if it was held in his absence, he now thought would be inevitable:

Madrid, June 17th 1726 N.S.

Dear Sister,

My name has been so often mentioned of late in the public prints, and consequently become the subject of private conversation, that all my personal friends (you particularly) may with reason expect to know from myself what steps I have taken, or intend to take; and what were the true reasons of my present resolutions...

Can a High Commission Court at present, or a secret committee, tarnish the honour of a family? Is it a real disgrace to be condemned by Macclesfield, Harcourt, Townshend or Trevor? Is it a dishonour to be robbed of a private fortune by those who have stripped the widow and the fatherless? Who have sold their country? Who have plundered the public? No! My dear sister, assure yourself that this unjust prosecution is a lasting monument erected to the honour of our family...

No change in my circumstances shall lessen my tender concern for you, or my sister Lucy, to whom I desire you will present my love, and charge her, as she values my friendship, never to marry without my consent. Be assured that no distance of place nor length of time shall abate my affection for you. And my enemies shall find, whenever I return to England, it shall be with honour to myself and joy to my friends...And wherever I am, I shall be always, dear sister,

Your sincere friend and brother,
Wharton. [13]

Love and the Fall

In his days in the Capuchin convent, he had kept up his correspondence with the ministers of Madrid who succeeded Ripperda in power, but he did not try to call on them because he was out of favour at court and because he now saw little of anybody. He took a house for a period of six months in a village outside the city, where he proposed to spend the autumn with his new Duchess, and he told King James:

> The present tranquillity of my mind and the happiness I enjoy with the Duchess of Wharton (whose good nature and easy temper every day gain more and more upon my affection) give me a calm of spirit I never felt before. [14]

King James, at Rome, was in doubt as to how he should react to the tales he heard of the Duke. From Liria and from Zeck Hamilton he now heard nothing but bad about him; Ormonde's occasional, very short and badly scrawled notes did not contradict them; and Philip told him nothing serious at all. Bishop Atterbury from Paris showed his pain at Philip's betrayal of Anglicanism by saying that he could no longer support him. So King James and Lord Inverness told Philip by letter that he could not possibly do any good for them in Spain. He could go to Flanders, if he liked, in order to contact his friends in England and try to beg a pardon and save his estates. But they said that he could not come to Rome because James was leaving for Bologna for the winter, and in any case they did not want to see him. They asked the Duke of Ormonde to investigate whether the worst of what Liria and Zeck Hamilton said about Philip was true, and in particular whether he had jeopardised the Jacobite cause at the Court of Madrid. Ormonde replied that he had no evidence that Philip had said anything that could have offended the King of Spain, and certainly the King had taken no such offence. To this small extent Philip's name was cleared.

He himself was spending a quiet summer being weaned off brandy by his new Duchess, until during August he fell ill. He had a weakness in the stomach and was spitting blood. It is impossible to tell today what the cause of it was. But it seems to have passed, on this occasion, quite soon. By the end of September his poverty was more of a problem.

His allowance from his trustees was still being remitted to Rotterdam, where John Graeme used it all to pay his debts to the banker Mr. Sorrel. The money that had been given him by the Jacobites had all run out. The 250 pistoles that Maria-Theresa was owed as the dowry of a Camarista had never been paid, although Philip had already borrowed 150 pistoles (over £100) on the strength of it. So by November he was begging James to let him come and live quietly with him at Court, promising not to meddle in any public business, but pointing out that if he came he would be the only English (as opposed to Scottish) nobleman there. If he could not come, he said, he and his Duchess would starve.

With ill grace James and Lord Inverness relented a little, saying that they might visit Italy briefly provided that they soon went on the Flanders, and Inverness commented coldly on the impracticality of the plan:

> It will be inconvenient travelling if her Grace falls with child upon the road. [15]

And they sent him no money, suspecting that he would spend it on paying his Spanish debts rather than travelling to Rome or Bologna. He, now desperate to assert that he was still a person of some political importance, wrote expressly to say that his confessor Father Clarke, the rector of the Scottish College at Madrid, had been made confessor to the King, which gave him Court influence once more. Then he sent to England a deed repudiating the Dukedom that King George had given him. (It is said that as a joke he had sold the title for a few pistoles). This curious behaviour caused some amusement in England, but did not move the cold hearts of the men at Rome.

So, making the best of things as usual, he decided to pass the winter on the Mediterranean. Shortly before the end of November when the lease of his house outside Madrid was to expire, he left with a train of unpaid servants for Valencia. Here, in the temperate climate between the mountains and the sea, the Duke and Duchess of Wharton set up their matrimonial household.

Here he had time to contemplate another falling meteor, the Duke of Ripperda, who had betrayed him. Ripperda had been

Love and the Fall

removed from William Stanhope's house by a deputation headed by Don Louis de Cuella Alcaide de la Carta and backed up with the squadron of Castilla of Santiago. He was put in the castle of Segovia, under close watch, and was charged with high treason. But from this difficult situation he escaped, (probably with the connivance of the British) and wandered Europe before straying down to the north coast of Africa and enjoying the hospitality of the Moorish princes who ruled there. He found employment at the end as the chief adviser to the ruler to Tetuan in Morocco, and there he died.

The sudden and catastrophic fall of Ripperda from the highest rank in Spain to disgrace and flight made Philip ponder on the uncertainty of his own future. But he himself had the advantage of youth. After he had settled down with his beloved wife at their pleasant house in Valencia he was only just twenty-seven.

CHAPTER SIXTEEN

War

> Why beats thy bosom with illustrious dreams
> Of self-exposure, laudable and great?
> Of gallant enterprise, and glorious death?
> Die for thy country? Thou romantic fool!
> > Edward Young, *Night Thoughts,* Book 7.

> I had rather carry a musket in an odd-named Muscovite regiment than wallow in riches by the favour of the Usurper.
> > Wharton to Lord Inverness, 8 June 1726
> > (State Papers in the Royal Archives Vol. 94 fol. 90.)

The war for which the Jacobites had been waiting broke over Europe early in 1727 when Spain commenced hostilities against Britain. The first guns were fired at the British from a battery which the Spaniards were building near the town of Gibraltar on February 21st at four in the afternoon. The Spanish Queen had decided to attack England by besieging Gibraltar rather than by invading Devon or Ireland partly to save money and partly to snub James. But in any case King James's followers were still unprepared for war. They had solved none of their long-standing problems. Their ranks were ludicrously divided. The squabbles of the King and his ministers against the Queen and the Pope and Spain, of the Catholics against the Protestants, of the Scots against the Irish, of Atterbury against Mar and Dillon, and of the Madrid Jacobites against Wharton, had not been settled. Most of their best military commanders — and the Jacobites had some very good ones — were unavailable for service. Marshall Berwick, James's illegitimate half-brother, was now irredeemably devoted to the fortunes of his adopted country France. Lord North and Grey, the veteran of Blenheim, was in the process of turning Catholic, and so for this tactlessness he was almost as blamed as Philip had been, though nobody doubted his sincerity. General Dillon was still out of favour at Court for supporting Lord Mar. The Duke of Ormonde was now well into his sixties. The Earl Marischal, who had led the abortive 1719 invasion attempt, and his brother James Keith, who later became one of the greatest European soldiers of the century, were stuck purposelessly at Cordova with only sixty pistoles between them. The exiled Scottish highland chieftans in Paris, always touchy and vain, were growing disillusioned with Jacobitism generally. Lord Seaforth had been bribed by the Whigs to surrender his principles in return for a pardon and his land, but had told James that he had left the Jacobites because of their inactivity:

Paris. July 30 1726

...Whether the kingdom be conquered or not, I think I am. If any is so loyal as to judge otherwise, let him do more than I have done, if he can. And that man and no other is more justly entitled than myself to be esteemed,

Sir,

Your Majesty's most dutiful humble servant and subject,

Seaforth [1]

His discontent was echoed by the other Jacobite leaders whose recent euphoria had ebbed: they had no money, no troops, and although Spain was beginning a war, neither Russia nor Austria looked like helping her. James himself, the centre of the whole movement, only half wanted war; half of him wanted to be left in quiet at Bologna, away from all these political problems, with his precocious Prince of Wales, whom he called his "Carluccio", and little Henry, Duke of York, who now had three teeth and who hardly ever cried.

The Spanish military effort was soon proving as inept as the strategy behind it. Although its commander, the Conde de las Torres, had rashly boasted that his campaign would be over in six weeks, Gibraltar was proving almost impregnable by land. By sea it was supplied and guarded by the squadron of Sir Charles Wager which had sped hither from watching the Russians in the Baltic.

Because the British fleet was blockading the Spanish treasure galleons in Cartagena in South America, there was no money to pay Spain's troops. Philip, whose health had been restored by Valencia's gentle climate and his wife's nursing and who was chafing at inactivity, cynically reckoned that it would be easier for Spain to seize Whitehall than to seize Gibraltar. But when he heard that his friends the Earl Marischal and James Keith were making their way from Cordova towards Gibraltar to join Las Torres's army, he decided to do the same. He took Maria-Theresa down the coast and over the rocky inland road across Murcia to Granada, where he left her and pressed on alone. But his hastening carriage was overturned a few miles later, and he was badly bruised and shaken, so he could not finish his journey to Gibraltar until March.

The army of the Conde de las Torres was not a very imposing sight. It was ill-equipped, and already it had lost a quarter of its men through incapacity or desertion induced by the torrential rain, disease and lack of pay. Its cannon, which had not all arrived, numbered only thirty pieces. But it was still an army, and its thirteen thousand regular soldiers had been briskly set to work building two strong batteries. When these were finished, two thousand men were entrenched in the flat sandy isthmus which separates the Rock from the mainland. Unfortunately their excavations could not be deep, because the lowness of the ground and the wetness of the weather filled them with water.

Although more numerous, they were worse prepared and organised than the British. Sir Charles Wager had almost doubled the strength of Colonel Jasper Clayton's garrison by disembarking a thousand men and ten 24-pound guns from his ships. The fortifications around the town were not in perfect repair, but Clayton kept three hundred men busy at improving them. And the enemy gunfire was not particularly effective: when the Spaniards' "Thessé" battery opened up at one of Wager's ships, the Portland, on February 21st, it did no harm to it at all.

Philip, not discouraged by finding that the Earl Marischal and James Keith had been given insignificant posts in the army (ostensibly because they were Protestants), enlisted as a cadet in the ranks of the Spanish Guards. His enemies and those who knew of his famous cowardice smirked at this, and Zeck Hamilton wrote from Madrid that:

He may chance to finish his history in this expedition if he has not the sense to keep out of harm's way and reserve himself for greater exploits. A true Knight errant must not confine himself altogether to the service of the ladies. [2]

But everyone was surprised when Philip was immediately appointed A.D.C. to Las Torres and Colonel-Aggregate, or Lieutenant-Colonel, to the Hainault, one of the Irish regiments in the Spanish service, whose notional Commander was the Marqués de Castelar. This provided him with liberty to take time off for hunting, and with a uniform and a salary of seventeen pistoles per month, about fifteen or twenty pounds. Very pleased, he sent for the Duchess to join him in the camp, and with the Keiths and the Spanish officers he made himself as comfortable as he could.

Unfortunately, his new rank soon made demands upon him. After he had been at the siege only a few weeks he was appointed to command a battery or small fort which guarded the Spaniards' land route to their front-line trenches. Shortly after his appointment, the British at a Council of War decided to send a naval expedition to destroy his small emplacement. This was soon clear to Las Torres and Philip, who saw two men-of-war being specially equipped so that they could sail close enough to flatten the fort with cannon fire or land marines to capture it. But Philip and his men had no choice but to defend it as best they could, however slim their chances of survival seemed to be, and he fortified himself with brandy accordingly. Luckily just as the two British ships weighed anchor, the wind dropped and a dead calm ensued. It lasted for days. By that time the British had decided to cancel their attack altogether, since the whole ailing Spanish onslaught was really not worth counter-attacking.

The Conde de Las Torres had indeed ordered his men to advance and build new fortifications even closer to the town, within close range of the British guns. This order had so exasperated his engineers that they almost mutinied, and they actually demanded that his order should be put in writing. They were right in thinking the advance desperate, for after they had lost three hundred men a day from the accurate fire of the new 18-pounders that Wager had unloaded from the lower decks of H.M.S. Rossario, the order had to be countermanded and the men withdrew to their old lines.

Then Las Torres tried an artillery bombardment. He employed his thirty-odd cannon full-time firing 70 or 80 exploding shells each night into the British lines. But the defences on the Rock itself were so high that they were out of shot for most Spanish guns, whose touch-holes became so worn from over-use that they became useless. But however shaken Philip may have been from his proximity to death, his Commander was still loath to give up the siege. And shortly afterwards he received some encouraging news from Madrid. The treasure-galleons carrying eight million pieces of eight, had escaped from the British blockade in Colombia and were now safely at anchor in Spain. So he now had enough money to pay his troops, and in a determined but inefficient way his attack went on.

Philip had discovered that brandy could make him quite brave. Once he left his own trenches and approached the British lines, wearing his uniform of Colonel-Aggregate and either incited them to fire at him by shouting "Vive le Prétendant!", or tried to persuade them over to Jacobitism. In any event, with-holding their fire because they reckoned him drunk, the sentries allowed him to return unharmed to his own ranks.

He was soon notorious in the British camp, which was officered by many Scotsmen of high rank, such as Lord Charles Hay, who may have known him in London. During April Lieutenant Clark of H.M.S. Tiger was sent to parley with Las Torres, and after his interview he dined with the Duke and Duchess, who sent him back to the beleagured Rock afterwards laden with gifts, including a basket of fish and a whole wild boar. The fish turned out to be bad, but the boar was eaten by the garrison officers with relish the next day.

But now diplomatic movements in the capitals of Europe began to overtake the slow and rain-sodden progress of the siege. The Queen of Spain was beginning to lose her nerve. It was clear that the Austrians were not going to help her storm Gibraltar, and that without foreign aid she would find the place impregnable. So she allowed preliminary talk of a new peace treaty to begin.

An older dispute was being settled at Bologna. There King James under threats from the Pope, at last agreed to compromise with his Queen by allowing Prince Charles to be tutored by Catholics, stopping the Anglican service being held in his household, and replacing his Secretary of State Lord Inverness (who had long been begging for permission to resign) by Philip's old secretary John Graeme. At this, Clementina left St. Cecilia's convent, where she had been heartily bored, and rejoined him without loss of face. Then he knighted Graeme, gave Liria (who was jealous) the Garter, and prepared for his court to relapse into its usual quiet insignificance. With the Spanish war going so badly, nothing would remove the sixty-seven year-old King George from the throne of England, it seemed, except a natural death.

But on the night of June 11th George I died, overtaken by an apoplexy at Osnabruck, in his dear native Hanover. James was electrified by the news. It was a God-given chance for his peaceful Restoration. In a flurry of activity which was unusual to him he prepared to leave Bologna and to throw himself on the mercy of the common people of England. Putting from his mind the inauspicious news from Gibraltar and the ever-interesting details of Prince Charles's bowel movements, he set out boldly with his court to cross the Alps for Avignon and England.

But few Jacobites in England and France shared his optimism. Before James had jogged a dozen dusty miles towards France George II had peacefully succeeded to the throne of Britain, Sir Robert Walpole was back in power and England was as little expecting a Jacobite Restoration as ever. While James obliviously rode northwards, Lord Orrery wrote desperately to tell him of the absurdity of an invasion at the present time. Charles Cesar from the House of Commons, old Lord Strafford from the Lords, and Atterbury from Paris all urged him to delay. He received their pessimistic letters phlegmatically. They forced him to admit that he had missed another opportunity; and he settled down to spend the autumn at Avignon.

Meanwhile, Philip had tried his new-found bravery once too often during the siege of Gibraltar. One day during May, as he was inspecting the troops in their waterlogged trenches, a shell from the town of Gibraltar landed near him and exploded. Its splinters shattered his foot. His men carried him back to his quarters, where surgeons cauterised the wound and bound it up with splints. But they told him that his days as a soldier were over. So he retired honourably from his regimental duties and was carried to Cadiz to convalesce with his patient Duchess.

The siege activity was ending anyway. On June 24th Las Torres agreed with Sir Charles Wager that armed conflict at Gibraltar was to cease. The Earl Marischal and James Keith, in despair at the news, followed Philip to Cadiz. By the time that they arrived they found Philip hobbling the hot streets in as bad a temper as they were. His wound had ended his hopes of regaining Jacobite confidence by soldiering. And he felt, with some reason, that he had been hard done by. It was barely a year since he had been the greatest of King James's subjects. Now James treated him as a drunkard and a fool. He blamed Inverness and Dunbar and the other Scotsmen who surrounded James at Rome for not protecting him against the jealousy of the Spanish Jacobites of Madrid. And when he heard that such a low-born Scotsman as his former secretary Graeme was now the King's Secretary of State, he gave vent to his feelings in a long letter to James (which was never sent, but which was discovered amongst his papers years later), complaining about Inverness, Dunbar and Graeme and all their views and policies including their complaints about the Queen which he himself had always supported:

> What extremely surprises us is that your Grace should be so far deluded as to excuse the evidence of crimes of a set of upstart ministers who would endeavour to fly to integrity and virtue, that was never their distinguishing characteristic, in order to screen themselves from the just resentments of a wise and an injured Queen, armed with a just indignation to see the lives and fortunes of the greatest men of England lodged in the hands of two poor younger brothers of Scotch families, hated by the King's real and great friends in their own country and in some measure unknown to England, whom His Majesty dragged from obscurity to place at the head of his affairs... [3]

Perhaps this spiteful draft letter reflects a mind disordered by a painful wound, rather than a political attitude that Philip could reflectively maintain. At any rate by August the pleasant company and warm sea air at Cadiz had mended both the broken foot and his jaudiced mood, for he was once more drinking brandy and joking at the Earl Marischal, who was killing time in the outlying countryside shooting quail with his brother James Keith.

Unfortunately, they were not amused by one of Philip's "frolics". Marischal wrote soberly back in cypher to King James at Avignon to report a practical joke:

Cadiz   Sep 22nd 1727
Sir,
The Duke of Wharton is still here in bad health and rarely sober; he fraughted a ship ten days ago for England and three or four days after told me of it. He said he had a letter from the Duke of Hanover inviting him home, in which he said there was this expression — "You left England because it was governed by Germans but you shall find me entirely English..."

In half an hour after he pretended to laugh at my brother and me for believing he had received such a letter, yet said he was going to England, but it was to raise his men to die nobly with them fighting under your standard...

He bid me tell you he was going to Madrid and not to England and entreated I would not tell what he told me...I will not promise him that, and therefore by this very post I acquaint the Duke of Ormonde and Bishop Atterbury with what passed.

I am all duty and respect, Sir,
Your Majesty's most obedient subject and servant
MARISCHAL [4]

Before this letter was sent Philip had written to James asking him again for permission to visit him in Italy to ask for employment and, more important, for pay. After waiting a few months for a reply to this letter which never came, he set out with the Duchess to Madrid to see if he could borrow money there with which to travel to Rome uninvited.

At Christmas 1727, James was still staying in the antique Papal palace at Avignon where Philip had first met him over eleven years before. Because it was north of the Alps he seemed much closer to Britain than at Bologna or Rome, and because it was not the resident city of the Pope he did not feel the oppressive nearness of the paymaster whose pensioner he was. Unfortunately, if he was happy, his courtiers were not. In Rome they had learnt to live on macaroni. But in Avignon macaroni was unknown, the proper flour for making it was unobtainable, and other food was expensive. Their shortage of money became acute. King James even permitted Sir John Graeme to go to Madrid to seek a pension for himself there to eke out his Royal pay. And there, by chance Graeme once more met Philip who had just arrived from Cadiz. In the interview which followed, humiliating for Philip, Graeme at last convinced him that the Jacobites did not want him. Such a snub from one who had been his own private secretary only eighteen months before was hard to bear. But harder still came the whisper from his Madrid friends that either the embarrassing reputation his carefree manners gave him at Court or — more likely — the English diplomats' demands at the newly-convened peace conference, would make the Monarchs ask him to leave Spain within six months. His prospects looked blacker than ever.

Oddly, historians of the Freemasons persuasively claim that during this stay in Madrid Philip founded in his lodging "in a French hotel" the first Spanish Lodge of Masons, the first lodge ever to be "warranted or constituted in Foreign Parts by the Grand Lodge of England."[5] There is no other evidence that Philip had returned to Freemasonry after leaving the Masons in England and founding the Gormogans four years earlier. But the theory that he founded a Spanish Lodge in those early days before Masonry became anti-Catholic, seems to be supported by the fact that only four years later the Grand Master of Andalusia was called Comerford, which was the surname of Maria-Theresa's half-brother or brother-in-law. And certainly only seven years later the Earl of Wintoun was the Master of a lodge at James's court at Rome itself.

Two months after his lodge was allegedly founded, and in spite of Graeme's opinions and advice, Philip wrote to tell James bluntly that he was coming to visit him. In vain James hastily ordered Philip to stay away, and begged Lord North and Grey, who was staying at Barcelona, to intercept the Duke and Duchess when they arrived there.

Philip and Maria-Theresa took ship to Leghorn late in April. James, who had returned from Avignon to Bologna, then accepted in his passive way that a meeting with Philip was inevitable. But he resolved to keep it as secret as possible. He pretended that the reason for this was that he wanted to protect Philip from a treason charge in England. But the truth was that he did not want the other Jacobites to know that he was seeing him. So low had Philip's reputation amongst them sunk.

CHAPTER SEVENTEEN

A Dream of Home

"And wanting nothing but an honest heart..."
Pope on Wharton, *First Moral Essay* 193.

By the end of May 1728 Philip had befriended the Duke of Parma, at whose court he and Maria-Theresa had arrived after landing at Leghorn. From a hired house here he wrote to James, who was back at Bologna, asking for an audience. James, who only wanted to see him secretly, sent to him a discreet gentleman of his court called J. O'Brien, one of many Irish Jacobites of that name, to bring him through Modena to Samoggia, in Papal dominions, roughly thirty miles from Parma and ten from the court of Bologna. Here James came out to meet them.

During the interview which followed Philip was refreshed by James's apparent gratitude to him for past services. As James reported to Ormonde, "All passed with great submission on his side and friendliness on mine." [1] But the King did not promise Philip a job or a pension. This confirmation that he was redundant stung him more deeply when James thoughtlessly mentioned that other Jacobites whom Philip had once pitied or patronised were now being usefully employed. Lord North and Grey was a Spanish Lieutenant-General and was arranging with Britain that his British peerages and land would not be prejudiced by it. Atterbury had retired from Paris, but his place had been taken by his French-educated secretary Colonel Daniel O'Brien. Liria was Spanish Ambassador to Moscow, where he was protecting the Earl Marischal and helping James Keith to become a Major-General in the Czarina's army. And priggish Sir John Graeme, as James's Secretary of State, was master of them all. Philip alone had no role. James suggested that he should go to Madrid, where his congé could be postponed, or to Normandy whence he could try to settle his financial affairs in England. James promised to write to the Jacobite leaders in France to tell them that Philip would not be betraying them even if he corresponded with the Whigs.

Philip rode back to Parma contemplating the chance that he might successfully negotiate with the Whigs in England and save the remains of his estate. After three years of wandering, he might return to be a quiet country Jacobite in his own land. He might spend his life as a dilettante at Twickenham or hunting in the deer-park with Phil Lloyd and Kit Musgrave at Wharton Hall. And the long-suffering Maria-Theresa could be an English Duchess in form as well as in name.

On his return to Parma he found her ill with a sharp fever. It passed leaving her very weak, which made it impossible for them to set out on the road to France. Not that they had enough money to pay for carriages to take them anywhere else anyway. Philip had written to Waters, the Jacobite banker at Amsterdam, to send him such money as his account there still contained, but this would take weeks to arrive if it arrived at all. So they remained at the pleasant court of Parma.

This annoyed King James who had intended visiting Parma himself during the next fortnight, and who thought it undesirable to be seen in the same town as Philip. He sent them a sharp note telling them that they should hurry on to France for their own good — lest the Whig Secret Service should discover they were associating with him again. Philip replied firmly:

> The Duchess of Wharton is just recovering from a violent ague and is so weak that she cannot possibly undertake a journey without the greatest hazard...Being in the same town as the King won't be worse than wearing the Garter or serving Spain...The other point that detains me at Parma is want of money, for I have not enough by me to pay my expenses here, much less to think of setting out to France. [2]

So when James arrived and was greeted by the Duke of Parma with all the honours due to a reigning monarch of Great Britain, Philip was still residing in the city. He optimistically sent James a note asking for another secret interview. James again told him to move on. But by then Philip had found enough money to pay his bills and to hire carriages for their journey towards Lyons. So two days after James's arrival Philip took his leave of the Duke of Parma, who tactfully left

James in his opera-box to step out and give Philip his good wishes for the journey. Then they were off on the road to Piacenza, following up the valley of the river Po towards Turin.

After ten days their little party had passed Milan, had crossed Piedmont, climbed the Savoy Alps, descended into the French district of Dauphiné, and had halted at Lyons. Here Philip, tired by the journey, fell ill with his old stomach complaint, and although the inns were expensive, they had to wait a day or two while he recovered his strength. But by the morning of June 30th he was writing letters, and in the afternoon they were on the road once more.

One of his letters was to King James at Parma. The other was despatched to His Excellency Horatio Walpole, British Ambassador to France. By writing to him, Philip was anticipating events. Because he had gathered from King James that he could expect neither employment nor pay in the foreseeable future, he knew that he must try to save his English estates. But to deal with England without taking precautions was dangerous. The Walpole government had exiled the Bishop of Rochester and confiscated his property for lighter crimes than Philip's; so Philip decided to temporise. He was not ashamed of lying to the Walpoles; Sir Robert Walpole had once flagrantly betrayed him. He decided to claim that he was no longer a Jacobite, and to seek such a pardon as Bolingbroke had been given without betraying any such secrets as Bolingbroke had done. And he could tell them that he wanted to live quietly, and dabble no more in politics. The Walpoles would like to hear this. They had always been afraid of the Jacobites; they were always ready to welcome back, on terms, anybody they could wean from the Jacobite party. Here, thought Philip, there was room for negotiation. But however disillusioned he might be with James, and however much he hated some of James's ministers, he would never betray any of them. The Walpoles might deal in personal betrayal, he thought, as he and old Lord Cowper had been betrayed when the Prince of Wales was reconciled to George I back in 1720. But Philip stood above such behaviour. For all his faults and idiocies, the Duke was a man of honour.

This is what he had written from Lyons to Horatio Walpole:

Lyons. June 28th O.S. 1728

Sir,

Your Excellency will be surprised to receive a letter from me...

Since His Present Majesty's accession to the Throne I have absolutely refused to be concerned with the Pretender or any of his affairs...

I am coming to Paris to put myself entirely under Your Excellency's protection...If Your Excellency would permit to me to wait upon you for an hour I am certain you would be convinced of the sincerity of my repentance for my former madness, and would become an advocate with His Majesty to grant me his most Gracious Pardon, which it is my comfort I shall never be required to purchase by any step unworthy of a man of honour.

I do not intend, in case of the King's allowing me to pass the evening of my days under the shadow of His Royal Protection, to see England for some years, but shall remain in France of Germany as my friends shall advise, and enjoy country sports till all former stories are buried in oblivion.

I beg of Your Excellency to let me receive your orders at Paris, which I will send to your hostel to receive. The Duchess of Wharton, who is with me, desires leave to wait upon Mrs. Walpole, if you think proper...[3]

The Ambassador was as pleased to hear from the Duke as he was surprised. He had long been interested in Philip's activities. The Duke was as blatant as any traitor north of the Alps. The government could have him convicted and hanged, drawn and quartered if they found him in England. Even if he stayed abroad, an outlawry for treason might deprive him of his estates. The Ambassador had been kept informed of his movements to a certain extent by John Sample, his wretched Jacobite spy who heard about them through the Paris grapevine. But to receive such a letter from the Duke was still startling for him.

Philip and Maria-Theresa reached Paris three or four days after this letter, on the morning of July 5th. As soon as lodgings had been found for themselves and their few servants — in an attic, Philip said, which was all they could afford — he sent a footman to Horatio Walpole's residence for news. He was told that the Ambassador would see him at eight the following morning.

It was strange for him to be amongst Hanoverian Englishmen once more, hearing the couriers and footmen talk about Westminster politics and London society. But it was stranger for them to see his lanky figure, his face grown pink and puffy from drink, and to hear that this was the dangerous Duke of Wharton "coming in". If he had discarded his Spanish Colonel's uniform for civilian clothes they would have noticed that the cut of them was three years out of date, his coat and wig being both too long and heavy to be fashionable now. But they did not have long to stare, because the Duke was promptly ushered in to a room in which he could speak privately to Horatio Walpole.

Philip began by professing great friendship for each of the Walpole brothers. The irony of this was lost on the Ambassador who was an intelligent but not imaginative man. Then Philip said that he had left the Jacobites more than a year before, and now wished to fling himself at the feet of King George II, "which he expressed," as the Ambassador later reported, "with that eloquence which is so natural to him." [4] But he said he would only reveal to him Jacobite affairs "as far as was consistent with his honour, in not betraying or doing the least harm to any person that had been concerned with him." [5] Then he told the Ambassador some witty anecdotes about James; charmed him with his apparent sincerity; said that he would be retiring to Rouen, and would hope to hear from him there; and then he left. The same evening he sent a formal letter to the Ambassador, repeating his declarations and his request for a pardon. It was bundled up that night in the Ambassador's express despatch to the Duke of Newcastle in London.

The Ambassador suspected that Philip was now politically harmless, which was a good reason for pardoning him. But when he retired to his bed that night, a thought is likely to have struck him. Philip wanted to remains of his estates to be saved, and his own name to be cleared by a pardon. But in return for all this, what had he offered? Such tales of the Jacobites as would incriminate nobody and were "conistent with his honour". It amounted to nothing at all.

Philip settled at Rouen, in Normandy, fifty or sixty miles from Paris, because it was cheap, excellent hunting country, and convenient for the port of Dieppe, where posts might easily be sent to England. Here he hired the numerous servants that he always found necessary, and set up house as gaily as if he had been back at Winchendon. Meanwhile the Ambassador's despatch enclosing his letter was gone from Paris on July 7th, O.S., and within two days it was in London. It reached Sir Robert Walpole in Norfolk the next morning, where it was read with great interest, doubtless before the Houghton gamekeeper's reports that Walpole boasted that he perused before any state papers. He returned it with his remarks on it to Lord Townshend at Whitehall the same afternoon. The Duke of Newcastle then laid it before King George II personally, to give his royal Opinion on it in his usual laborious and finicky way. Newcastle wrote back to Horatio Walpole on July the 12th with an answer for Wharton. The King and the Ministers, he said, would not give Philip a pardon; they would not even accept any more letters from his saying why he might deserve one. He could remain an exile. Horatio Walpole immediately sent this melancholy news to Philip at Rouen.

Worse news from England followed this. Walter Pryse, his longstanding man of business in London, reported that the Government prosecution for his treason at Gibraltar was pressing ahead. It seemed certain that his remaining estates would be confiscated. He would then be left with no hope of any income at all. Even now he seemed the last person entitled to the income of his own estates. His £2,500 a year which had been settled upon him by his trustees in 1722, was subject to various deductions. Out of it he still owed several hundred pounds to Mr. Sorrel who had lent him so much money at Vienna. He was probably still paying for the education of young Richard Coningsby, old Lord Coningsby's grandson, at Amsterdam. He was certainly still paying twenty florins a month to Scipio, his black valet, at Vienna. What had happened to Harry, his other valet who had also been left there, we do not know, Perhaps he had made his own way across Europe to Rouen.

Although for the last three years he had neglected to do anything to help Lord Orrery, Walter Pryse and Sir Kit Musgrave redeem his over-mortgaged land, they had done well. Wooburn had been cleared of its mortgage to Francis Charters and sold; Aske had been bought by Sir Robert Sutton, Horatio Walpole's predecessor at Paris; some land at Brigham and Whinfell in Cumberland had been equally well disposed of. Cheered by this, Philip let his household at Rouen grow extravagantly. He and the Duchess had been joined there by some servants from Spain and several Jacobite gentlemen of small means such as the affable Irish captain Brierly who become Philip's indispensable friend, and by Sir Harry Goring, who had been an exile in France since the days of the Atterbury plot. He entertained them at Rouen and in Paris on a ducal scale, having:

> ...made a calculation, in which there appeared to be but one mistake: that is, His Grace proportioned his disbursements not according to the extent of his fortune, but agreeable to the size of his quality. [6]

He had just collected from a banker in Paris £600 of his allowance which his trustees still sent, but this would not support his household long. He was not on good enough terms with the chiefs of the Jacobites to be able to expect any money from them, even if they had money to spare. Their opinion of him was unfortunately lower than ever. When he called on Atterbury whom he had not seen for five years, the old Bishop could only demand of him what he meant by his change of religion; and when Philip, taken aback, answered hastily that it was no true change but they "might as well think he was a Turk," [7] Atterbury was appalled. Other Jacobites agreed with him that if the Duke was insincere in religion he was probably insincere in politics as well. Even Lord North and Grey believed that Philip was selling Jacobite secrets to Horatio Walpole in exchange for a pardon, as many Jacobite leaders had done before. Although Atterbury's successor as Resident in Paris, Colonel Daniel O'Brien, would occasionally correspond and exchange visits with him, most Jacobites shunned him as a traitor or (worse) one about to become a traitor.

Philip claimed that he had King James's permission to see the Ambassador. But this was not strictly true. He only had James's permission to try to save his estates. There can be no doubt that Philip had taken this to mean that he might try to get what he could from

Horatio Walpole. And it is certain that he never contemplated betraying the Jacobites. But James had not told his supporters to expect Philip in France negotiating with his trustees, although he had promised Philip at Parma that he would warn them of this. So the Jacobites had every reason to be suspicious of the Duke's curious behaviour when he appeared in Paris. It was all very unfortunate.

However unpopular he might be abroad, Philip was as interesting as ever to England. The whole course of his foreign travels had been followed with a colourful disregard for accuracy by the London press. That grandfather of English pornography, Edmund Curll the bookseller, who had just produced a volume of verses called *"Whartonia"* containing some of Philip's less tasteful poems, now sneered at his Catholicism:

> Pray isn't it queer
> That a wild peer
> So known for rakish tricks,
> That Wharton should
> At last be good
> And kiss a crucifix?... [8]

Others concocted a correspondence between him and a Quaker of Aylesbury, in which the Quaker accused him of decadence, treason and popery, and Philip (allegedly from Madrid) replied roundly that:

> ...I left your Canaan because it was fallen into wickedness, and the sin of Sodom began to take root in the metropolis; I quitted a religion which no longer subsisted than in theory: but this is no rule for my having quitted my pretension to common sence and rejecting the dictates of reason... [9]

When his old friend Nathaniel Mist, the redoubtable Jacobite proprietor of *Mist's Weekly Journal,* arrived hot-foot in Paris with an assistant called Bingley during July, fleeing from the effect of their latest libel on the Government, Philip relieved the destitute Mist of the expense of maintaining Bingley by taking the latter back to join his household at Rouen. He wrote to King James that Mist:

Paris July 26
...has singly maintained the spirit of the people at the expense of his fortune, his liberty, and at the hazard of his life, for several years. [10]

Mist told him that in London discontent with the Government had reached a new peak. Not merely were the unruly Jacobite watermen on the Thames angry at the prospect of the bridge being built at Putney reducing their trade. In the City both of the sheriffs elected this year, Brocas and Levett, were Jacobites. If only a certain Colonel Robinson in London was given the word, Mist said, James could be restored by a rebellion of the men of London alone. Philip told James this in a series of despatches. But James and his advisers, who placed all their hopes on a foreign invasion of England, had largely lost interest in English home politics, and were accordingly glum at news of how well the peace-conference at Soissons was going. Philip's despatches were ignored.

Philip and Mist took up the struggle alone. They decided to publish, from the security of French soil, pamphlets that would (in their opinion) show up Whiggery in its true light. Both were experienced propagandists, and Philip soon found that his gift of satire had not been blunted by disillusionment or brandy. He composed a long letter purporting to describe the government of Persia — clearly Britain — to be printed in *Mists Weekly Journal*, which was still appearing in London in spite of its owner's exile, under the courageous editorship of a printer called Wolfe.

But on August 18th, before it had appeared, there arrived at Rouen a deputation from England comprising his old friend Phil Lloyd and a companion called Room. Lloyd had been Philip's M.P. for Saltash, but after Philip's disappearance abroad he had lost his seat and all other prospects, and so he had turned for support to Walpole, whose mistress, Molly Skerret, lived in his house in London. And in return for several hundred pounds provided by Sir Robert Walpole out of public funds, he had tacitly undertaken to support Walpole in the Commons as Walpole's M.P. for Aylesbury. Now Lloyd had been sent by Walpole [11] to Rouen to make Philip an offer for a pardon. Its terms provoked mixed feelings in Philip and in Sir Harry Goring, who witnessed its reception at Philip's house. Lloyd offered Philip, Mist and Bingley total forgiveness for all their Jacobite activity — even for Philip's open treason at Gibraltar. Philip's estates might yet be saved, he said, and could yield six thousand pounds a year. His rank and titles could also be preserved, and he could return to England. All that Philip need do, he said, was openly to submit himself to the Government and ask for a pardon. Robert Walpole's only condition was that Philip should not henceforth attack the Government in Parliament or himself personally in the press.

These terms were so generous that Philip at first suspected a trap. He asked the two men what proof they had that the Whigs would honour their word by pardoning him if he gave himself up. They answered that his pardon could be proclaimed publicly in England before he need set foot there, as proof that the Government was sincere. But still it was all very odd: why was Walpole now offering him the very thing that they had refused earlier in the summer? The truth of the matter as Sir Harry Goring realised, was that Walpole was frightened by Philip's rhetoric, his pen and the power of a printing-press. From Rouen Philip and Mist could flood England with libellous propaganda. But if they were pardoned and allowed to return to England, they could be kept under control.

Philip's rumination on the offer Lloyd presented to him, and its discussion with Mist, Bingley, Captain Brierley, Sir Harry Goring and the other Jacobites who thronged his house was not aided by sneers from the London press which had heard rumours of the pardon. A mock *Humble Petition of His Grace Philip Duke of Wharton* appeared on the streets:

> Sir, may it please you but to hear
> Wharton, a poor petitioner;
> With pity on a vagrant look —
> Wax-chandler, citizen and Duke;
> Humble remission I entreat
> To Kiss, if not your hands, your feet,
> And, rather than the favour miss
> I sue for, anywhere would kiss...
>
> Ah, pity but my birth and rank,

> I freely offer a chart blank;
> I'll witness what design you please
> — Unheard, unthought, discoveries —
> Whatever schemes you set your heart on
> I'll sign with Philip Duke of Wharton... [12]

It took him only a few days to make up his mind about Walpole's offer; then he turned it down flat. He would never ask for a pardon subject to conditions, he said, because doing so amounted to being bribed. He would not be bought. He would not even allow his valet-de-chambre to write to the English ministers on his behalf to ask for such a pardon. Only if they granted him a pardon gratis, he said, without him asking for it and without any obligation to end his vociferous opposition, then he would accept it and consider himself morally bound to stop attacking them.

The distinction he drew was a fine one; but Lloyd and Room had no authority to agree to what he demanded. Urge him as they might — and they stayed trying for nine days — Philip still rebelled from the comfortable course which was now laid open to him. However broke he might be, he would never bow before the Walpoles. He chose exile, poverty and the name of a traitor at home, instead of wealth, power, pardon, safety and perhaps a great new political career in Hanoverian Britain. He was not yet thirty; he could still have shaken off his Jacobite past, calling it another youthful indiscretion. But he chose the hard path of pride and of moral virtue partly because he was proud or vain, and partly because he wanted to uphold what he believed were the old Whig standards of political "honesty". By refusing the dishonourable option he felt he stood for his father's principles. Actually he was taking a far higher moral stand than anyone else in his father's day or his own would have done.

At the end of August Phil Lloyd, whom he never saw again, set out for London again puzzled and hurt, hoping he would change his mind or say he had been joking. At Dieppe, whilst waiting for a favourable wind, he forwarded a letter which had arrived from England for Philip, and wrote a touching covering letter:

We are just going to hoist sail; and wherever I am, I shall

always be, as far as is consistent with my duty to my king and country,
>My dear Lord,
>>Your Grace's most obedient servant,
>>>Phil. Lloyd [13]

The English letter he forwarded to Philip from Dieppe did not bear good news. It was from John Jacob, one of Philip's trustees, and another friend of Walpole's. It said that because of his prosecution for treason:

>>>>>Lothbury Aug 28
>I find I am disabled from sending you any more money, and I dread the consequences... [14]

Henceforth Philip and Maria-Theresa were penniless.

CHAPTER EIGHTEEN

The Duel

> Sure there is not anybody like him, [Wharton], all that I can say of him is, if he is not capable of being a friend, he is capable of being a severe enemy.
> Sir Harry Goring to Colonel Daniel O'Brien, Sep. 1728.
> State Papers in the Royal Archives, 120. f25.

As long as the tradesmen at Rouen were happy to remain unpaid, Philip and Maria-Theresa were perfectly comfortable. He liked being a Normandy country gentleman, visited by friends and visiting Paris to dine at the Spanish Embassy or with such Jacobites as still tolerated him. Although English noblemen passing through France on the Grand Tour whose money he borrowed regarded him merely as a curiosity, the French nobility treated him with sympathy. They felt for distressed Dukes more than the English did. The Duc de Luxembourg gave him permission to hunt deer in Normandy, so he sent over to England for some deer-hounds, a request which was predictably ignored. But in September the Duc d'Harcourt, who was away at Versailles, lent him his own hunting lodge at La Mailleray, which was provided with all the hounds, horses and grooms in livery that even Philip's ostentation demanded. So his tall, gaunt form could often be seen spurring over the fields of Normandy, hotly followed by a band of French gentlemen and British Jacobites. And when he was neither hunting nor driving in the coach-and-six he had bought, but was quietly at home with the Duchess, he would tell his listeners that he was happier than he had ever been in his life.

Scipio, his black valet-de-chambre, now re-appeared from Vienna to remind him of better days, and Sir Harry Goring came to stay at Rouen for long periods. Straightforward, blustering Sir Harry was by nature a simple middle-aged sporting Tory squire rather than a Jacobite plotter; his family in England had recently burnt both his Jacobite military commission documents and his Jacobite patent of nobility creating him Baron Buttinghill and Viscount Goring, for fear of them being discovered by the Whigs, and his anguished requests to James for replacements for them amused Philip much. But he was a good influence on Philip, because he was beginning to wean him off excessive port, burgundy and brandy, which had been ruining his health for the last ten years. Sir Harry taught him to need only a pint of burgundy at dinner and a quart-sized bottle at supper. Both of them wrote to Rome to boast of this remarkable exercise in abstinence.

Other problems remained: whether Philip's standing in James's eyes might improve, and whether his Duchess's "pin-money" might be saved when his own income and estates were confiscated, which depended upon whether his hostile trustees and enemies in England would discover that Scipio, whose signature he had forged on her jointure deeds, had not been in Madrid when they had been signed. Worst was his own pennilessness: he wrote to King James again asking for money or promotion in the Spanish Army or for a recommendation to the Russian Court at Moscow. And with his usual wild optimism, as soon as he had asked he assumed that James would oblige, and his spirits rose accordingly, and were raised higher when he now heard of the effect on London of his Persian satire. It had appeared as a letter signed "Amos Dudge", addressed to the editor of *Mists Weekly Journal:*

> Mr. Mist...
> I observe you have been often under confinement for having disobliged the present Government, and I must say that I hope for the future you will avoid all occasions of giving offence to the ministry: A ministry! equally esteemed for their abilities in domestic, and their great experience in foreign affairs; and whose leniency, of which we have the strongest proofs, render their administration as amiable at home, as it is formidable abroad.

It proceeded to describe Persia as a land where a foreign princeling had deposed a lawful monarch and introduced despotism and outlandish fashions at Court:

> The usurper and his followers have changed the Persian

habit, and appear in dresses that are proper decorations to adorn the persons that wear them: the fashion of them is so singular that the courtiers look like pantomines that strut upon the stage of life to represent Vanity and Folly.

It concluded:

If the Turks [i.e. the French] should listen at last, as no doubt they will, to the cries of an injured oppressed and plundered nation, who implore their protection, then, and then alone, a peace will ensue in the East, which will make the Halcyon days return, and the temple of Janus may be shut for ever.[1]

It was said that Queen Caroline burst into tears of fury and Sir Robert Walpole was sullen with rage when they saw the letter. The whole issue of the *Journal* which contained it was soon sold out, and hand-written copies of it were sold at half a guinea apiece. But the Ministry retaliated immediately. They smashed the offending printing-press and tried to imprison the printers. Although Wolfe, who was printing the *Weekly Journal* in Mist's absence, escaped to Rouen, his wife and children were caught and Nathaniel Mist's whole London household, his servants, their wives and children and even a baby only four weeks old, were arrested and put in custody. But Amos Dudge, whose real identity was soon guessed by Walpole, had been privately assured by the French Court that he was safe writing in France provided that he published nothing under his own name. The leaders of the other Jacobites in France, by contrast with him, had suffered miserably at pamphleteering. When they had begun to print a manifesto in Paris which they proposed to distribute to the delegates at the peace conference at Soissons, the British formally complained to the Court of France and as much of the impression as had been printed was seized and destroyed by the Garde des Sceaux.

Philip, cheered by the Whigs' anger, wrote a mock Will of George I, which was published by the courageous printers of the *Weekly Journal* as soon as they had found a new press. The Will (pretending to be the actual one which had been burnt by George II with its contents unread) announced that the new King was illegitimate. Philip followed this with some letters to the *Weekly Journal* purporting to be from Wolfe, complaining of his treatment by the Government:

> How precarious then must the life, liberty and daily bread of every historian, poet and printer be in Great Britain, if panegyric and satire be declared High Treason, as often as vice happens to prevail and virtue be in distress. Consider these things, and show pity to thy
> afflicted servant
Wolfe [2]

Next Philip sent to England in manuscript a lewd poem about the relations between Sir Robert Walpole, Phil Lloyd and Molly Skerret, hinting at Walpole's impotence:

> Dear Lloyd, they say you're Walpole's ferret
> To hunt him out poor Molly Skerrett...
> Molly, 'tis said, by you inclined,
> Received his offers, and resigned;
> But Walpole, long by vice decayed,
> Unable was to please the maid;
> But none his fury can describe
> (Unlike his wretched voting tribe)
> To find one *member* scorn a bribe.
> And happy were it for the land
> If corrupt members ne're could stand... [3]

Then he produced a serious essay in self-justification, defending his political views under the title, *The Duke of Wharton's Reasons for Leaving His Native Country, and Espousing the Cause of His Royal Majesty King James III. In a letter to His Friends in Great Britain and Ireland*

> *Friends, Countrymen and Fellow-citizens:*
> ...I shall begin with expressing the greatest regard for the

memory of the best of fathers. I have endeavoured to model my life accordingly to the principles he gave me, as the unerring guides to direct my steps in every public as well as private action. He taught me those notions of government that tend to the preserving of liberty in its greatest purity...

Imbued with these principles I entered upon the stage of life, when I beheld the Triennial Act repealed, standing armies and martial law established by authority of Parliament, the convocation of the Clergy prevented from meeting, the orthodox members of the church discouraged, schism, ignorance and atheism become the only recommendation to ecclesiastical benefices...

When I reflected upon these dreadful scenes, I saw the reasons which my father gave for the support of the Hanoverians succession fall to the ground, and those who follow the maxims of the old Whigs are obliged to resist such destructive tyranny, unless they forget their principles and grow obdurate in guilt and tenacious in iniquity...

The severest frowns of fortune, in the cruel, ungrateful manner in which I am treated by a set of men whom my father dragged from obscurity, shall never be able to deter me from pursuing the King's Interest with steadiness and perseverence...And when I reflect on the generous dispositions that adorn the King's mind, His Majesty seems to be pointed out by providence to free us from usurpation and tyranny and to restore our constitution to its primitive glory...

Let us, therefore, with unwearied zeal, labour to support the cause of our King and country, and to shake off the ignominious load of foreign fetters.

Wharton [4]

This Old Whig political testament circulated privately in England, and became about as seriously received as his dirty poems.

As he pamphleteered at Rouen, deserters from amongst the Spanish Troops who had served with him at Gibraltar waited in the Tower of London to be used as witnesses in the indictment against him for treason. If his remaining estates and all his titles and honours were forfeited, as seemed certain, his only consolation was that he was personally out of the reach of Whig justice, and would not have to join that select body of men from various political persuasions whose extrovert lives had been ended with the axe on Tower Hill. But an outlawry would make his financial situation impossible; and in September 1728, at Rouen, it was already very bad indeed:

> Though the Duke was in the way of being degraded of his titles in England, yet some certain marks of nobility began to appear more and more every day at Rouen, till he became overloaded with such sort of honours. Particularly, he was attended every morning with a considerable levée, made up of the tradesmen of the town, such as his butcher, poulterer, baker, wine and brandy merchant, etc. The Duchess had also her milliner, manteau-maker, tire-woman, etc. The Duke received their compliments with an air suitable to his quality, till they grew too importunate, and then he set out for Paris, leaving his horses and equipage to be sold and the money appropriated as there was found occasion. [5]

Philip, Maria-Theresa, Scipio and their other servants and Bingley fled their creditors late in the evening. They travelled by night so that they would spare themselves the expense of an inn. When they arrived at Paris, they temporarily parted. Maria-Theresa had an elderly uncle called Captain O'Neill, her mother's brother, living down-river from Paris as a survivor of the old Jacobite Court at St. Germain, and he was prepared to accommodate her. So Philip sent her to stay there with a maid or two who had escaped from Rouen and 1800 livres, about a hundred pounds, which he borrowed from a kind Irish exile called Sir Peter Redmond. He, Scipio and Bingley found an English surgeon named Birmingham who agreed to lodge and feed them and a few servants for two thousand livres a year, rather over two pounds a week for them all. Here they settled to wait for their luck to turn.

Meanwhile, James had realised that something must be done about Philip, partly because news of his starvation would not encourage other English peers to risk themselves for him, and partly lest desperation might make Philip sell Jacobite secrets to Horatio Walpole. So he sent him the first instalment of an irregular financial allowance, via Colonel Daniel O'Brien the Jacobite agent in Paris, on October 25th 1728. And after O'Brien had deducted what the Duke owed him personally, there was about a thousand livres, or sixty pounds, left. Philip was grateful for it although bad news came in a covering letter with the money: Philip was not to go to Russia, James said; if he insisted on going anywhere, he could go back to the Court of Madrid, where his congé (his expulsion) had been postponed, and James had asked that whatever Philip's rank or pay in the Spanish army might be, he should not actually have to engage in active duties for it. This much James would do for him; this much and no more.

So Philip wrote to his old acquaintance the Marqués de la Paz, the new Prime Minister of Spain, but in reply received mere promises of help in the future. He chafed, and took up drinking once more. He spent some time looking for a suitable printing press and workers who could help Bingley print the *Reasons for Leaving his Native Country*, copies of which were already circulating in London in manuscript form. He loitered at the English coffee-house, the usual meeting place for Paris Jacobites, dined with Lord Cranstoun and Sir Peter Redmond, (where he saw Lord Mar carried out by two footmen from the dining-table to bed, monstrously drunk), and paid calls at the Spanish Embassy. And here, at the Embassy, a curious incident occurred.

Maria-Theresa had an admirer amongst the Parisien Jacobites; a Scotch peer, who can probably, though not definitely, be identified as Lord Cranstoun. Philip, because of his wit and rank and fame, still held social pre-eminence amongst the Jacobite noblemen who gathered at the Spanish Embassy. One drunken evening there he dropped one of his white gloves and Lord Cranstoun, out of courtesy, stooped and picked it up for him. The Duke pretended that it had been dropped intentionally; he asked Cranstoun, laughing, if Cranstoun "would take it up in all its forms?" "Yes, my Lord", replied Cranstoun, "In all its forms." [6]

This was not all jest, for Cranstoun had boasted amongst the Jacobites of the affection which the Duchess of Wharton held him in, which annoyed Philip very much; not because he suspected the

Duchess's fidelity — but because he was insulted that anyone would touch his reputation in a place where he had touched so many other men's. The matter came to a crisis when after a few weeks' separation from the Duchess he received his few hundred livres from Rome and decided to give a ball in her honour for the French nobility of St. Germain. That he should embark upon entertaining the most extravagant aristocracy in Europe in the most opulent way available to him shows how little thrift he had learnt from poverty. The Jacobite nobility from Paris were all there. The Duke seemed happy and at ease until a tactless guest loudly asked him if it was true that he had forbidden the Duchess to dance with Lord Cranstoun?

The implication behind the question was obvious. But Philip contained his anger, entertaining and amusing the company, until an hour or two before the winter dawn. Then at five o'clock he slipped away back to Paris, arriving in the middle of the morning to join Captain Brierley, who had consented to act as his second, and to compose a short challenge which he sent by a footman to Cranstoun's lodgings, summoning him to Flanders outside the French criminal jurisdiction:

> ...His Lordship might remember his saying, "That he took up his glove in all its forms"; which, on reflection, he looked upon to be such an affront, that he could not put it up; he therefore desired him to meet at Valenciennes, where he would expect him, with a friend, and a case of pistols, and if he failed, he would post him a coward...[7]

This message, although sent at about mid-day on Wednesday, did not reach Cranstoun until Thursday afternoon, because he was away from his lodgings making preparations to move from Paris. But everyone else in Paris and at Versailles had soon learnt that Philip had challenged him, so as soon as he returned to his lodgings he was put in protective custody by the Duke of Berwick, who, as Marshal of France and commander of the Guards, was responsible for preventing bloodshed over affairs of honour. Meanwhile, Philip and Brierley waited at Valenciennes with growing impatience, oblivious of the stir at court, and with only about seventeen pounds between them; they had not anticipated any delay, but expected Cranstoun to have been hot upon their heels for all the hundred miles from Paris. They had to wait until a servant arrived from Paris on Thursday night or Friday morning, and announced that he was one of Lord Cranstoun's household, and asked for the Duke of Wharton. Philip's nerves by this time were unsteady. He had had no sleep on the night of the ball, and for two days since then he had been under strain, so he understandably assumed without enquiry that the servant was Cranstoun's second, and that Cranstoun himself was nearby. He had only one thought: that he might fight the duel with a pistol and not with a sword, because he had always been bad at swordsmanship. With more dignity than truthfulness, "Sir", he said, "I hope my Lord will favour me so far as to let us use pistols, because the wound I received at Gibraltar, in my foot, in some measure disables me for the sword".

"My Lord Duke", replied the servant, "You may choose what you please. My Lord Cranstoun would fight you with any weapon, from a small pin to a great cannon; but that is not the case, my Lord has an Exempt of the Guards put upon him by order of the Marshal Berwick."[8]

The rules of honour demanded that Philip should now return to Paris and pretend that he still wanted to fight Cranstoun. But when he arrived he was immediately arrested by Berwick's Guards for the same reason as Cranstoun had been.

Then the friends of the antagonists sought to patch their quarrel up. Cranstoun asked that the Duke should apologise. The Duke still demanded satisfaction. Berwick, who was used to calming down pugnacious gallants and who knew Wharton from of old, eventually visited Philip in gaol and persuaded him to agree with his adversary that "There was no challenge nor difference between them." Having then declared a truce, honourably if not amicably, they were both released from the custody of the guards.

This sorry business was made sorrier by the conflict of rival accounts of what had happened. Philip said that Cranstoun had always had ample time to come to Flanders, but for cowardly reasons had evaded doing so. Philip's enemies said that Philip himself had tipped off Berwick's Guards, so that Cranstoun would be arrested and the duel never fought. The latter account was widely believed in England, where the *London Journal* and the *London Evening Post* printed versions

The Duel

of it.

By early 1729 French society had begun to regard Philip as a buffoon. Although he had never been very thoughtful about what he was wearing, his one or two surviving suits were now ludicrously old and seedy, and scruffiness was not a common vice amongst Dukes in early eighteenth-century Paris. He usually wore his Spanish Colonel's uniform, this with two year's wear, embellished with a very tarnished silver star of the Order of the Garter. But during the winter of 1728/9 he acquired a new suit in curious circumstances. Sir Peter Redmond had invited him to a dinner of the Portuguese Order of Knights of Christ. It was customary for all present to wear a black velvet suit. Sir Peter politely suggested Philip should get one to wear not only at this dinner but also on other occasions. Philip thanked him, but said that he knew no tailor in the city. Sir Peter said that he would send round his own. The tailor duly arrived, and the clothes were made, and Philip appeared at the dinner in black velvet, remarkably decently dressed. A week afterwards the tailor appeared at Philip's lodgings with the bill. "Honest Man", said Philip with heavy irony, "You mistake the matter very much. You are to carry the bill to Sir Peter Redmond; for, be pleased to know that whenever I put on another man's livery, my master always pays for the clothes."[9]

His pride no longer prevented him sponging whatever he could. Once he met a rich young Irish peer when he was visiting the Duchess at St. Germain, and asked him to lend him his coach for a ride to Paris on important business, and to accompany him as well since he wanted a companion, his business being so pressing that it preyed on his mind. The Irishman agreed, and off they drove together at about nine at night, arriving in the city by midnight. Here the Duke hired another coach-and-four, and he bribed six or eight musicians from the opera-house to get in it and follow him back to St. Germain, which they reached at five in the morning. Then he arranged his band on the steps before the castle, and ordered them to start playing. They were there in the dawn to serenade some pretty young ladies who had attracted Philip's attention.

As morning broke he packed the band back into the two coaches and drove to the gates of Poissy, three miles away, for more work. Here the musicians began to complain. They said that they would not be back at the Paris opera in time for the performance that afternoon, which would cost them a forfeit of more than their daily wage, half a Louis d'Or each, about eight English shillings. Philip was not impressed. "Half a Louis d'Or?" he laughed: "Follow the Duke of Wharton, and all your forfeitures shall be paid." [10]

He lined them up in military formation outside Poissy, with the drummers and trumpeters at the front, and marched them into the town, playing martial music, until they reached a house belonging to an English acquaintance of his. The inhabitants of the town thought they were being invaded by an army and turned out to stare (to the embarrassment of the Englishman whose house seemed to be under siege) but Philip rose to the occasion by delivering an impromptu speech telling them what a compliment he was paying them by his behaviour. When he ended, he stopped the musicians playing, disbanded them, and he told the Irish peer that his "business" was finished.

But the musicians and their hired coach had not been paid for. "My Lord", he said to the Irish peer, "I have not one livre in my pocket, therefore I must entreat you to pay the fellows, and I'll do as much for you when I am able." [11] The Irishman paid everything, which amounted to twenty-five Louis d'Or, about twenty English pounds. Perhaps it was not a large sum to him. It was more than Philip had in the world.

In January, James had sent him, via O'Brien, a second installment of £2,000. But after O'Brien had deducted the cost of the ball from it the balance Philip received was small, and by the end of Lent it was gone. So he had to leave the lodgings of Birmingham the surgeon, being unable to meet even the small charges there, and he and Scipio became nomadic, sponging off any Jacobite who thought that duty or decency required that he put them up, or begging accommodation with any rich young Englishman who passed through Paris on the Grand Tour.

A few weeks of this undignified life and the continued separation from Maria-Theresa soon plunged his spirits very low, and (to the relief of his friends) he turned to the Church for support. Shortly before Easter he went into a religious retreat. Those who saw him announced to incredulous outsiders that he seemed to be sincere, and

The Duel

was seeking to reform his whole life. He dazzled the simple Brothers with his enthusiasm and wide learning. It is said that the more pious of the priests suspected that he might actually be a saint. In such a virtuous state of mind, so unusual for him, he passed Easter in 1729.

CHAPTER NINETEEN

The Road to Poblet

> The Modes of the Court so common are grown,
>   That a true Friend can hardly be met;
> Friendship for Interest is but a loan
>   Which they let out for what they can get.
>   'Tis true, you find
>   Some Friends so kind
> Who will give you good counsel themselves to defend;
>   In sorrowful ditty;
>   They promise, they pity,
> But shift for your Money, from Friend to Friend.
>   (To the Air of *Lilliburlero*)
>   John Gay, *The Beggar's Opera*, (1728) Act II Scene II.

He did not stay in a religious retreat for long. However much the monks admired Philip, he did not think much of them. Soon after Easter he was out in the streets of Paris again; still penniless, still scruffy, often drunk, and always pursued by a band of duns and creditors. English noblemen passing through France regarded him with interest:

> The Duke of Bedford is here, and had conferences with the Duke of Wharton, up two pair of stairs at the English coffee-house, over a bowl of punch. And those that have seen the latter tell me that no theatre-discarded poet was ever half so shabby, and that none of Shaquespears strolling Knights of the Garter had ever so dirty a Star and Ribbon.[1]

In England he had been convicted of High Treason in his absence for "Appearing in arms before and firing off cannon against His Majesty's town of Gibraltar". So less than twelve hectic years since the grant of his Whig Dukedom, he had been outlawed, stripped of all his peerages and deprived of all his estates. The remains of his land (but luckily not Maria-Theresa's jointure and pin-money charged on it) was forfeited to the Crown. It was soon sold off; his ancestral estate at Wharton Hall went to the Northern family who had previously won his Cumberland and Westmorland electoral interest from him, the Lowthers. He himself was left destitute.

He was soon shunned by many of his old friends in Paris. He could not even call upon Colonel Daniel O'Brien for fear of meeting Jacobites he owed money to or tradesmen who hoped to ambush him there. Bingley had now found lodgings of his own and put him up whenever possible. Otherwise he was forced to stay with any odd acquaintance — one was called Walsh — who would tolerate him. But soon his debts forced him to leave the centre of the city altogether, and to go and stay in small villages in the suburbs where his title would still get him credit. Now he drank more brandy than ever, not only to forget his troubles but also to take away his appetite. Gone were the days when he could survive on a mere two bottles of burgundy a day. And drunkeness showed clearly on his face and in his manners. He looked white and middle-aged and sank into pathetic bouts of self-pity, complaining sourly to anyone who would listen to him that he had been monstrously mis-used. He was in danger of losing his wit, which was the last asset besides his Spanish commission and some Jacobite titles that his fate had left him with.

It is hard to see how Scipio, his black valet-de-chambre, was provided for during these difficult days. He was probably inseparable from the Duke. He fitted into an attic or cupboard wherever Philip happened to be staying. It was a sad fall from the style he had lived in when he was the Duke's favourite servant at Leicester Fields or at Winchendon. He had lived far more comfortably then than the Duke did now. But he stood by Philip to the last.

Nor was the Duchess's position very hopeful. Her jointure and pin-money from England were not being paid. She had been given a little money by O'Brien early in the year — part of the two thousand livres which James had sent for Philip's sustenance. But soon it ran out. The uncle she lodged with disliked Philip, his pranks and the odd hours that he kept, and was exasperated when Philip sent the wife and eight-year old daughter of Wolfe the printer to stay with him because they had arrived destitute in Paris looking to Philip for help. In the middle of May, Maria-Theresa managed to spend a night or two with Philip in the village where he was then lodging. They decided that they must move. Life in a country where they had no money was intolerable. So they sent Bingley into Paris to borrow all the money that he could for them — about twenty-five pounds sterling — and with this and one servant, a single clean shirt and cravat for Philip and a small box of clothes for Maria-Theresa, they set out on the road for Orleans, fifty miles South-West of Paris. To hide from their creditors they travelled under the assumed names of M. and Mme. Durant.

They had shared discomfort together already, but they had never shared a servant. They were terribly ignorant about everything which servants had always done for them. So before they reached Orleans, Philip wrote to Colonel O'Brien at Paris to ask him to send the Duchess's ladies-maid from St. Germain with some more clothes, because the Duchess "n'a pas une chemise avec elle". [2] He also asked that Captain Brierley and "mon more Scipio" [3] and a second servant should be put on the public coach that left Paris at midnight for Orleans. It was the last request for Philip that patient O'Brien carried out. Philip's party met up as planned at Orleans. They were a sorry bunch. Philip looked ill, and the Duchess tired and worried, and their followers scruffy and dispirited and hungry.

Bingley had flatly refused to accompany them. Since he had fled to France he had stood loyally by Philip, but as a friend and confidante and not a servant. He saw that if he followed Philip from Paris, like Captain Brierley, he would become a mere hanger-on, a spaniel: and he was growing popular with Colonel O'Brien and the Jacobites who appreciated his witty writing. There was some sort of a future for him with them. With the Duke there seemed to be none.

But Philip's small entourage was joined by one or two more of his old servants at Nantes, which they reached after following the river Loire westwards for over a hundred miles, and here he received enough money (probably from Maria-Theresa's uncle at Paris) to pay for the passage of the Duchess and her maids on board a small coastal vessel across the bay of Biscay to Bilbao. But this left him with no money to pay for his own fare and those of the others. So he persuaded the ship's master that Brierley and the menservants were recruits for

The Road to Poblet

his Spanish regiment, whose passage the Spaniards would pay on arrival. They were let on board accordingly, and made the crossing and arrived at Bilbao uneventfully during June. Here they had no friends, no credit, no influence and no acquaintances. Nor was Bilbao, in the summer of 1729, a particularly pleasant little port to stay in: it was hot and noisy and smelly. But the Duchess and most of the servants were put in lodgings there which they all knew she could never pay for and Philip pushed on without them. His destination was Lérida, across the neck of Spain beside the Mediterranean in Catalonia, where the Hainault regiment of which he was still Colonel-Aggregate was in garrison, and where his board and lodging at least would be free.

On the stony road across Navarre and Arragon, which led to the bridge over the Ebro at Saragossa, he heard news from Madrid. The Government, in an effort to reform the incompetent administration of the army, had issued a new ordinance requiring all Colonels-Aggregate to take personal command of their own regiments when the Colonels "en pied" were absent. The Colonel "en pied" of the Hainault was at Court, and was unlikely ever to see his regiment, let alone to command it. So Philip was required to be on duty. This did not affect his present circumstances or his desire to reach Lérida in the least, but it altered his dreams for the future. He had hoped that he might one day keep his military rank and pay but still work for the Jacobites. Now this would be impossible. As long as he kept his commission, he would have to be on duty with his regiment. So when he reached his old comrades-in-arms from the Gibraltar siege at Lérida during July, he had to make the best of being a soldier of fortune.

Meanwhile, after some weeks had passed at Bilbao and it was clear that the Duchess was penniless, she found herself a prisoner of a growing army of creditors in her lodging-house. Philip was no more neglectful of her than he was of himself, and intended to bring her to Lérida as soon as he could afford a carriage for her, but his salary of eighteen pistoles (less than twenty pounds) a month, never gave him the chance. She stayed frugally at Bilbao for ten weeks, hoping to be sent money by him, and running up debts, which she hated. By then word of her reached the old Duke of Ormonde who had always been a patron of the O'Beirnes' at Madrid. He sent her a hundred pistoles, which was enough to pay all that she owed and the expenses of travelling with her two maids to Madrid, where she was re-united with her family late in the summer.

Philip and Brierley, for whom he seems to have found a place in his regiment, settled down contentedly to the interminable drilling of two scruffy battalions in the very town through which he had ridden so grandly only four years before, as King James's Ambassador to Spain, accompanied by one of the King of Spain's Couriers Extraordinary. Times had changed. He was glad to be given enough to eat and drink and to enjoy the temperate weather of the Mediterranean coast. It is true that he was still acutely short of money, but he was seldom actually forced to beg from his brother officers or to leave unpaid the brandy-merchants of Lérida. His scanty wardrobe was large enough: the winters at Lérida were not very cold. It is said that when he eventually needed a new uniform he was helped by some funds sent out from England, perhaps from one of his sisters.

His lot was better than that of other Jacobites. Some of his contemporaries literally starved. John Sample, the wretched Paris spy, who had sold such principles as he ever possessed for a few Hanoverian shillings, was ill rewarded in the end. The Jacobites discovered that he had betrayed them, and they expelled him from their circle. When the Whigs discovered that because of this he was no longer of any use to them, they proposed to drop him. Horatio Walpole, the Ambassador, consulted Sir Robert Walpole about this. Sir Robert said that there was no point in wasting any more money on him. His desperate appeals for sustenance were therefore ignored. His skinny corpse was found soon afterwards in a dirty street in Paris, wasted away for want of food.

Philip wrote fairly regularly to James at Rome and to Maria-Theresa at Madrid, and returned to literature as a pastime. He finished the tragedy of Mary Queen of Scots which he had begun in Twickenham years before, and for which Lady Mary had written a prologue, but no copy of it has ever reached England. He translated Fénélon's *Télémaque*, a graceful narrative in admirable French about the imaginary wanderings of Telemachus, and then put the whole of its first book into English verse. He thought more and more of the past and of his glories and his suffering, and began to melodramatise himself a little. In a letter he wrote home to England he quoted the lines that the ageing Dryden had addressed to Congreve thirty years before:

> Be kind to my remains, and oh! Defend
> Against your judgement, your departed friend...[4]

In Madrid the Duchess of Wharton's mother died early in 1730, which was more than merely a personal loss to Maria-Theresa, for it meant the end of the court pension upon which her family lived. King James heard of this and sent her his good wishes and a few Spanish pistoles, but the Duke of Ormonde did more by using his influence on their behalf and both Maria-Theresa's sisters were duly taken into the Queen's care as Maids-of-Honour. They earned enough to continue to keep the Duchess.

This reassuring news reached Philip during the Spring of 1730 and found him cheerful for other reasons. First, he thought that there would soon be a war between Spain and Austria over Parma, in which case the Catalonian regiments of Spain (being nearest to Parma) would be the first into the fray. Secondly a copy of John Gay's *Beggar's Opera* had reached him from London, where it had run with enormous success at the theatre in Lincoln's Inn Fields in 1728.

John Gay had incurred great ministerial displeasure by writing it. The Duchess of Queensberry was banned from Court for supporting John Gay. She sent George II a note thanking him:

> "The Duchess of Queensberry is surprised and well pleased that the King had given so agreeable a command as to stay from court, where she never came for diversion, but to bestow a great civility upon the King and Queen; she hopes that by such an unprecedented Order as this the King will see as few as he wishes at His Court, particularly such as dare think or speak truth..."

It was said that the Duchess of Marlborough was thoroughly jealous of her good fortune in being excused from Hanoverian Court functions.

The Beggar's Opera was a satire on all that the English had thought holy in the early years of the 1720's: money, political sharpness and Whiggery. Its success showed an improvement in the way that London society was thinking. Its hero, Macheath, was an honest rogue: the leader of a gang of highwaymen. Its villain, Peachum, was a fat hypocritical handler of stolen goods who repaid the thieves he employed by betraying them and seeing them hanged: he was drawn from Jonathan Wild, the famous receiver who had died at Tyburn in the year Philip left London; but the comparison between him and Sir Robert Walpole was clear. Philip thought of himself as Macheath. The little group of friends that collected around him in Catalonia — Brierley, a servant or two, and some officers of Spain (probably Irish) — were his gang. He called them his pick-pockets, cardsharps and pimps. He liked the idea that he was a sort of Robin Hood, persecuted by pious hypocrites. Although it is believable that some exiled Jacobites had turned to crime for support, it is unlikely that any of them were led by the Colonel-Aggregate of the Hainault. His days as a leader, whether of treason or "frolics", were now over. He was left with his dreams alone.

But the late Spring of 1730 gave him little time for dreaming. War being expected, the regiment was marched to Balaguer. The Marqués de Torremayor, inspector-general of infantry for Catalonia, had announced that there was to be a review of each of his regiments late in May, and that any officers unfit for service were to be removed. This inspired or alarmed Philip into activity, and his two battalions of infantry suddenly saw some of his old energy. By the time of the inspection on May 23rd he had polished and barracked them into smartness, and took some pride in doing so, calling them, "two battalions that are as fine as any troops in Europe."[5] But he seldom had cause to be proud. He was no longer a person of much importance in the world. At a ball which was given when he was garrisoned at Barcelona he was insulted — in what way is not stated — by a mere valet employed by the Governor of Barcelona, the Marquis de Risburgh.[6] With a courage and ferocity unusual for him, he beat him thoroughly with a cane. But the valet's master, Risburgh, although he had been pleased enough to entertain Philip five years before when the latter was King James's ambassador, now imprisoned him summarily for two days in the fortress of Mont-Joi which stands above the town.

Philip could hardly believe that he could be treated with such insolence. So when his short imprisonment was up he refused to leave the fortress, and demanded that an account of the whole business be sent to Court. He hoped to embarrass Risburgh by this behaviour, and to have him rebuked. But the Court at Madrid, hearing the Marquis's story rather than the Duke's, said that the Governor was right, and ordered Philip to leave the fortress and not to enter the town again.

This decided him that he was not likely to be promoted on his merits alone for years to come, so he pressed King James to help him: influence at Madrid was what he needed. Or, he asked James, might he have money to travel to Madrid to see his old acquaintance the Marquis de Castelar, and to get a promise out of him of future promotion? Late in June 1730, James warned him that there were dozens of Irish Jacobite offices in the army all hoping for promotion, and many were more experienced in warfare than Philip, but that Philip was welcome to try his luck at Madrid, and he sent fifty pistoles to pay the expenses of travelling there.

It was a journey that Philip dearly wanted to make. He had not seen the Duchess for months. And he heard that Bingley had come from France to be Ormonde's secretary in Madrid. But the pressures of his duties in Catalonia were too heavy for him to set out before winter. And then, in January 1731, his old sickness came upon him again. Military food and too much brandy had ruined his stomach. By February he was only able to eat a thin egg broth, and he was too weak to be able to walk from his bed to his fireside without help.

For two months he was near death, and then, in May, he partly recovered. He accompanied his regiment when it moved to Tarragona, on the Mediterranean, where in a composed frame of mind he wrote his will, in French. He took to riding up the mountain road towards Lérida, to enjoy the waters at some mineral springs which lay near to the road and which were reputed to be healthy. But on one of such visits he suffered a relapse and the stomach cramps came upon him again, in a sudden fit. He could not ride back to Tarragona, but was carried to a house in the village nearby. Here there was no accommodation suitable for the poorest officer of Spain, let alone a sick one. Word of him was therefore sent to the Fathers of the great Cistercian monastery at Poblet, which lay less than a mile away. They came and collected him and bore him back to their hospital.

The monastery at Poblet was one of the most lavish monuments of the Spanish Catholic church. It was enormously rich, and most of its inmates were from noble families. It bore little resemblance to the shabby little home of "poor monks" that it has been called in some accounts of the life of the Duke. It lay in pleasant, hilly and cool countryside. Such was its magnificence that in the revolution a century later the peasants of the nearby villages thoroughly desecrated it.

In the monastery hospital Philip lingered on, well looked afer, for a week. On the 31st May it was clear that he was dying. His exhausted body and mind seemed easy at the prospect. When the Abbot and a handful of monks gathered around his death-bed to give him the last rites of the Church, he indicated that he had something to say. He had one last request. In two writing-cases which were in his quarters at Tarragona and which comprised almost the whole of his wealth, there were papers which should be returned to their owner. He asked the Abbot to seal them and to despatch them, after his death, to Rome, to be delivered to King James III of England.

When Philip was dead he was carried with full solemnity to be laid in a corner of the chapel of the Holy Sepulchre. It was an insignificant place, for he had left no money to pay for a better, but his grave was guarded by the great monuments and altars of alabaster and lapis-lazuli which marked the tombs of the medieval Arragonese kings. The monks, at their own cost, raised for him a plain memorial:

Hic jacet Exmus Dnus Philipus de Wharton Anglus Duc, Marchio et comes de Wharton, Marchio de Malsburse et Carthlock, Comes Rathfarnum, Vice-Comes de Winchindon, Baro de Trim, Eques de St. George (alias de la Gerratiera). Obit Populeti die 31 Maii 1731 in fide Ecclesie Catholicae Romanae.

Philip himself had asked, in his Will, that other words be cut on his tombstone:

Vixi et, quem dederat cursum fortuna, peregi

[I have lived: I have finished the course that fortune gave me]
and
Thy fame shall live when pyramids of pride
Mix with the ashes they were raised to hide.

He did not deserve such arrogant epitaphs. The words that were taken later that year by his first biographer as the motto for the *Life of Philip late Duke of Wharton* were the lines from Othello, which Philip used to quote to English strangers in Catalonia:

When you shall my unhappy deeds relate,
Speak of me as I am — Nothing extenuate,
Nor set down aught in malice.

EPILOGUE

> Philip...was a person of unbounded genius, eloquence and ambition: he had all the address and activity of his father, but without his steadiness: violent in parties, and expensive in cultivating the arts of popularity; which indeed ought in some measure to be charged to his education under such a father...In a word, if the father and son had been one degree higher in life, and had lived in Macedonia at the time of Philip and Alexander, they would have done just as Philip and Alexander did.
>
> Joseph Nicholson and Richard Burn: *The History and Antiquities of Westmoreland and Cumberland (1777)*
> Vol. I. p.560

The news of Philip's death reached Madrid a fortnight later. From there the Duke of Ormonde told King James of it in one of his short, atrociously scrawled despatches to Rome. The tidings reached England a few weeks afterwards. Little interest was aroused. The Duke had too long ceased to be the light of English politics and literature which he had once been. The little world of his hey-day was already gone and its actors dispersed. He died without many friends, and even his enemies had half forgotten him. No-one remembered the grand Old Whig principles on which he had prided himself. He had outlived the days when the existence of a Jacobite party in Parliament was possible, and the days when the success of a Jacobite invasion seemed probable. And it was better for him that he was now dead, rather than condemned to the life that some of his contemporaries were to lead: kicking their heels at Rome, ever growing poorer, always living on dreams, always knowing their dreams were hopeless. Philip's pride could never have borne such shame.

Lord Orrery died within three months of Philip's death, and Atterbury within seven months. Three years later Major-General Lord North and Grey was laid to rest beneath the chapel of the crucifix in the church of St. Madin in Madrid. But Sheridan lived to see his pupil, Bonnie Prince Charlie, capture half of Britain, and stood beside him at

Culloden. The Earl Marischal outlived the Duke by almost half a century and died pardoned by George II, an intimate of Frederick the Great and a friend of Voltaire and Rousseau. Even he, however, was over-shadowed in glory by his brother James Keith, who became a Prussian Field-Marshal and fell at Hochkirk acknowledged the finest soldier in Europe. Frederick the Great wept over his body. Perhaps in his fortunate latter days he was able to do something for those lesser Jacobites with whom he had shared desperate hardship years before. Of the fate of the many Irish officers who befriended Philip so well, Captain James Butler, Barry, Captain Brierley and the others, we know nothing. It is improbable that they ever returned to their native land.

Sir Robert Walpole died immensely rich as the Earl of Orford; his brother Horatio as Lord Walpole of Wolterton; and William Stanhope, the Ambassador in Madrid, as Earl of Harrington. Edward Young, now a clergyman, married one of the daughters of Philip's old crony the Earl of Lichfield. Colonel Francis Charters died in the same year as Philip, universally hated and envied, but keeping his enormous fortune to the end. Lady Mary Wortley Montagu, tired by the fickleness and triviality of English Society and disappointed by her family, went abroad in 1739 to seek rest and quiet. She only returned to England a few months before her death in 1762. Lady Jane Wharton died shortly before her, having outlived her unattractive husband, John Holt, and subsequently marrying the Earl of Leicester's brother Robert Coke. Lady Lucy Wharton, her sister, obedient to her brother's wishes, never married until after his death. She then chose badly, for she soon ran away from her husband Sir William Morrice to live in sin with Lord Augustus Fitzroy, and was divorced for adultery in 1737. Within two years she died at Bath.

More fortunate in later life was Philip's widow. Maria-Theresa Duchess of Wharton, whom he had called in his Will "my dearest spouse" and constituted his "universal heiress", accepted his death with the calm courage that was characteristic of her. King James gave her permission to go to Britain, and fifty pounds for her maintenance. Although she was wholly without friends in England, she sailed there eighteen months later to claim the unpaid annuity and the pin-money to which she was entitled out of his estate. At Dublin in 1736 she proved his Will. Thereafter she lived in Frith Street, then at 9 Soho Square, then at Golden Square, an unfashionable part of the town, but by careful economy she provided comfortably for herself, and kept a small household of servants. If she could find means to communicate with King James at New Year, she sent him the compliments of the season. Lady Jane, her sister-in-law, would occasionally visit her. She died on February 13, 1777, after a widowhood almost nine times as long as the length of her marriage to Philip. One week after her death she was buried as she had requested, "very privately" in St. Pancras's church.

Philip's reputation, which had reached its lowest ebb at the end of his life, began to revive soon after his death. A volume of his writings called *"Select and Authentic Pieces"* appeared in London that year under the false imprint "BOULOGNE: printed by J. Wolfe at the Duke of Wharton's Head."

His first biographer, (perhaps Young, but more likely Nathaniel Mist or Bingley) wrote the *Life of Philip late Duke of Wharton by an Impartial Hand*, only a few weeks after the news of his death had reached London. It was instantly popular, and was republished the following year with the Duke's *Life and Writings,* and subsequently as a preface to his *Poetical Works.* By 1740, less than ten years after his death, it had run to numerous reprintings and was in its third edition.

The world, which had so maltreated Philip during his lifetime, came to be haunted by him when he was dead. Many in the eighteenth century were moved by the story of the rise and fall of Philip Wharton, who had inherited so much, who had risen to the highest honours, and had lost them all and his life as well at the age of only thirty-two. Those who had known Philip and those who had heard of him were moved by the moral that could be drawn from his grand successes and his grander failure. Edward Young was said to cast in his image the tragic character of Lorenzo in the *Night thoughts;* Horace Walpole wrote a life of him in his *Royal and Noble Authors;* Samuel Richardson is said to have taken him as the model for Lovelace, the ignoble seducer in *Pamela;* and Charles James Fox allegedly quoted his example when he tried to show that drunkeness and gambling could be consistent with great statesmanship. Alexander Pope, who was so jealous of him, constantly abuses him, and Sam Johnson expresses disgust at him. To the eighteenth century he was always a mystery. He possessed so much that his century admired, and he had thrown so much away. What should we think of him? Perhaps simply that he was a hopeless romantic; he had great talents, but his imagination would always soar far beyond the reach of the highest of them. He was a man who was condemned by his own excesses, and by the boundlessness of his dreams.

NOTES

Place of publication is London, unless otherwise stated.

ABBREVIATIONS

Cobbett: W. Cobbett (ed), *The Parliamentary History of England* (1806-20).

Glover: J. H. Glover (ed.), *Stuart Papers* (1847);

SP. Stuart Papers in the Royal Archives at Windsor Castle.

BIBLIOGRAPHY

CHAPTER ONE — THE ELOPEMENT

1. So described in a kind letter to the author from Sir Oliver Millar, Keeper of the Royal Collection. For an account of the Van Dycks see G. Vertue *Notebooks* published Walpole Soc., 1947, i, 109.
2. *Lord Whig-Love's Elegy* (1715) 2nd ed.
3. Swift's note on Macky's *Remarks on the Characters of the Court of Aueen Anne:* Thomas Warton; *Works of Swift,* ed. Sir Walter Scott, x, 307 (Edinburgh 1815).
4. *History of England* (1855) IV p. 456.
5. Unpublished mss in the possession of L J Stratton, Esq.
6. *Life of Philip late Duke of Wharton* (1731) p.3.
7. *Remarks and Collections of Thomas Hearne* ed. C E Doble (Oxford 1885-9).
8. *Life of Philip late Duke of Wharton* (1731) p.2.
9. Notts. Univ., Portland Mss Hy 1516.
10. *Life of Philip late Duke of Wharton* (1731) p.5.
11. *A Dictionary of the English Language* (1755).
12. *Letters of Joseph Addison* ed. Walter Graham (Oxford 1941): 12th April 1715.
13. *The Last Will and Testament of Thomas Marquis of Wharton* (1715).

See also:-
    Rev. Mark Noble ed. *A Biographical History of England;* a continuation of Rev. J. Granger's work, III (1806).
    Cockayne *The Complete Peerage,* sub "Wharton".
    Mary Cathcart Boyer *The Years of Grandeur, The Story of Mayfair* (1975).
    John Carswell *The Old Cause* (1954). This contains a biography of the Marquis of Wharton.
    George Lipscombe *Buckinghamshire* (1847).

Westminster City Library: Rating books for the parishes of St. Anne's, Soho and St. Martin's-in-the-Fields 1718 8c.
Sir R. Steele (?) *Memoir of Thomas Marquis of Wharton* (1715).
Joseph Spence *Observations, Anecdotes and Characters of Books and Men* ed. James M. Osborn (Oxford 1966).

CHAPTER TWO — DESCENT TO AVIGNON

1. (1847) ii 633.
2. *Notebooks* — published by the Walpole Soc. (1947) ii 98.
3. iii 28.
4. Introductory anecdotes to Lady Mary Wortley Montagu's *Works* ed. Lord Wharncliffe (1837).
5. Durham County Record Office D/Ch/F Chaytor 1534; 12th April 1715.
6. *Verney letters of the Eighteenth Century* from the mss at Claydon House.
7. Glover iv 66.
8. *The Life of Philip late Duke of Wharton,* (1731).
9. Glover ii 390.
10. Glover ii 473.

See also:-
Sir Charles Petrie *The Jacobite Movement* (1959).
Diary of Mary, Countess Cowper, (1864), 194.
Survey of London (L.C.C.) 1914.
Strype's edition of Stow's map of London, C.1720.

CHAPTER THREE — TREASON

1. From Mar, Avignon Oct 7 1716; Glover iii 37-8.

2. Glover iii 61-2.
3. Glover iii 149-50.
4. Glover iii 243.
5. Glover iii 165.
6. *Verney letters of the Eighteenth Century* from the mss at Claydon House: Jack Baker to Lord Fermanagh, 15 Nov 1716.
7. Glover iii 306 Nov 29 1716 to Lord Mar.
8. as (6) Mrs Vickers to Lord Fermanagh 8 Feb 1717.
9. Glover iv 558 July 20 1717.
10. Swift's note on Bolton in Macky's *Remarks on the Characters of the Court of Queen Anne; Works of Swift* ed Sir Walter Scott, (Edinburgh 1814) x 301.
11. Aikin's *Life of Addison* ii 207, Eustace Budgell to Addison 28 Aug 1719.
12. *Remarks and Collections of Thomas Hearne* ed C E Doble (Oxford 1885-9).
13. Patrick Delany *Observations on Swift* (1754) p 216.
14. *Letters of Joseph Addison* ed Walter Graham, Oxford 1941: Addison to Bolton 12 Sep 1717.

See also:-
H.M.C. Portland Mss V 555.
Brian Williams *The Whig Supremacy* (1939).
Peter Smithers *The Life of Joseph Addison* (Oxford 1954).
Walter Sichel *Bolingbroke and his times* (1902).
Bishop Percy *Anecdotes* (1792) ii 348-53.

CHAPTER FOUR — THE HELL-FIRE CLUB

1. Durham Record Office: Chaytor D/Ch/F 1405.
2. Mrs Eliza Haywood *Memoirs of a certain island adjacent to the Kingdom of Utopia* (1725) i 220.
3. Christchurch, Oxford, Ch Ch ccxlii vol ix Canterbury Docs iv 1721-4 ff 37r/38r, f38r. I am indebted for this reference to John

Redwood *The 1660-1750 Enlightenment* (1976), and to the governing body of Christ Church for liberty to quote it.
4. Joseph Spence: *Observations, Anecdotes and Characters of Books and Men* ed James M. Osborn Oxford 1966. This edition, taken from Spence's ms, incorporates many original corrections not previously published. The book is now considerably more valuable than it was in previous editions.
5. Edward Young *Night Thoughts,* book 5.

See also:-
Complete Letters of Lady Mary Wortley Montagu ed Robert Halsband (Oxford 1967).
Geoffrey Ashe: *Do What you Will* (1974).
The Spectator; The Tatler [J. Addison and Sir Richard Steele].
The Hell-Fire Club, kept by a Society of Blasphemers. A satyr to Macclesfield (1721).
R. J. Allen: *The Clubs of Augustan London*
John Murray Graham: *Annals and Correspondence of the Viscount and First and Second Earls of Stair* (1875).

CHAPTER FIVE — THE HEIR

1. *Diary of Mary Countess Cowper* (1874) i 286.
2. House of Lords Committee Books.
3. To Bishop Nicolson of Carlisle: *Letters of William Nicolson D.D.* (1809) p. 507.
4. Daniel Defoe, *"A Tour through the whole Island of Great Britain"* (1724-27). Contents.
5. Durham County Record Office, Chaytor D/Ch/F 1412.
6. Herts Record Office, Panshanger MSS; Cowper D/EP/F 57 24th April, 1720.
7. *Diary of Mary Countess Cowper* p.194.

See also:-

J. H. Plumb *Sir Robert Walpole* ii (1972).
William Cobbett: *Parliamentary History of England* (1806-20) vii.
Joseph Nicholson and Richard Burn *The History of Westmorland and Cumberland* (1777)

CHAPTER SIX — THE BUBBLE

1. *Letters of William Nicolson D.D.* (1809). From Bishop Downes.
2. Swift, *Works*, (1824) xvi 311, where the letter is wrongly dated 1717.
3. Aug. 2nd 1720, to Abigail Harley. *HMC Portland MSS V, 601.*
4. Thomas Hearne, *Remarks and Collections,* ed C. E. Doble p. 442.
5. Herts Record Office, Panshanger MSS; Cowper D/EP/F 57 2nd Jan. 1721.

See also:-
William Cobbett ed. *The Parliamentary History of England* vi & vii.
John Carswell: The South Sea Bubble.
The Committee Books of the House of Lords.

CHAPTER SEVEN — THE END OF THE HELLFIRE CLUB

1. *Cobbett* vii Jan 9 1721
2. ibid Feb 4th
3. Ballard MSS Bodleian Library
4. *HMC Miscellaneous Collections* Vol. 8 Anne Viscountess Irwin to Charles Ingram.
5. Aug. 30th 1790
6. *Cobbett* vii p 893

7. *Cobbett* vii p 806
8. ibid p 808
9. *Verney Letters of the Eighteenth Century from the MSS at Claydon House.*

Cobbett — *The Parliamentary History of England* ed William Cobbett, Lon 1806-20.

See also:-
George Vertue: *Notebooks* (ed Walpole Society) 1947.
T. B. Macaulay: *Essay on Atterbury.*
Herts Record Office. *Panshanger MSS.*
Samuel Johnson: *Lives of the Poets: Edward Young,* London 1810 III p 290.

CHAPTER EIGHT — THE ELECTION

1. L. Melville *The Life and Writings of Philip Duke of Wharton,* (1913) p93.
2. Herts Record Office *Panshanger MSS* Cowper D/EP/F 57 9 Aug 1721.
3. ibid. 24 Aug.
4. Cumberland Record Office D/Lons/W/Agents letter books 39. 1 Sep 1721.
5. Cockayne: *The Complete Peerage,* sub "Kent".
6. Notts Univ: *Portland MSS* PVW 490. Dated 3 Feb 1724 but wrongly, for Earl Harold died 21 July 1723. It has been suggested that Lloyd wrote the poem, but I know no evidence for it.
7. Erasmus Philipps' diary: *Notes and Queries,* x 2nd. 445.
8. HMC *Portland MSS* V 625 William Bromley to Lord Oxford 22 Aug 1721.
9. HMC *Stowe MSS* 242 f 209.
10. Durham County Record Office D/Ch/F Chaytor 17 Nov 1721.
11. Herts Record Office *Panshanger MSS* Cowper D/EP/F 57 2 Dec 1721.

12. HMC *Portland MSS* VII 310.
13. *The Constitutions of the Freemasons* (1723).
14. *Family Memoirs of Stukely*, Surtees Soc., ed. W.C. Lubeis (1882).
15. HMC *Bagot MSS,* from Colonel James Graham, 14 April 1722.

See also:-
J. H. Plumb, *The Growth of Political Stability in England 1675-1725* (1967).
C. B. Bealey, *The Early Opposition to Sir Robert Walpole 1720-27* (1927).

CHAPTER NINE — TWICKENHAM

1. *The Constitutions of the Freemasons* (1723).
2. *London Journal* 16 June 1722.
3. *The Constitutions of the Freemasons.*
4. Pope *Imitation of Horace*, Epistle VI, 85 ff. See note in Elwins & Whitewell's ed. (1889).
5. Cobbett viii 47.
6. HMC Appendix to Second Report, p.26.
7. Cobbett viii 273.
8. Cobbett viii 308 ff.
9. ibid.
10. Cobbett viii 348.

See also:-
John Nichols, *Bibliotheca Topographica Britannica*, x, *History of Twickenham* (1717) p 78.
G. V. Bennett: *The Tory Crisis in Church and State* (1976).
R. S. Cobbett: *Memorials of Twickenham* (1872) p 256-7.

CHAPTER TEN — THE TRUE BRITON

1. Nottingham Univ., Portland MSS P W V 492.
2. B M Add MSS 34, 744 f 123.
3. Printed in No. 43 of *The True Briton*.
4. *The New Foundling Hospital for Wit*, (1743).
5. *The True Briton*, No. 22, 17 Aug 1723.
6. B M Add MSS 32,686 f266.
7. The Wax Chandlers Company's books are on loan to the Guildhall Library.
8. B M Add MSS 32,686 f266.
9. *The True Briton* No. 40, 18 Oct.
10. HMC Lowther MSS 123.
11. *The True Briton*, No. 35 30 Sep 1723.
12. *The True Briton*, 14 Feb 1724.
13. *The True Briton*, 3rd ed. (1740) ii 606 ff.
14. *Works*, 5th ed., iii 134; 31 Oct 1723.
15. *Complete Letters*, ed R. Halsband (Oxford, 1967); March 1724.
16. *Family Memoirs of Stukely* (Surtees Soc., 1881) ed W.C. Lubeis.
17. *Daily Post*, Sep 1724.
18. *The Merrythought*, (late 1720's).
19. It was republished in two volumes with a *Life of the Duke* in 1732.
20. *The Parliamentary HIstory of England* ed Cobbett, viii 386.
21. (1807) p 288 ff.
22. Wharncliffe's *Letters*, ii 161 (1837).
23. *Correspondence of Jonathan Swift*, ed Williams, (Oxford 1963), to Charles Ford.
24. H.M.C. Rawdon, Hastings MSS to Earl of Huntingdon, June 24 1724.
25. Horace Walpole, *Royal and Nobel Authors*, 125
26. *The New Foundling Hospital for Wit*, i 228.
27. Lady Louisa Stuart's *Introductory Anecdotes* to Lady Mary's *Works* ed Lord Wharncliffe (1837).
28. Pope to Caryll, 23 Oct 1733.
29. *First Moral Essay*, 180 ff.

30. *Correspondence of Edward Young,* ed Thomas Pettit (1971).
31. *Complete Letters* 42.
32. ibid. to Lady Mar, undated.
33. State Papers of the Jacobites in the Royal Archives at Windsor Castle, 82 f 50.
34. ibid. 80 f167.
35. John Lekeux to Lord Molesworth's son, HMC Polworth MSS II (1911).
36. *Anecdotes of his own Time* (1819) p 34.
37. See No. 35 above.
38. *Complete Letters:* 10 June 1725 to Lady Mar.
39. *Ralph, Miscellaneous Poems by several Hands.* (1729) p. 130.

CHAPTER ELEVEN — VIENNA

1. SP 81 f 129.
2. *Complete Letters* ed Halsband. 8 Sep 1726.
3. SP 83 f 104.
4. SP 83 f 135.
5. B.M. Add. MSS 32, 743 f 207.
6. B.M. Add. MSS 32,502. 10/21 July to Robinson at Paris.
7. SP 85 f 8.

See also:-
   J. F. Chance *The Alliance of Hanover* (1923).

CHAPTER TWELVE — THE INVASION OF ENGLAND

1. SP 85 f18.
2. SP 85 f139.

3. SP 85 f82.
4. ibid.
5. Wharton to Lord Inverness, SP 85 f150.
6. SP 86 f19.
7. SP 86 f52.
8. SP 86 f55 22 Sep.
9. SP 86 f53.
10. SP 86 f80.
11. SP 86 f12.
12. SP 86 f60.
13. SP 86 f151.
14. SP 86 f136.
15. SP 87 f9.
16. SP 86 f66.
17. ibid f66.
18. SP 86 f109.
19. SP 87 f4.
20. SP Nov 3, SP 87 f48.
21. SP 87 f66, Nov 10.
22. ibid.
23. to Lord Inverness, SP 87 f111.
24. to Lord Inverness, SP 86 f2, probably Nov 10. Wrongly dated Sep. 10.
25. SP June 17 1727 94 f129.

See also:-
  Hubert Cole *First Gentleman of the Bedchamber.*
  Gabriel Syveton *Une Cour et un Aventurier.* (Paris 1896).

CHAPTER THIRTEEN — ROME

1. SP 87 f83.
2. SP 89 f28 5 Jan 1726.
3. SP 90 f80 6 Feb.

4. B.M. Add. MSS 32,745 f76 Thomas Robinson to Newcastle 4 Feb N.S.
5. SP 89 f115, 19 Jan.
6. SP 88 f144 31 Dec 1725 O.S.
7. SP 88 f143.
8. SP 90 f80.
9. SP 90 f21.
10. SP 90 f98; dated 10 Feb, but I think wrongly for 15th.
11. SP 91 f15 12 Feb.
12. SP 91 f63.
13. SP 90 f145.
14. SP 91 f102.
15. Toda y Guel, *Curiositats de Poblet: Enteno d'un Adventurer Inglis.*
16. SP 92 f29, Barcelona 23 May 1726, to Lord Inverness.

CHAPTER FOURTEEN — MADRID

1. Wharton to Lord Inverness, 23 March, SP 92 f29.
2. ibid.
3. SP 92 f136.
4. SP 90 f16 16 Feb.
5. B.M. Add. MSS 32,744 f283 28 Sep 1725.
6. B.M. Add. MSS 32,745 f495.
7. B.M. Add. MSS 32,745 f539.
8. SP 90 f143 Graeme to Lord Inverness 23 Feb 1726.
9. ibid.
10. SP 91 f134.
11. *Hardwicke State Papers* ii 636-8, 5 April O.S., to T. Robinson.
12. SP 92 f139, 13 April.
13. SP 92 f16 20 April.
14. SP f92 f114.

CHAPTER FIFTEEN — LOVE AND THE FALL

1. To Lord Inverness 6 Sep 1726 SP 96 f162 and 20 Sep SP 97 f62.
2. *Memoirs of the Count de Beauval,* p.62.
3. SP f90.
4. To Lord Inverness 8 June SP 94 f90.
5. *Memoirs of the Count de Beauval,* p.64.
6. To Lord Inverness SP 95 f128.
7. To Lord Inverness 20 July SP 95 f110.
8. SP 95 f128.
9. 96 f8.
10. 96 f128.
11. Journal in the possession of the Duchess of Alba at the Palacio Liria in Madrid quoted by Sir Charles Petrie, *The Jacobite Movement.*
12. June 7 SP 94 f82.
13. SP 94 f126.
14. SP 96 f40.
15. To Liria 22 Oct 1726 SP 98 f75.

CHAPTER SIXTEEN — WAR

1. SP 95 f140.
2. SP 102 f103 to Lord Inverness.
3. SP 93 f52 & 53.
4. SP 110 f90.
5. R. F. Gould: *The History of Freemasonery* (Edin) N.D. c.1880.

See also:-
   George Hills *The Rock of Contention* (1974).

CHAPTER SEVENTEEN — A DREAM OF HOME

1. SP 116 f85 24 May 1728.
2. SP 117 f23 8 June 1728.
3. HMC Weston-Underwood MSS.
4. B. M. Add. MSS 32,756 f417 Paris 6 July.
5. ibid.
6. *Life of Philip late Duke of Wharton.* p.26.
7. Williams, *Life of Atterbury,* ii p 308. Surenne 14 Aug.
8. E. Curll B. M. 839 m 23.
9. B. M. Add. MSS 12,331 ee 31.
10. SP 118 f105.
11. "from a certain house in Norfolk" *vide* n.6. *supra,* ch.3.
12. (1730) B. M. Vet. A4 e 358.
13. SP 86 f61.
14. ibid.

CHAPTER EIGHTEEN — THE DUEL

1. *Mist's Weekly Journal* 24 Aug 1728.
2. *Mist's Weekly Journal* Sep 1728.
3. *The New Foundling Hospital for Wit,* 1743.
4. B.M.C. 38 g 14.
5. *Life of Philip late Duke of Wharton,* (1731) p 31.
6. ibid. p.38.
7. ibid. p.38.
8. ibid. p.42.
9. ibid. p.36.
10. ibid. p.34.
11. ibid. p.35.

CHAPTER NINETEEN — THE ROAD TO POBLET

1. *A Duke and his Friends,* ed Earl of March (1911): Duke of Richmond to Martin ffolkes.
2. SP 128 f72 23 May.
3. ibid.
4. J. Grainger, M. Noble. *The Biographical History of England,* iii (1806) sub "Wharton".
5. *Life of Philip late Duke of Wharton* p 51.
6. *Memoirs of the Count de Beaval,* Marquis d'Argens, p.68.

See also:-
   Eduart Toda y Guel *Curiositats de Poblet* (Tarragona 1922).

Index

A

Abell, Richard. 70.
Abingdon, Lord. 21.
Addison, Joseph. 13, 18, 21, 32, 33, 34, 40, 49, 50, 99.
Aislabie, John. 69.
Alexander, Mr. a Jacobite, 29.
Alexander, Pope. 225.
All Souls College, Oxford. 59, 60.
Amsterdam. 66, 196.
Anglesey. 59.
Anne, Queen. 9, 10, 14, 23, 61, 81, 118.
Appleby. 11, 24, 78, 81, 85.
Aranjuez. 167.
Arbuthnot, Dr. 12, 41.
Archangel. 145.
Argens, Marquis D'. 173.
Argyll, John Duke of. 68, 71, 93, 138.
Aske, Near Richmond, Yorks. 69, 76, 104, 124, 197.
Atholl, Duke of. 162.
Atterbury, Francis Bishop of Rochester. 59, 65, 81, 82, 91, 93, 94, 95, 96, 98, 99, 100, 103, 110, 114, 123, 124, 129, 131, 132, 140, 146, 155, 156, 162, 163, 178, 181, 186, 188, 191, 193, 197, 225.
Austria. 133.
Avignon. 26, 27, 28, 30, 33, 34, 124, 160, 186, 188.
Aylesbury. 11, 32, 199.
Aylesbury, a Quaker of. 198.

B

Bains, Mr. the Wharton's Westmorland agent. 24, 79.
Balaguer. 221.
Bangor. 59.
Barcelona. 158, 159, 189, 221.
Barrington. 11.
Barry, Captain. 226.
Bath. 226.
Bathurst, Lord Allen. 65, 68, 71, 91, 94, 114, 118.
Beauclerck, Dr. 116.
Beaufort, Duke of. 162.
Bedford, Dukes of. 13, 215.
Bedford, Rev. Hilkiah. 57.
Beggars Opera, the. 215, 220.
Belvedere Palace. 128, 132.

Belvedere Upper and Lower. 145.
Berkley, Bishop George. 87.
Berkley House. 12.
Bernard Street, Madrid. 164.
Berwick, James Duke of. 156, 181, 210, 211.
Bicester races. 80.
Bilbao. 217.
Bingley, a printer — Jacobite. 198, 200.
Bingley, Robert Lord. 65, 68, 94, 208, 216, 217, 223, 227.
Birmingham, Mr. an English surgeon in Paris. 208, 213.
Bishops and Judges, on the. 97.
Black Mass, 45.
Blandford, Marquis of. 162.
Blenheim, battle of. 91, 121, 181.
Blenheim Palace, 126.
Bletchingdon marble 59.
Blunt, Sir John. 66.
Bologna. 178, 179, 182, 185, 186, 189, 191.
Bollingbroke, Henry St John Viscount. 14, 23, 25, 26, 29, 114, 118, 193.
Bolton, Duke of. 12, 33, 35, 52.
Bond Street. 37.
Boscobel. 73.
Boughton. 21.
Bowes, Mrs. subject of poem by Lady Mary. 112.
Boyes, Colonel, Jacobite agent. 31.
Boyle, Robert. 83.
Bracegirdle, Mrs. 111.
Braemar. 23.
Brett, "Mother" Elizabeth. 42, 98.
Brierly, Captain. 197, 200, 210, 217, 219, 221, 226.
Brigham, Cumberland. 197.
Britannicus. 68.
Briton the. 105, 110.
Brocas, Sheriff of London. 199.
Bromley, William. 81.
Brooke, Lord. 114.
Brutus, Norman patriot. 67.
Buckingham. 11, 74, 85.
Budgell, Eustace. 33.
Burleigh House. 47.
Burlington House. 12.
Burn, Richard. 225.
Bury Street. 44.
Bute, Earl of. 68.
Butler, Captain James. 124, 126, 151, 226.
Buttinghill, Baron. 204.
Buttons coffee house. 21, 93.

243

C

Cade, Miss, later Mrs. Lloyd. 111, 125.
Cadiz. 186, 187, 189.
Cadogan. 145.
Calais. 31.
Caligula. 174.
Campden House. 61.
Canterbury, Archbishop of. 45, 53.
"Careless" 12, 20.
Carlisle, Charles Earl of. 22, 76.
Caroline, Princess, later Queen. 51, 55, 61, 87, 205.
Cartagena. 182.
Cassel. 29.
Castelar, Marquis de. 176, 184, 222.
Castle Howard. 22, 76.
Castle Tavern the, in Fleet Street. 109.
Catherine I. 145, 191.
Catherine the Great. 139.
Catherlough. 34.
Catherton. 104.
Cavan, County. 58.
Cave, Sir Thomas. 23.
Centileore, Susannah. 68.
Cervantes. 90.
Cesar, Charles. 119, 189.
Chardin, George. 151.
Charles I. 9, 59, 101, 122, 139.
Charles II. 29, 72, 102, 139, 142, 155, 157.
Charters, Francis, Colonel. 37, 50, 88, 117, 138, 226.
Charters, Sir Francis. 197.
Chatham. 145.
Chatham Harbour. 142.
Chatworth. 21.
Chelsea. 12.
Chéron, Louis. 21.
Chesterfield, Earl of. 84.
Chetwynd, Lord. 58.
Chery, Chase. 79.
Child, Francis. 101.
Churchill, Charles. 45.
Cibber, Colley. 41, 68.
Cicero, M. Tullius. 47, 90, 98, 113.
Cirencester. 70.
City of London Constitution. 102, 118, 133.
Claremont. 99.
Clarendon, Trial of the Earl of. 95.
Clarissa, Harlowe. 99.
Clark, Lieutenant. 185.
Clarke, Father. 179.
Claudius, Emperor. 67.
Claydon. 73.
Clayton, Colonel Jasper. 183.
Clementina, Queen. 116, 131, 147, 148, 154, 156, 164, 166, 168, 171, 181, 186, 187.
Cobbett, William. 95.

Cockermouth. 11, 50, 77, 78.
Cockpit, the. 67.
Code. 115, 124, 153, 188.
Coke, Hon. Robert. 226.
Collier, Captain. 160.
Comerford, Grand Master of Masons of Andalusia. 189.
Common Council of City of London. 102.
Commons, House of. 52, 55, 62, 63, 69, 94, 119, 160, 186, 199.
Conduit Street. 44.
Congreve, William. 220.
Coningsby, Richard. 196.
Coningsby, Thomas, Earl. 196.
Conolly, William. 104.
Constantinople. 87.
Constitution of the Freemasons, the 89, 90, 100.
Conyers, Sir Gerard. 102.
Cordova. 182, 183.
Covent Garden Theatre. 40.
Coverley, Sir Roger de. 41.
Cowper, Earl. 50, 55, 56, 60, 62, 64, 69, 71, 76, 77, 81, 82, 92, 94, 96, 103, 110, 134.
Cowper, Mary, Countess. 51, 56, 94.
Cowper, William, First Earl. 65.
Craggs, James. 69.
Craggs, James, the younger. 61, 69, 87.
Cranstoun, Lord. 209, 211.
Craven, Lord. 94. 162.
Crew, a Royal messenger. 170.
Cripplegate Ward. 102.
Croglin. 103.
Cromwell, Oliver. 10.
Cross, Sir Thomas. 16.
Crown Tavern. 102.
Cuella Alcaide de la Carta, Don Louis de. 180.
Culloden. 226.
Curll, Edmund. 168.

D

Daily Post. 109.
Dalkieth, Earl of. 84, 89, 100.
Danvers House. 12, 21.
Danvers Street. 21.
Darcy, Conyers. 85.
Dashwood, Sir Francis. 45, 46.
Defoe, Daniel. 54, 83.
Denton, Alexander. 70.
Derwentwater, Lord. 24.
Desagliers, Dr. John Theophilus. 90, 100.
Devonshire House. 12.
Dieppe. 196, 201.
Dillon, General. 148, 163, 181.
Dilston, Mr. of Woodstock. 62.
Doddington, Bubb. 46.
Don Quixote. 154.

Dorset, Sackville Duke of. 68.
Dover, 32.
Dover Street, 12, 14, 16, 17, 19, 21, 32, 33, 41, 42.
Downes, Bishop of Killalla. 53.
Drury Lane Theatre. 40.
Dryden, John. 220.
Dublin. 33, 36, 37, 44, 58, 72, 84, 226.
Dubourdieu, J. A. 111.
duelling. 11, 117.
Duke of Wharton's Ballad, the. 97.
Duke of Wharton's Reasons for his Leaving his Native Country, the. 206, 207, 209.
Dunbar, James Murry, Earl of. 147, 159, 163, 176, 187.
Durant, M. and Mme. 217.
Dusoul, M. 24, 25, 27, 30.
Dutch Gazette, the. 160.

E

Earle, Colonel. 183.
"Eclipse" 20.
Eden Hall. 54, 79.
Edgar, Jemmy. 156.
Edgehill, Battle of. 9.
Election, General, of 1722, and see names of individual boroughs. 85.
Elizabeth I, Queen. 54.
Eloquence of the British Senate. 111.
Emperor, Holy Roman, Charles VI. 121, 122, 125, 126, 130, 133, 135, 137, 145, 148, 152, 153, 163, 165, 167, 174.
Empress. 136.
Erskine, an A.D.C. 28.
Escorial Palace. 169.
Eugen, Prince. 121, 128, 130, 144, 145, 155.
Exeter, Earl of. 47.
Exchange Alley. 56, 57.

F

Farnese, Elizabeth, see Spain.
Faro. 42, 44.
Feast, Mr. Alderman for Cripplegate. 102.
Fénélon, François de Salignac de la Mothe. 90, 219.
Fenton, Elijah. 87, 112.
Fermanagh, Lady. 73.
'Fifteen, the. 23, 24, 25, 26, 50, 59, 123, 141.
Figg. 42.
Fitzroy, Lord Augustus. 226.
Fleet Prison. 16.
Fogs Weekly Journal. 73.
Forster, Tom a servant of second Duchess. 151, 159.

'Forty-five, the. 50, 141.
Fox, Charles James. 227.
Frankfurt. 124.
Frederick the Great of Prussia. 226.
Freemasons. 189.
Freemasons, Order of. 41, 83, 84, 88, 90, 100, 101, 109, 172.
Freind, Dr. John. 41, 91, 93, 94, 119.
Frith Street. 227.

G

Galloway, Earl of. 59.
Garda, Lake. 154.
Gardiner, Rev, Rector of Hawarden. 59.
Garter, Order of the. 157, 161, 164, 165, 186, 192, 212, 215.
Gascoigne, Benjamin. 117.
Gay, John. 41, 215, 220.
Geneva. 25, 27, 30.
Genoa. 157.
George I. 14, 21, 23, 24, 25, 26, 30, 35, 42, 49, 50, 51, 53, 55, 61, 67, 71, 73, 79, 82, 84, 99, 121, 122, 129, 133, 141, 161, 171, 179, 186, 205.
George II. 51, 52, 55, 61, 80, 87, 103, 118, 186, 194, 195, 205, 221.
George III. 119.
Gibraltar. 122, 141, 181, 182, 183, 185, 186, 196, 200, 207, 211, 215, 218.
Gibson, Mr. the banker. 151.
Gibson, Thomas. 70.
Gilling, Near Richmond Yorks. 76, 104.
Glenshiel, skirmish at. 50.
"*Glorious Revolution*" the. 14, 25, 27, 51, 134, 172.
Golden Square, Soho. 227.
Goose and Gridiron Tavern, St Pauls churchyard. 84.
Gordon, Mr. Wine merchant in Bordeaux. 162.
Goring, Sir. Harry. 94, 197, 199, 203.
Goring, Viscount. 204.
Gormogans, the. 110, 189.
Gower. 94.
Graeme, John. 136, 142, 143, 145, 149, 150, 153, 155, 163, 179, 186, 187, 191.
Graeme, Sir John. 189.
Graham, Colonel James, 78, 85.
Grammont, Conte de, 90, 157.
Granada. 183.
Grand Master of Freemasons. 83, 88, 90, 100, 109.
Great George Street. 51.
Great North Road. 75.
Greenwich. 33.
Greyhound Tavern. 44, 46.
Grimaldi, the Papal Nuncio to Vienna. 128, 135.

"Grumbletonians" 60, 62, 65, 70, 72, 73, 78, 81, 82, 94, 133.
Guy, Thomas. 37.
Gwynn, Mr. Jacobite agent. 26.

H

Habeus Corpus Act, suspension of. 92, 133.
Hainault, a Spanish regiment. 184, 218.
Hamilton, Colonel James. 81.
Hamilton, James, a Jacobite agent. 121, 124, 125, 132, 141, 149, 150, 155, 161, 170.
Hamilton, Major Zeck. 160, 166, 169, 170, 173, 174, 176, 178, 183.
Hampton Court. 34.
Handel's *Water Music*, 33.
Hanover. 25, 30, 49, 61.
Hanover, Electors of. 14.
Hanover Square. 42, 44, 108.
Harcourt, Duke de. 203.
Harcourt, Simon Viscount. 177.
Harley, Hon Edward. 61.
Harold, Earl. 78.
Harry, one of the Duke's valets-de-chambre. 121, 124, 153, 163, 196.
Hartley Castle, Westmorland. 54.
Hawarden. 59.
Hawksmoor, Nicholas. 39. 59.
Hay, John, Earl of Inverness, see Inverness.
Hay, John, Secretary of State to James. 115.
Hay, Lord Charles. 185.
Haymarket Theatre. 40.
Hazlitt. 110.
Healaugh, Yorks. 77.
Hearne, Thomas. 15, 33.
Hell-Fire Caves. 45.
Hell-Fire Club. 44, 46, 62, 71, 72, 83, 84, 172, 174.
Hell-Fire Club, Proclamation against. 71.
Henrietta Maria, Queen. 139.
Henry, Prince, later Cardinal of York. 116.
Herbert, James, M.P. 73.
Hermitage Palace. 139.
Hesse, Landgrave of. 25, 29.
Hibernia, Spanish regiment. 169.
Highgate, maid at. 15.
Highlands of Scotland. 118.
High Seat. 76.
Hillsborough, Earl of. 44.
Hillsborough, Lord. 139.
Hillsborough, Viscount. 34, 42, 62, 80, 85, 103, 107, 108.
Hochkirk, Battle of. 226.
Hofburg. 125.
Hofburg Palace. 132.
Hogarth, William. 46, 84.
Holdernesse, Lord. 85.

Holland Street, Soho. 115, 170.
Holmes, Major General, Richard. 16.
Holt, John. 177, 226.
Holyhead. 33, 36, 59.
Holy Roman Emperor, see Emperor.
Honeycombe, Will. 41.
Houghton. 139, 196.
"*Humble Petition of His Grace Philip Duke of Wharton.*" 200.
Hungerford, John. 97.
hunting. 130, 136, 203.
Hyde Park. 12, 91.

I

Ilchester. 11.
Innsbruck. 154.
Inverness, Earl of. 123, 131, 132, 136, 139, 142, 148, 150, 155, 156, 160, 163, 166, 170, 174, 176, 178, 179, 181, 186, 187.
Inverness, Lady. 147, 148.
Irwin, Lady. 68.
Islay, Earl of. 71.

J

Jacob, John. 70, 138, 143, 201.
Jacombe, Thomas. 70.
James I. 9.
James II. 10, 14, 78, 134.
James, Stuart, Titular James III and VIII "The Old Pretender" 14, 23, 25, 26, 27, 29, 31, 32, 34, 93, 104, 107, 116, 118, 119, 121, 122, 124, 126, 127, 130, 132, 135, 137, 141, 142, 144, 147, 148, 152, 154, 155, 156, 161, 163, 166, 169, 170, 172, 175, 178, 179, 181, 182, 185, 186, 187, 188, 191, 192, 198, 204, 208, 213, 216, 219, 222, 223, 225, 226.

K

Keene, Benjamin. 164.
Keith, James. 182, 183, 187, 188, 191, 226.
Kelly, George. 91, 93.
Kenmure, William, Viscount. 24.
Kent, Duke of. 78.
King Dr. 117.
King, William Archbishop of Dublin. 18.
Kingston, Evelyn, Duke of. 11, 22, 52, 84, 87.
Kingston, Lord. 84.
Kinnoull, Earl of. 68, 94, 122.
Kirkby, Stephen. 76.
Knight, Robert. 66.
Knights of Christ, order of. 212.
Königsegg, Count. 167.

L

La Ciotat. 158.
Laguerre, Louis. 21.
La Mailleray. 203.
La Paz, Marquis de. 176, 209.
Las Torres, Conde de. 182, 184, 185, 187.
Laud, Archbishop. 66, 139.
Launceston. 91.
Lawson, Sir Wilfred. 78.
Layer, Christopher. 91, 92.
Lechmere, Nicholas. 17, 22, 24, 61.
Lee, Anne. 11.
Lee Family. 12.
Leeds, Peregrine, Duke of. 26.
Leghorn. 190, 191.
Leicester Fields. 51, 55, 60, 101.
Lely, Sir Peter. 20.
Lérida. 160, 218, 222.
Levens Hall. 78, 85.
Levett, Sheriff of London. 199.
Lichfield, Earl of, 42, 44, 65, 68, 80, 114, 116, 226.
Life and Writings of Duke of Wharton. 227.
"*Life of Philip Late Duke of Wharton by an Impartial Hand.*" 15, 37, 223, 227.
"Lilliburlero" 10, 215.
Limerick, siege of. 11.
Lincoln's Inn Fields, Theatre at. 40, 220.
Lipscombe's *Buckinghamshire.* 20.
Liria, Duke of. 156, 163, 164, 170, 176, 178, 186, 191.
Lloyd, Phil. 78, 93, 111, 192, 199, 201, 106.
Locke, John. 44, 83.
Lockhart, George, of Carnwarth. 32, 33.
Lockwood, Mr. Tory candidate for Shrievalty of London. 101.
Lodge of Masons, Spanish. 189.
London Evening Post, the. 211.
London Journal, the. 89, 211.
Londonderry, Thomas, Lord. 70.
loo. 42.
Lord Whig Love's Elegy. 9, 10.
Lords, House of. 51, 54, 55, 63, 65, 66, 71, 74, 81, 92, 94, 110, 186.
Lothbury. 202.
Louis XIV. 12, 14.
"Lovelace". 99.
Lowther Family. 78, 216.
Lowther, Sir James. 78, 104.
Luxembourg, Duke de. 203.
Lyons. 27, 29, 192.

M

macaroni. 189.
Macaulay, Thomas, Lord. 11.

Macclesfield, Lord. 118, 119, 177.
Madrid. 127, 144, 152, 157, 159, 160, 163, 166, 167, 169, 171, 172, 173, 176, 178, 183, 187, 188, 189, 191, 204, 209, 218, 219, 222, 225.
Mall, the. 41.
Malmesbury. 11, 74, 85, 104.
Malmesbury, Thomas, Marquis of. 49, 53, 54.
Malplaquet, Battle of. 91.
Maltsters of Edinburgh and Glasgow. 129.
Malt tax. 129, 162.
Mar, Countess of. 115.
Mar, John Earl of. 23, 27, 28, 29, 30, 32, 107, 123, 124, 148, 163, 181, 209, 226.
Marischal, Earl. 162, 167, 182, 183, 187, 188, 191.
Marlborough, Charles Duke of. 50.
Marlborough, John Duke of. 121, 126.
Marlborough, Sarah Duchess of. 124, 138, 221.
Marriage Act 1763, 17.
Marseilles. 158.
Mary Queen of Scots. 112, 219.
Masquerades. 106, 107.
Mayor, Lord of London. 102.
Mayerlin. 125.
Mayfair, 13.
Meade, Dr. 116.
Meath, County. 34, 58.
Menzies, John. 32.
Merry Thought, the. 110.
Milan. 193.
Minorca. 122.
Mist, Nathaniel. 72, 83, 198, 200, 205, 227.
Mist's Weekly Journal. 72, 99, 110, 198, 204, 205.
Modena. 191.
Modena, Mary of. 30.
Molesworth, Robert, Viscount. 34, 52, 58, 62, 69.
Montagu, Duke of. 84, 88, 90.
Montagu, Lady Mary Wortley, see Wortley Montagu.
Montrose, Duke of. 42.
Moore, Sir Thomas's House. 12.
Mornington, Earls of. 58.
Morrice, Sir William. 226.
Morris, John and Thomas Street, hosiers. 88.
"*Mr. Higgs Merry Arguments from the Light of Nature.*" 52.
Murray, James. 131.
Musgrave, Sir Christopher, 'Kit'. 54, 77, 78, 104, 117, 138, 151, 155, 192, 196.
Muti, Palazzo. 147, 148, 155.

N

Nantes. 217.
Needham, Elizabeth, "Mother". 21.

247

Nero. 174.
Newcastle, Duke of. 50, 80, 99, 102, 150, 162, 195.
Newgate. 13.
Newmarket. 12, 55, 81.
Newstadt. 136.
Newton, Sir Isaac. 44, 83.
Nicholson, Joseph. 226.
Night Thoughts. Poem by Young. 47, 49, 131, 181, 227.
Nine Standards Rigg. 76.
Norfolk, Duke of. 91.
North and Grey, Lord. 55, 63, 65, 91, 93, 94, 114, 124, 136, 145, 148, 181, 189, 191, 197, 225.
Nottingham, Earl of. 71.

O

O'Beirne, Colonel. 169.
O'Beirne, family. 218, 220.
O'Brien, Colonel Daniel. 191, 197, 203, 209, 213, 216.
O'Brien, James. 191.
O'Brien, Sir Ed. 44, 80.
Oldisworthy, William. 99, 105.
O'Neill, Captain. 208.
On Robbing the Exchequer. 98.
Onslow, Lord. 71.
Opera, Paris. 213.
Orford House. 61.
Orleans. 217.
Ormonde, James Duke of. 23, 27, 28, 101, 124, 145, 156, 160, 161, 163, 166, 172, 178, 181, 188, 191, 218, 220, 222, 225.
"Ormonde" Mob. 101, 141.
Orrery, Earl of. 57, 91, 93, 94, 117, 119, 124, 139, 145, 162, 186, 196, 225.
Osnabruck. 186.
Ossory, Lady. 69.
Ossory, Lord. 65.
Ostend. 121, 144, 145.
Othello. 224.
Oxford. 59, 60, 114, 177.
Oxford, Edward Harley, Earl of. 59, 118.
Oxford, Robert Harley, Earl of. 14, 23, 26, 81, 82.

P

Paisley, Lord. 84.
Pamela. 227.
Panshanger, Hertfordshire. 63.
Panton. M. 29, 31.
Paris. 25, 26, 30, 37, 123, 162, 186, 210, 211, 217, 219.

Parker, Lord Chancellor. 57.
Parker, Thomas, and see Macclesfield. 97.
Parliamentary History. 95, 110.
Parma. 192, 220, 221.
Parma, Duke of. 191, 192.
Parsons, Humphrey, Alderman. 101, 129, 155.
Parsons, Humphrey. 162.
Paterson, Dr. 140.
Payne, printer of the True Briton. 100.
Peering, Jane. 11.
Penrith, Cumberland. 54.
Persian Satire, the Duke of Wharton's. 204.
Perth, Duchess of. 165.
Peter the Great, Czar of Russia. 25.
Peterborough, Earl of. 71.
"Philibert". 157.
Piccadilly. 12, 40.
Piggott, Nathaniel. 117, 138, 140.
Pitt, Thomas. 70.
Poblet, Monastery at. 223.
Poetical Works of Duke of Wharton. 227.
Poissy. 213.
Pomfret, Countess of. 113.
Pontacks Coffee House. 21.
Pope, Alexander. 34, 41, 44, 57, 61, 66, 75, 87, 88, 90, 94, 112, 118, 147, 159, 191, 227.
Pope, The. 136, 147, 148, 155, 156, 168, 171, 181, 185, 189.
Portland, H.M.S. 183.
Portugal Street. 12.
Preston, Battle of. 23, 99.
Privy Seal, Lord. 16, 17, 170.
Privy Seal, the. 161, 170.
"Protesting Lords". 94, 162.
Pryse, Walter. 101, 116, 124, 139, 196.
Purcell, Henry. 10.
Putney Bridge. 199.
Pyrmont. 99, 129.

Q

quail shooting. 188.
Quainton. 19, 20.
Quainton racecourse. 11.
Queensberry, Catherine Duchess of. 221.
Queensberry, Duke of, 46, 84.
Quinn, Mr. one of the Duke's gentlemen. 121, 143, 153.

R

Rabelais's Gargantua. 46.
Radcliffe, Dr. 59.
Rank, General, chief minister of Landgrave of Hesse, 30.

Rathfarnham Castle. 13, 20, 34, 58, 72, 88, 103, 166.
Ravenstonedale. 104.
Rawlins, "Lord". 68.
Redmond, Sir Peter. 208, 212.
Richardson, Samuel. 99, 100, 105, 111.
Richelieu, Duc de. 143, 144, 149, 150, 152.
Richmond, Duke of. 84.
Richmond Palace. 61, 87, 113.
Richmond, Yorks. 11, 23, 38, 70, 76, 85, 104.
Rimini. 154.
Ripperda, Jan William Duc de. 126, 127, 129, 135, 137, 141, 142, 144, 145, 148, 150, 155, 156, 159, 160, 161, 163, 165, 166, 167, 170, 172, 175, 178, 179, 180.
Risbourg, Marquis de. 159, 221.
Robespierre. 48.
Robinson, Colonel, a freemason. 100, 199.
Rochester, Wilmot Earl of. 113.
Rome. 91, 124, 127, 128, 130, 131, 134, 142, 147, 150, 153, 155, 157, 159, 166, 171, 175, 176, 178, 179, 188, 189, 204, 210, 219, 223, 225.
Room, Mr. 199, 201.
Rossario, H.M.S. 184.
Rosse, Earl of. 84.
Rotterdam. 49, 121, 122, 124.
Rouen. 195, 197, 198, 199, 201, 203, 205, 208.
Rousseau., Jean-Jaques. 226.
Roussilion, Gabriel. 68.
Royal Archives at Windsor. 70.
Royal and Noble Authors, by Horace Walpole. 121, 227.
Royal Society, the. 110.
Rupert, Prince. 139.
Rushout, Sir John. 85.

S

Sacheverell, Henry. 15.
Sade, Marquis de. 46.
Saint-Saphorin, Baron de. 127, 129, 130, 149, 152, 164.
St. Albans, Duke of. 84.
St. Cecilia, convent of. 147.
St. Germain-en-Laye. 14, 30, 208, 210, 212, 217.
St. Giles-in-the-Fields. 21, 42.
St. James's. 40.
St. James's coffee house, the. 21.
St. James's Park. 12, 40.
St. Leger, Elizabeth. 84.
St. Pancras' Church London. 227.
St. Petersburg. 152.
S. Germains, Madrid. 165.
San Ildefonso. 160, 164.
Salisbury Court, off Fleet Street. 99.

Saltash. 93, 199.
Salzburg. 153, 154.
Samoggia. 191.
Sample, John. 91, 194, 219.
Sandwich, Earl of. 45.
Saragossa. 160.
Satanic rituals. 45.
Scarborough, Lord. 118.
Scarsdale, Lord. 65, 94, 114, 118, 152.
Schaw, Sir John. 93.
"Schemes" the. 106.
Schönbrunn. 125.
Schönen. 25.
Scipio. 16, 24, 26, 31, 58, 121, 124, 153, 163, 171, 193, 203, 204, 208, 213, 217.
Scone. 24.
Seaforth, Lord. 162, 182.
Segovia. 180.
Sejanus. 67.
"Select and Authentic Pieces." by Duke of Wharton. 227.
Selwyn, George. 36.
Shaftsbury, Lord. 101.
Shakespeare, William. 90.
Shepherd's Market. 12.
Sheridan, Thomas. 126, 130, 131, 132, 134, 136, 147, 148, 155, 225.
Sheriffs of City of London. 99, 100, 101, 102, 199.
Sheriffmuir, Battle of. 23.
Shrewsbury, Duke of. 9.
Skerrett, "Molly". 114, 199, 206.
Smailes, family. 23, 38, 75.
Smailes, Matthew. 81, 103, 104, 138.
Soho Square. 227.
Soissons, peace-conference at. 199, 205.
Solomon, King. 84.
Somerset House. 44.
Song Made at York Races. 75.
Sorrel, Mr. English banker at Vienna. 150, 153, 179, 193.
South Sea Bill. 55.
South Sea Company. 55, 61, 63, 65, 66.
South Sea Scheme. 55, 57, 63, 65, 69, 91, 103.
South Sea Stock. 56, 57, 61.
Southesk, Lord. 30.
Spain, Elizabeth Farnese Queen of. 122, 123, 127, 147, 148, 156, 165, 167, 168, 170, 173, 181, 185.
Spain, Philip V King of. 122, 137, 141, 147, 148, 156, 165, 168, 170, 173, 175, 178.
Spanish Succession, war of. 122.
Spectator The. 41.
Spedding, Mr. the Lowthers agent. 78.
Spence, Joseph. 47.
Spenser, Lord. 49.
Spillers Head tavern in Clare Market. 63.
Stair, Earl of. 30, 31, 32, 37.

249

Stanhope, Charles. 69.
Stanhope, James Earl, 16, 50, 53, 65, 66, 67, 69.
Stanhope, Philip Dormer, later Earl of Chesterfield. 68.
Stanhope, William. 127, 161, 164, 167, 170, 180, 226.
Stapleton, Ensign. 117.
Stapleton, Sir William. 117.
Stationers' Hall. 84, 88, 89, 100.
Stecho, Michael. 121, 143, 153.
Steele, Sir John. 41.
Steele, Sir Richard. 21, 41, 84.
Stephansdom (St Stephan's Tower). 125, 163.
Sterne, John, Bishop of Clogher. 166.
Steuart, Hon. William. 59.
Stiles, Benjamin Haskins. 104.
Strafford, Countess of. 40, 108.
Strafford, Earl of. 32, 63, 65, 68, 94, 103, 114, 119, 145, 161, 186.
Strickland, Abbé. 136.
Stuart family. 147.
Stuart, Prince Charles Edward: 'Bonnie Prince Charlie'. 130, 131, 147, 155, 162, 166, 182, 185, 186, 225.
Stuart, Prince Henry. 182.
Stukely, Dr. William. 84, 89, 109.
Stukely, Thomas. 90.
Sunderland, Charles Earl of. 16, 49, 50, 53, 61, 62, 63, 65, 66, 67, 69, 70, 71, 72, 81, 82, 85.
Sutton, Sir Robert. 197.
Swaledale, Yorks. 38, 76, 93, 104, 138, 171.
Swift, Jonathan, Dean of St. Patricks (Dr). 11, 33, 36, 58, 66, 87, 93, 111, 118.

T

Talman, Thomas. 39.
Tarragona. 222, 223.
Tatler, The. 97, 99.
Télémaque. 219.
Tencin, Claudine de. 25.
Tetuan. 180.
Thanet, Earl of. 79.
The Earls Defeat. 79.
The Luck of Eden Hall. 79.
The Revenge, Play by Young. 47, 68, 90.
Thompson, Ned. 139.
Tiberius, Emperor. 67.
Tickell, Thomas. 114.
Tiger, H.M.S. 185.
Torremayor, Marqués de. 220.
Tower Hill. 208.
Townshend, Charles Viscount, 16, 50, 55, 61, 71, 89, 96, 99, 102, 129, 177, 196.
train-bands, the city. 101, 134.
Trevor, Thomas Lord. 72, 170, 177.
True Briton, The. 97, 99, 100, 102, 103, 105, 107, 110.

Tunbridge Wells. 69.
Turkey. 157.
Turkey, Sultan of. 112.
Twickenham. 61, 86, 87, 90, 93, 99, 103, 104, 112, 113, 192, 219.
Tyburn. 13, 221.

U

Utrecht. 49.
Utrecht, Treaty of. 121.

V

Vanburgh, Sir John. 22, 39, 76, 88.
Van Dyck, Sir Anthony. 9, 20, 68, 139.
Valencia. 179, 180, 182.
Valenciennes. 210.
Vanhutyt, Madame. 49, 140.
Versailles. 76, 129, 203.
Vertue, George. 20, 21.
Vienna. 121, 124, 125, 126, 127, 129, 131, 134, 136, 141, 143, 144, 148, 151, 152, 155, 161, 163, 165, 166, 169, 203.
Villeneuve. 28.
Voltaire. 144, 226.

W

Waddesdon. 138.
Wager, Sir Charles, 182, 183, 187.
Waldegrave, Lord. 84.
Walpole, Dolly. 11.
Walpole, Horace. 69, 87, 227.
Walpole, Horatio. 129, 141, 193, 195, 197, 209, 219, 226.
Walpole, Mrs. Horatio. 194.
Walpole, Robert, later Sir. 11, 12, 16, 42, 50, 55, 61, 62, 63, 65, 69, 80, 81, 82, 91, 94, 95, 96, 97, 98, 99, 103, 114, 118, 121, 122, 133, 135, 139, 140, 150, 162, 165, 172, 186, 193, 195, 199, 201, 202, 205, 219, 221, 226.
Walsh Mr. a Paris Jacobite. 216.
Ward, Ned. 41, 46.
Walters, the Jacobite banker at Paris. 117, 124, 192.
Wax Chandler. 209.
Wax Chandlers Company. 101.
Wellington, Duke of. 58.
Wendover. 11, 50.
Wesley, Mr. 58.
Westcot. 104.
Weston, Bishop of Bath and Wells. 65.
Westport. 104.
Wharton, family, 77.

250

Wharton Hall. 13, 20, 24, 54, 69, 76, 77, 88, 104, 192, 216.
Whartonia. 198.
Wharton, Lady Jane. 11, 119, 177, 226.
Wharton, Lady Lucy. 11, 119, 177, 226.
Wharton, Lucy (née Loftus) Marchioness of. 11, 16, 19, 32.
Wharton, Maria-Theresa, second Duchess of. 169, 171, 178, 179, 180, 183, 184, 185, 188, 190, 191, 192, 194, 197, 202, 203, 204, 208, 209, 212, 213, 216, 217, 219, 222, 226.
Wharton, Martha, (née Holmes) First Duchess of. 16, 32, 43, 49, 52, 53, 63, 77, 80, 114, 115, 116, 119, 124, 139, 151, 169, 171.
Wharton, Philip Duke of.
his birth 9; his christening 9; styled Viscount Winchendon 10; his mother 11; his childhood 12; meets Addison 13; his education 13; early precocity 14; his appearance and character 15; disinherited 18; his guardians 22; travels to Germany and France 24; connected to Jacobitism, with Avignon 26; asks for Garter 28; meets James III and is promised Dukedom of Northumberland 29; leaves Paris for England 31; contracts smallpox 32; travels to Ireland 33; admitted to Irish House of Lords 33; created Duke of Wharton 35; returns to London 37; his life in London 42; founds Hell-Fire Club 44; travels to Rotterdam 49; joins Leicester Fields party 51; takes his seat in House of Lords 51; his son dies 53; the South Sea Scheme 55; sells his Irish estates 58; and All Souls' College 59; attacks those responsible for South Sea Bubble 63; attacks ministry in Parliament 65; orator in House of Lords 67; as political speaker 69; his debts 70; visits Wharton Hall 77; leaves Grumbletonian party to join Sunderland 82; joins Freemasons 84; his electoral failure in 1722 General Election 85; in Twickenham 88; becomes Grand Master of Order of Freemasons 89; defends Atterbury 95; as poet and pamphleteer 98; and City of London election 102; instances of his journalism 106; founds "the Schemes" 108; as patron of letters 111; Quarrells with Pope over Lady Mary 113; described by Pope 113; parts from Young 114, his distaste for duelling 117; goes abroad 119; arrives at Vienna 124; delivers memorial to the Emperor 135; crosses the Alps to Rome 154; receives Garter from James 157; at Madrid 161; his conversion and re-marriage 172; his ill health 179; at Gibraltar 183; is wounded and retires to Cadiz 187; founds Spanish Freemasons 189; sees James III in Italy 192; ill at Lyons 193; sees Horatio Walpole at Paris 195; his request for a pardon refused 196; the subject of popular interest in England 198; pamphleteers from Rouen 199; refuses offer of a pardon 201; drinks less at Rouen and health improves 204; flees from his creditors to Paris 208; is convicted of treason and outlawed 216; his death 223.
Wharton, Philip 4th Lord. 9, 20, 54.
Wharton, Thomas First Lord. 77, 225.
Wharton, Thomas Marquis of. 9, 10, 11, 14, 17, 19, 20, 31, 37, 49, 134.
Wharton, Village of. 77.
"Whens", the Duke of Wharton's. 97.
Whinfell, Cumberland. 197.
Whitehall. 12.
Whitehaven. 77, 78.
White's. 75.
Wild, Jonathon. 98, 221.
Wilkes, John. 46.
William III. 9, 10, 134.
Williams, Sir John. 101, 102.
Williams, William Peer. 38.
Winchendon. 11, 13, 14, 16, 18, 19, 20, 27, 32, 33, 37, 50, 52, 62, 63, 68, 69, 73, 77, 88, 124, 138, 159, 196.
Winchendon, Over, Manor. 104.
Winnington, Thomas. 26, 27, 28, 29, 31.
Wintoun, Earl of. 189.
Woburn Abbey. 13.
Wolfe, Jacobite printer. 199, 205, 216, 227.
Wooburn. 13, 16, 19, 20, 37, 50, 68, 69, 74, 104, 117, 138, 196.
Wooburn House. 63, 88.
"Woods half-pence". 162.
Woodstock, racing at. 62.
Workington. 78.
Wortley Montagu, Edward. 16, 112.
Wortley Montagu, Lady Mary. 22, 32, 39, 61, 87, 90, 104, 106, 107, 109, 111, 112, 113, 114, 119, 125, 177, 219, 226.
Wycherley, William. 40.
Wycombe. 11, 45, 140, 151, 160.
Wyndham, Sir William. 114, 118.
Wynn, General. 58.

Y

York. 75.
York, Archbishop of. 52, 76, 97.
York Races. 75, 76.
Yorke, family of. 76, 85.
Young, Dr. Edward. 34, 36, 42, 47, 49, 52, 58, 59, 68, 70, 88, 91, 114, 131, 140, 181, 226, 227.

251

Z

Zindendorf, Abbé, son of the Count. 153.
Zindendorf, Count. 128, 130, 132, 135, 136, 141, 143, 144, 145, 148, 152, 153, 155, 156, 163.